CONTENTS

MEDIA AND AUDIENCES
New Perspectives

Karen Ross and Virginia Nightingale

OPEN UNIVERSITY PRESS

Open University Press
McGraw-Hill Education
McGraw-Hill House
Shoppenhangers Road
Maidenhead
Berkshire
England
SL6 2QL

email: enquiries@openup.co.uk
world wide web: www.openup.co.uk

First published 2003

A catalogue record of this book is available from the British Library

ISBN 0 335 20691 3 (pb)   0 335 20692 1 (hb)

Library of Congress Cataloging-in-Publication Data
CIP data applied for

Typeset by RefineCatch Limited, Bungay, Suffolk
Printed in the UK by Ashford Colour Press Ltd., Gosport, Hants.

SERIES EDITOR'S FOREWORD

'There are in fact no masses,' Raymond Williams once famously observed, 'only ways of seeing people as masses.' This notion of 'the masses', from the vantage point of today at least, seems strangely anachronistic. And yet, by a similar logic, what happens to certain familiar conceptions of 'the audience' when subjected to closer scrutiny? To render problematic 'the audience' as a singular, cohesive totality, is it not necessary to recognize that a multiplicity of audiences exist where typically only one is being acknowledged?

In *Media and Audiences*, Karen Ross and Virginia Nightingale explore precisely these sorts of thorny questions. In their view, the increasing centrality of mediated information in modern societies, together with the interactivity engendered by new media technologies, mean that there are unprecedented opportunities for innovative, highly engaging media experiences to emerge. Pertinent here, for example, are the ways in which some internet users pursue common goals, seek out information, track down contacts, and share ways to circumvent the rights of content producers, copyright holders and hardware suppliers. Creatively negotiated practices such as these ones, Ross and Nightingale contend, underscore the necessity of examining afresh certain longstanding assumptions about media audiences, and the academic concepts used to characterize their actions. Thus it is this book's aim – together with the accompanying text, *Critical Readings: Media and Audiences* – to provide a careful elucidation of several major strands of the research literature on audiences. Future lines of enquiry, Ross and Nightingale point out, will be empowered by an understanding of the history of the field, one which recognizes not only its advances, but also its limitations, gaps and silences.

The *Issues in Cultural and Media Studies* series aims to facilitate a diverse range of critical investigations into pressing questions considered to be central to current thinking and research. In light of the remarkable speed at which the conceptual agendas of cultural and media studies are changing, the series is committed to contributing to what is an ongoing process of re-evaluation and critique. Each of the books is intended to provide a lively, innovative and comprehensive introduction to a specific topical issue from a fresh perspective. The reader is offered a thorough grounding in the most salient debates indicative of the book's subject, as well as important insights into how new modes of enquiry may be established for future explorations. Taken as a whole, then, the series is designed to cover the core components of cultural and media studies courses in an imaginatively distinctive and engaging manner.

Stuart Allan

ACKNOWLEDGEMENTS

When we began the planning of this book – which now seems an awfully long time ago – we realized that we had both been teaching and researching audiences for almost all our academic lives. We also realized that we still had things to say about our field that had yet to see the light of day, and so we embarked on this collaborative enterprise, across continents and cultures, time zones and academic years. For both of us, this book was our first writing collaboration with a colleague on the other side of the globe and as we crafted our work we felt at times that the media visionary, Marshall McLuhan, must have been chuckling quietly in some time-warped corner of cyberspace. This book is first and foremost, a product of the information technologies with which we engage daily. Writing it would have been unimaginable without email in particular, since email made the distance between our respective geographical spaces almost irrelevant, and working to deadlines possible. Equally important, however, have been the international people networks, like the International Association of Media and Communication Research (IAMCR) and its associated conferences which created environments where it was possible to share ideas and develop this and other international projects. IAMCR introduced us to each other and made it possible for us to develop the collegial relationship that eventually produced this book. The other network we share is the loose one of feminist media scholars and its more formalized structure in the shape of the journal, *Feminist Media Studies*, which keeps us focused on what we are doing and why it's important.

As always with a co-production such as this, each of Karen Ross and Virginia Nightingale has her own set of acknowledgements. Karen Ross would like to thank the colleagues and students who, in any number of big and small ways, have shaped my thinking about audiences, especially the lived realities of audiences as individual viewers, listeners and readers. I would also like to thank the various folks who have participated in my own audience research projects down the years whose insights have found their way into the writing of this book. Amongst my colleagues (who are also friends), I would like to specifically thank Carolyn Byerly, Sarah Hill, Katharine Sarikakis and Jennifer Tann for sustained friendship and support, and Annabelle Sreberny who started me off on my career as a media researcher. I would also like to thank my department (Communication, Media and Culture subject group) and School (Art and Design) at Coventry University for enabling me to find the time for this co-production and for providing funding for several writing meetings in several countries. Lastly, I would like to thank my partner, Barry, for all those large and small kindnesses which enabled me to prioritize this work when other things were vying for attention.

For Virginia Nightingale, in the course of writing my share of the book several colleagues, perhaps unbeknown to them, provided inspiration and encouragement through their work that should be acknowledged. The work of Richard Butsch and Henry Jenkins in the USA, and of Tom O'Regan in Australia showed definitively that audience research has and will continue to move in new directions. Richard's innovative historical research, Henry's cyber-community centred work, and Tom's ground breaking analysis of arts policy and arts audiences in Australia demonstrated the changing parameters of the field. Like Karen I owe special thanks to my Department (Communication, Design and Media) and to the University of Western Sydney for the travel funding and time allowances that enabled us to meet and plan. Last, but far from least, I give special thanks to my partner, Garry, and to my daughter, Anna, for sharing the highs and lows of this writing project with me, and to my work colleagues, Anna Gibbs, Hart Cohen and Tim Dwyer for their friendship and collegiality.

Having done the singular thing, there are people whom we both want to acknowledge: first Justin Vaughan kept us on message in the early days of the book's development; and Stuart Allan, a series editor who made serious demands of us which, in the luxury of hindsight if not at the time, we see were absolutely right and which resulted in a much better book; and for the editorial and production staff at Open University Press/McGraw-Hill who experienced considerable change during the lifetime of this project but who together have made this the book that it is.

1 | AUDIENCES TODAY

The audience is the best judge of anything. They cannot be lied to. Truth brings them closer. A moment that lags — they're gonna cough.
(Barbra Streisand, *Newsweek*, 5 January 1970)

When information rules

As the emerging information age begins its reorganization of everyday life, the study of media audiences has taken on renewed importance. This isn't just because *more* information is mediated, it's also because people are integrating both old and new media technologies into their lives in more complex ways. In his early discussion of the flow of television programming, Raymond Williams noted the demands made of viewers by the pace and rhythm of the incessant flow of diverse and sometimes discordant television programme fragments (Williams 1974). Today, being an audience is even more complicated. The media 'environment' is much more cluttered. Where once there was one television set and one radio in the average home, there are now several of each. Where once listening and viewing were group activities in the home, now individual listening and viewing is the domestic norm, with people sometimes using several different media simultaneously. It is not unusual today to find people reading a newspaper, book or magazine while listening to the radio or the latest MP3 track, or putting the latest interactive game on hold to take a call by mobile phone from a friend. Mobile telephony and mobile internet access have been added to the entertainment media mix, and in the future, streaming technologies for web radio and web television promise an intensification of this media layering. Today people actively add complexity to the range of information to which they are exposed by mixing media, media sources and media activities. If we compare this media environment with the traditional idea of an audience as the people present at a performance in a theatre or at a concert, it is obvious that there has been a rapid and dramatic expansion of what it now means to *be* an audience.

The frequency, range and immediacy of media engagements that link people to the information flows that are the life blood of the information society have obviously been precipitated by the proliferation of new technologies, the convergence of 'old' and 'new' media technologies and the globalization of communication environments. Separately and together, new technologies, globalization and convergence create new opportunities for people to access information — and they pose significant challenges for contemporary understandings of media audiences and the significance of their activities. Evidence of the type of impact this change has had on what counts as audience activity was demonstrated by the emergence in the 1990s of reality TV.

Audiences and reality TV

Reality TV was developed during the 1990s as a means to revitalize a world of jaded television viewers by adding new sensations of immediacy and agency to the TV viewing experience. This mock ethnographic genre aimed to exploit the interest of viewers in real-life stories. The ratings potential of the emerging genre had been anticipated by the depth of viewer interest in the stories and characters of 'ethnographic' documentaries like Michael Apted's, *Seven Up* series and by early 'fly on the wall' programmes like the successful British/Australian co-production, *Sylvania Waters*. This programme documented the everyday dramas of an 'ordinary' family living in Sydney, Australia. It offered viewers an opportunity to witness the daily dilemmas, thought processes, reasoning and reactions of ordinary people as they deal with the events of everyday life. Viewers witnessed these processes in lives other than their own, and responded by conferring celebrity status on the programme's participants. As 'fly on the wall TV' metamorphosed into 'reality TV', these early experiments were 'enhanced' with increasingly exotic locations, more glamorous, sexy, adventurous and willing participants, and increasing levels of producer control of and intervention in the fabricated 'TV reality'.

Reality TV reached the height of its popularity with programmes like *Survivor* and *Big Brother*. These programmes were franchised internationally and involved the production of local versions of a global TV 'product' in countries throughout the world. And, at the height of their popularity, they evoked unprecedented ratings and intensity of TV viewer involvement. Importantly, *Big Brother* offered viewers room to intervene in the onscreen world of the programme. At first this was limited to voting on which participant/contestant should be voted out of the Big Brother house and off the screen and this telephone voting constituted an added income stream for the production company. But viewer involvement did not stop at the telephone. In Britain, viewers gathered outside the Big Brother house to welcome out the contestants voted off the programme that week: other fans tried to evade security and invade the house itself. Many started dressing to look like contestants, or mimicked personal traits and characteristics of the participants, and by the time an Australian version of the programme was broadcast in 2001, these activities had been incorporated into the programme planning. In addition, participants inside and their support groups outside the house began to politicize the voting by engaging in rigging tactics, using mobile phones and automatic number redial techniques, to try and ensure their 'candidate' in the house emerged the winner.

The intensity of emotional involvement exhibited by viewers of reality TV led programme executives to consider new ways to monitor, channel and exploit viewer interest. The usual press, radio and TV promotion and programme-based news therefore expanded to include website and email initiatives, and the development of streaming technologies for TV and radio on the world wide web offered additional opportunities for actively recruiting and estimating viewer response to the programmes on a daily basis. The new strategies for engaging audiences invariably required unprecedented levels of interactivity between the production company and the public. Viewers were encouraged to visit the website, and for a small subscription fee, could buy additional access to coverage of the more intimate activities and interests of the participants. Viewers freely emailed opinions and reactions, likes and dislikes, directly to the programme websites. Internet technologies therefore allowed production staff more immediate, detailed and specific feedback from viewers than could be gained from syndicated ratings services (see Chapter 3), and provided them with the option of collaborating more closely with audiences in the provision of a greater viewing pleasure.

The *Big Brother* phenomenon was in many ways a watershed for our understanding of media audiences. It demonstrated forcefully one of the central tenets proposed in this book: that a mass media phenomenon cannot be explained by studying audiences or people factors alone. Viewing, listening and/or reading are events that invite participation, and people's participation in media events can take many and varied forms. Increasingly the ways of being an audience for a particular story or character set involves engaging with several media and seeking out or piecing together the story across multiple media. Being an audience now has an investigative dimension, and audience curiosity is subject to commercial exploitation. The *Pokemon* phenomenon is another case where the engagement of audience curiosity was opened up for commercial exploitation. It was possible to become a better *Pokemon* player by searching for additional information — by viewing the TV series, buying collector cards, and searching the internet for *Pokemon* cheats. Allegiance to the *Pokemon* phenomenon was also demonstrated by the acquisition of licensed merchandise. So, *being* an audience now extends well beyond viewing, listening or reading, and as a result, new approaches to audience research are needed, even if the research methods audience researchers call on remain fundamentally the same.

Naming audiences as people and groups

The word *audience* is so much part of our everyday talk that its complexity is often taken for granted. The word, after all, has a history that extends back into unrecorded time, and reflects pre-broadcasting modes of accessing information. In media studies *audience* is mostly used as a way of talking about people, either as groups or as individuals. It is used to refer to large groups of people, like the mass audience for television news, newspaper readerships, the general public, or even people attending a major sporting event or a rock concert. The people in such groups are seen as having little connection with each other, other than an interest in the event they are attending or witnessing.

The word *audience* is also used to refer to groups of people who are linked by ties of more enduring socio-cultural significance. These 'audiences' may be described as subcultures, taste cultures, fan cultures, ethnic diasporas, indigenous or religious communities, and even domestic households. Members of these 'groups' bring certain shared interpretative perspectives to their engagements with media and so are perhaps better described as *formations* rather than *masses*. Such formations are shaped by pre-existing social and cultural histories and conditions, and sometimes also by a sense of shared interests that incline them to repeatedly use particular media vehicles (like newspapers or radio programmes). These social formations exist independently of the media, however, and so participation in media events does not usually exhaust the range of their communal activity. Audience formations may combine or disperse to engage with the media, or be simultaneously together and apart — as is evident at major sports stadiums where audiences simultaneously watch the game on the field and the televised game on the big screen, and see themselves watching the screen at the game.

Then again, the word 'audience' may be used to refer to relatively small, local groups or congregations, like the people who attend a religious service, a school speech day, a theatre performance, or a poetry reading. These groups remind us that their purpose requires a designated space: a church, a school, a theatre. The conjunction of time and space is important in defining audiences. The expansion of access to the internet has created virtual spaces where even smaller groups assemble. Meeting in time, but separated in space, the micro-groups who frequent internet chat sites, gaming communities and other web-based activities are new members of the audience family.

Whatever the size of the group or the materiality of the space involved, it is obvious that *being an audience* has to involve more than just being in a group of people. After all, masses of people crowd into railway stations, airport terminals, holiday resorts and shopping malls, yet these people are not being 'audiences'. People meet in small groups for dinner and discussion, yet they are not described as audiences when they do so. Something else is required for people to be described as audiences. The *extra* required for a *gathering* to become an *audience* is for participation to be structured according to power relations governing the access to and use made of the informational dimension of the event. The guests at the dinner party become an audience when someone starts to tell a story, and the group contributes rapt attention for the telling. When talking about media audiences, the mediatization of information is often assumed to encompass the power and control dimensions of the media event. Yet the increasing complexity of the media environment, and the growing diversity of audience engagements, mean that it is time to re-examine such assumptions, and to expand our definitions of what 'media audience' means.

A media event perspective

Contemporary urban life depends on the media for the fast and efficient sharing of information. The media enable people who may otherwise have no direct contact to share access to the knowledge base on which their everyday lives are grounded. By being audiences, people navigate the complexity of con-temporary life, and enjoy a wide variety of active and satisfying social and cultural experiences. The changing media landscape has, therefore, enabled a dramatic expansion in the range and nature of the media spaces where com-municative engagement is practised. Being part of an audience, using the skills required to engage with mediated information, is now equal in importance with family and interpersonal interactions. These are all means by which people keep abreast of current affairs and contemporary trends, entertain themselves, relax, take time out, become involved with the cultural life of their communities and make themselves into interesting people. Everyone relies on being able to discuss the films, books or TV programmes they have seen that provoke comment or reflection about the world around us.

Generally speaking, being part of an audience means being part of a media event, where people engage with mediated information. People *are* audiences when they are *in an audience* and *in audience*. All media events are audience events since they require people to hang out in media time-spaces where they physically, mentally and emotionally engage with media materials, technologies and power structures. The audience event invokes the power relations that structure the media as social institutions and delimit the options available to people for involvement in the means of cultural production. Human groups have specified such arrangements for telling stories from time immemorial. For example, the anthropologist Bronislaw Malinowski (1954 [1948]) carried out fieldwork among the Trobriand Islanders of New Guinea in the 1920s. During his fieldwork he noted that the Islanders made special arrangements for telling different types of stories. Myths, for example, were regarded as true and sacred explanations of the origins of the world, and legends explained why certain clans held power and others did not, while the fairy tale was told for the amusement and enjoyment of the listeners and to promote sociability among them. Unlike the other story forms, he noted that for fairy tales:

> Every story is 'owned' by a member of the community. Each story, though known by many, may be recited only by the 'owner'; he may, however, present it to someone else by teaching that person and authorizing him to retell it. But not all the 'owners' know how to thrill and to raise a hearty laugh, which is one of the main ends of such stories. A good raconteur has to change his voice in the dialogue, chant the ditties with due temperament, gesticulate, and in general play to the gallery.
>
> (Malinowski 1954/1948: 102)

Even the telling of fairy stories can be surrounded by conventions that differentiate who is permitted to tell the story and who may listen, and by, in this case at least, communal endorsement of arrangements made to ensure that audiences can hear the story told well. It is this type of arrangement that we find, in a much more highly regulated and institutionalized form, in the relations between mass media and audiences. Rights to produce and to tell the stories that delight and entertain audiences have been licensed to the media industries. The power structure, evident in the media industries' control of media production, in turn governs who creates and who engages with media, and it presupposes the involvement of people's bodies, their physical being, in the time-spaces media create. In the complex communications environments and knowledge spaces that characterize the Information Age, audience events occupy an increasingly pivotal role as the means by which knowledge is transformed into social, cultural, economic and political action. The media event, then, involves simultaneously the minutiae of personal audience interests and actions and the complex sets of conditions that are brought into play to ensure the ongoing production of the culture's stories.

Broadly speaking five aspects of media events recur as sources of media research interest:

1. the audience participants as individuals;
2. the audience activities of the participants in the media event;
3. the media time/space of the event;
4. the media power relations that structure the event; and
5. the mediatized information with which people engage.

In all audience research, certain assumptions are made about what aspects of the media event are acting on audiences and about whether or not such 'influence' is likely to benefit them. In subcultures and fan research, for example, the aim is to trace the modes by which subcultural identity is maintained or threatened by the media and its patterns of representation, both of people and their perspectives on current events. Subcultures research considers:

1. who the subculture is in terms of its history and of its current socio-cultural situation;
2. what types of media activities members engage in or organize for themselves;
3. how media materials orient the group in time and space by assisting group members to better understand the past, the present or their future direction;
4. how the subculture is empowered (or not) by the power relations that structure the media event;
5. how the members of the subculture interpret — by accepting, negotiating or resisting — the meanings privileged by the textual structure of the media message.

In the case of subcultures, a fairly thorough overview of the media event is considered necessary to understand the event and the subculture's participation in mass culture.

In ratings analysis, by contrast, the aim is to produce an abstract map of the mass audience and of mass audience behaviour. To achieve the sort of measure of audience behaviour that can be used in statistical analysis, the media event and the behaviour of audiences have to be reduced to their most basic elements. In terms of our media event template:

1. only easily verifiable audience demographics (age, sex, and so on) are taken into account in determining audience 'composition';

2. one audience behaviour only, *exposure* or tuning in, is counted for the purpose of audience measurement;
3. analysis of the media time/space is limited to identification of the daypart (defined by hours of the day when viewing occurred, or by the type of content viewed – see Webster, Phalen and Lichty 2000: 240);
4. the structures of the media come into play only in terms of their capacity to offer a broadcasting service to the place where the viewer/listener is located; and
5. media content is considered a programming or scheduling matter, rather than a matter of concern to audiences.

Ratings analysis has a very specific purpose — audience measurement. Its purpose is best served by streamlining the sorts of information taken into account (ratings analysis is examined in detail in Chapter 3), so it defines the media event in a very abstract way.

These examples demonstrate that what we know about audiences is dependent on how the media event is defined and on what aspects of audience engagement with the media are being researched. By exploring the media event as a complex socio-cultural phenomenon, much more detailed and interesting information is developed about media audiences — about who they are and what they are doing, and about the long-term cultural significance of their activities. In Chapter 2, several studies that use historical research to examine the long-term implications of media events are introduced. These studies show that the repercussions of audience adoption of new media can be the catalyst for dramatic social and cultural change. The chapter then presents some of the key approaches to audience research (content and response analysis; personal influence; uses and gratifications; encoding/decoding) by examining the problems they address and the definitions of the media event they invoke.

From the perspective of the broadcast media industries, the most important thing about audiences is whether they are tuned in or not. The act of tuning in is called 'exposure' and the relevance of this behaviour as the basis for information about audiences is questioned in Chapter 3. As indicated above, exposure is the only audience act that is documented and statistically analysed by the commercially operated research firms who produce ratings analysis. In most parts of the world, the sale of audience exposures is used to fund broadcasting services. Since audience exposures are the only commodity produced by broadcasting, the ratings system doubles as a form of communication between broadcasters and audiences. However, the power balance in this system of communication favours the broadcaster, and because the information to which broadcasters pay attention, the exposure, is abstract, this system does not necessarily work in the long-term interests of audiences. For this reason it is important to understand at least the basic terms used in ratings analysis and to gain a better understanding of how broadcasters and advertisers think about audiences.

The basic principles and techniques of ratings research were developed in the early days of mass broadcasting. Syndicated ratings services have been available to the broadcasting industries since the mid-1930s (Beville 1988: 258). While the recording and processing of audience measurement has been transformed over the years, the basic procedures and formulae used have remained constant. Recently, however, the relevance of people meters and diaries has been challenged by new technologies for recording and analysing ratings data. New information technologies allow audiences to be monitored, and their consumer decision-making analysed, more quickly and more thoroughly than ever before. The internet allows people's net-surfing to be followed and analysed for commercial opportunities. The computing power of the Information Age has led audience measurement researchers to be able to embrace a new-found interest in the relationship between broadcast and internet service providers and their client audiences. Chapter 3 therefore concludes with some discussion of cyber activities where audiences and industry engage in the same or parallel activities, like 'data mining', software co-development, news production and file sharing. The internet is a media space where industry and audience rights are currently hotly disputed, while still in the process of being defined and developed. In this context, one aspect of the media event considered least relevant for ratings analysis in the past — that is the analysis of what audiences do with the information they gather from the internet — emerges as the site of contestation over future media growth.

The history of audience research is littered with the corpses of studies that have tried and failed to demonstrate, once and for all, a cause and effect relationship between media message and receiver behaviour. Chapter 4 therefore provides a journey through the 'effects' literature, moving from early concerns with propaganda through to the more contemporary debates that question whether mass media have any effect at all. Whilst there is little doubt, in the literature as much as amongst armchair philosophers, that the media play an important role in contributing to the social, economic and cultural environment in which we live, attempting to show precisely that this message causes that behaviour is rather a lost cause. Chapter 4 thus maps out the chronological development of the cause-effect paradigm and shows how researchers have come full circle from early audience theories which insisted that there was a simple one-way flow of influence from the media to the audience, through a rejection of audience passivity, back to a serious concern over the influence of, in particular, violent media content on criminal or violent activity. Along the way, we consider the still controversial view that watching violent films or

TV programmes is a pro-social act since it serves a cathartic function where the viewer can safely act out and identify with overt displays of aggression and can feel satisfied with the vicarious thrill of danger rather than have to experience it at first hand.

Early interest in the media/audience relation was provoked by a suspicion of news broadcasting and its propagandist tendencies in the pre- and immediate post-World War 2 period, and researchers have continued to be fascinated by news media, both print and broadcast. Much of the focus on news genres has been concerned with identifying bias, with traditional studies continuing to mine the now well-worn seam of political bias, whereas other work, especially researchers working with feminist and post-modern approaches, have tended to look at aspects of identity and representation. Chapter 5 considers all these approaches before moving on to consider the media's role in election campaigns, including negative 'attack' ads, the differential reporting of women and men candidates and the ways in which voters are enlightened (or not) by the media's election coverage. Crucially we explore the extent to which the media are influential in determining election campaign outcomes, finally arguing that the media are more likely to affirm voters in their pre-existing political beliefs than to change minds significantly. In other words, media do have an impact in elections but that impact is more confirmatory (of existing views) than revolutionary.

Fans are perhaps the most committed of all audiences in their loyalty to particular programmes or films or particular characters within programmes and film narratives, and fans are the principal focus of Chapter 6. In this chapter we examine the ways in which researchers have conceptualized the fan, both at the level of theorizing the difference between fans (low culture) and connoisseurs (high culture) as well as exploring how fans manifest their 'fandom'. In a review of the literature on established fan communities, especially those for programmes like *Star Trek* and *Coronation Street*, we also look at the newer groupings that have been enabled by the internet, and at the ways contemporary fans and fan groups communicate amongst themselves via virtual gateways. In particular, we look at the kinds of artefacts which fans produce, from handwritten fanzines to plotlines which are taken up by producers and worked into episodes, in order to explore the ways in which fans engage proactively with the object of their fascination, showing agency rather than passivity.

The final chapter looks at the ways in which new genres and new media are transforming the nature of audience interactions with media, which, in turn, means considering the new twists and turns of audience research. We suggest that the internet has opened up interesting new areas for research by requiring us to reconsider:

1. who is able to participate in the audience and who is not;
2. what types of (perhaps unexpected) activities do they now engage in;
3. how the time/spaces of the internet change the ways people think about their everyday interactions and the world around them;
4. do the questions traditionally asked about ownership and control and media regulation apply to the internet, or are new collaborations and contexts for the sharing of information making such questions redundant; and
5. what types of information are mediatized for the internet and how does their mediatization influence the ways the world is organized.

While the Information Age has introduced new media and new forms, and allowed people to organize themselves as audiences in novel ways, the tools available to the media researcher (for example, questionnaires, interviews, observation, focus groups) remain the same, even though we are now able to combine them and analyse them in different ways. Moreover, new media do not always consign older media to the scrap heap, and while the internet may suggest new challenges for audience research, the middle-aged technologies such as TV and radio are still the media most widely used. In fact, we can argue that the new technologies have stimulated innovative programme development for free-to-air television and talk-back radio by demonstrating the relevance of interactivity for mass media contexts.

Readers might want to note that there is a companion Reader to this book, *Critical Readings: Media and Audiences* (edited by Virginia Nightingale and Karen Ross 2003). Readings which appear there and which are relevant to chapters in this book are identified at the end of each chapter. We have also included a glossary of terms at the end of the book and these are indicated in the text by **bold italics**.

2 | AUDIENCES IN HISTORICAL PERSPECTIVE

There is a complicated interaction between the technology of television and the received forms of other kinds of cultural and social activity. Many people have said that television is essentially a combination and development of earlier forms: the newspaper, the public meeting, the educational class, the theatre, the cinema, the sports stadium, the advertising columns and billboards. The development is complicated in some cases by the earlier precedents of radio, and these will need to be considered.

(Williams 1974: 44)

Introduction

At some point in time, all media have been 'new', and all new media have offered more interesting, different, or proficient ways of achieving the communication goals human communities set themselves. In this chapter we concentrate on two processes associated with the introduction of new media and, for convenience, we use the terms **mediatization** and *industrialization* to describe them. These processes influence each other and in effect structure the time-spaces of audience engagement. In the case of television, for example — the medium most people still use most frequently — *mediatization* covers the ways that television amplifies the human capacity for sight and sound by allowing us to see and hear beyond our immediate surroundings, events occurring simultaneously or in the past; the *industrialization* of television, on the other hand, addresses the industrial structures and processes responsible for the delivery of low-cost television services. Television sets are designed for domestic use, sold relatively cheaply (most homes now have several sets) and the cost of using TV is met by the cost of a licence fee, a regular subscription to pay-TV channels and the inconvenience of viewing advertising. *Mediatization* and *industrialization* herald new audience research problems, of which they may well be the cause. They often lie at the heart of the public concern that calls for investigations into, and for the imposition of controls on, the media. This public concern has shaped the traditions of audience research that inform the knowledge we have of audiences.

More specifically, by *mediatization* we refer to the ways human cultures develop technologies that replicate, and usually also amplify, human senses and communicative power — as, for example, when the camera allows us to see people and events from the past or from inaccessible places, or when talk-back radio amplifies a discussion between two people so that it is heard simultaneously by thousands of other listeners. Media technologies allow us to transcend the limitations of presence, distance and time. But media technologies also impose interaction regimes on their audiences that physically limit what people can do while in the process of engaging with media technologies. So, for example, the screening of motion pictures presupposes a seated audience, a moratorium on conversation, and a darkened cinema, not to mention a positioning of the audience in a relation to the cinematic that engages the psychodynamic dramas on which personal identity is built.

By *industrialization* we refer to the impact of the commercial exploitation of media in a capitalist system, and the social and cultural changes the industrialized production and distribution of media bring. Industrialization has been the main driver for interest in and research about media audiences, and most of the audience research traditions outlined below have been developed to manage and control media audiences better — either as commodities for advertisers or as customers for information services — or to define and assess the social, cultural and political impact of the media on audiences. We argue in this chapter that this has occurred because audience research is a vehicle for monitoring the impact of both the *mediatization* of human senses and the *industrialization* of the productive capacity of the media.

Nightingale (1999) has pointed out that while people depend on media, media depend even more on people — on the co-optation of human bodies — for their very existence. New media, therefore, often initially proclaim their social utility or cultural benefit in terms of increasing the productive capacity of humans (allowing us to work faster, more accurately or more efficiently), by addressing the characteristics of media engagement and production that are most attractive to people as human beings (by being entertaining or amusing), or by promising to increase the body's physical powers. *Mediatization* in a sense encapsulates the enigma that informs our cultural myths and images of the cyborg (for example *Frankenstein*, *Robocop*, the *Terminator*). Heggs has defined the cyborg as referring to 'the extension or enhancement of the body through its fusion with technology' (Heggs 1999: 187). Such myths and images demonstrate the preoccupation with the ways the human body is empowered by media. But this preoccupation also masks the deep dependence of industrialized media on the co-optation of human bodies as the basis for their (the media's) continuing (industrial) viability. The clarification of this exchange — of audience body parts for communicative power — helps us to understand why the themes of audience research have continued for so long to alternate between 'audience activity' and 'media enslavement'. The image of the cyborg is ambiguous — are humans librated by the power gained from media or enslaved by being encumbered by these technologies? Audience research is a response to the concerns generated by the shifting balance between these two extremes.

Human bodies and mediatization

The changing conditions associated with being an audience today have sparked a resurgence of interest in media and media audiences by historians and art theorists (for example, Crary 1994; Manguel 1997; Butsch 2000) whose work has sharpened the focus on the ways human bodies are implicated in media use. Their explorations have touched upon how new media change the ways audiences engage with mediated culture, and provide historical contexts for understanding such changes, bringing the realization that, just as with the impact of new media on old media forms, new ways of being an audience can reactivate older patterns of engagement or prompt new adaptations of past and present modes of audience interaction (Butsch 2000).

Until recently, mediatization had mostly resulted in people being immobilized or inactivated by stationary interfaces (the printed page; the film screen; the television set; the computer screen). Media engagement imposed restrictions on people's physical activity while *in audience*. In some cases, for example reading a book or attending the cinema, the relative inactivity of the human body might be judged to stimulate thought or critical reflection — especially if justified by the authorial or auteur status of the work's creator. In the case of popular culture, however, the inactivity of its audiences, and the lack of reward directly observable for the time spent, means that it is often judged to be both physically and mentally detrimental. Yet by the early 1970s, the ubiquity of mass culture and the designation of many formerly popular cultural forms as art or literature led to widespread recognition that popular culture is a significant cultural phenomenon in its own right and worthy of investigation. The first response to this recognition was to analyse popular texts using methods adapted from literary and art theory (Berger 1976; Eco 1979; Fish 1980). It took longer, as we will see, for the role of the audience to be understood and accepted as an integral component of the communication process.

Photography and ways of knowing

The problem of explaining how the act of observation affects what is judged as attractive or excellent in popular culture (that is, the problem of understanding how *who* is observing *what* determines *what is seen*) surfaced in John Berger's analysis of images as 'ways of seeing' (Berger 1976). By choosing to analyse images from both advertising and art, Berger showed that a subtle shift had occurred in the sphere of critical appraisal of art that allowed artists and art critics to register that audiences play a role in making images meaningful. The critic's appraisal of a cultural work on the basis of the author's or artist's intentions, or on the basis of the formal qualities of the work, was challenged by the ways audiences judge the quality of cultural work. In other words, by whether audiences will pay to attend, buy or view the work. Berger situated images as diverse as classical oil painting and contemporary advertising in the same analytical frame and showed how art theory could be applied to the most commercial of popular cultural forms, the advertisement. His work, perhaps inadvertently, opened up the space between what an artist intends and how the image created will be 'read' by its audiences.

Engaging bodies: vision and observation

The question of how much of what we see is a product of our bodies and how much is defined by the outside world remains one of the central philosophical issues encountered in audience research. Just how do we explain people's engagement with texts? In what senses are audiences tied into patterns of response by the media and in what sense can they be said to be active? How, exactly, does audience activity affect what is observed and pattern interpretation? These questions lie at the heart of all cultural research about audience and indicate one of its key differences from research in the social science and other traditions.

Crary (1994) has tried to explain some of the confusions in this debate. He approached it by questioning the impact of the *camera obscura* on ideas about vision and how things are seen. The *camera obscura* (or pin-hole camera) is a darkened box that admits light through a tiny hole. This produces an inverted image of the scene outside the box on a surface inside the box. This image can then to be used as a template for more accurate sketches or drawings than freehand, or simply be enjoyed for its intrinsic qualities. Crary sees this issue, of seeing and vision, as a question about the relationship between observation and what is observed, and claims that the human-ness and physicality of the observer must be taken into account in order to understand the significance of the changing rhetoric of vision that followed the demise of the *camera obscura*. Crary argues that the technology of the medium is taken to stand in place of certain body processes that are part of the observer. The camera reveals things that are not apparent to the observer with the naked eye, thus appearing to increase the observer's capacity for vision. But it also suggests that the camera's capacity for vision is unencumbered by the prejudices and idiosyncrasies of the observer, and this leads people to mistakenly assume that the camera does not lie, and that mediated vision offers a superior account of the world. In audience research, this perspective often leads to the assumption that what people see when they engage with the media should somehow 'match' the text.

For hundreds of years before the invention of photography, the *camera obscura* had been the most accurate technology of representation and image production. Crary (1994: 25) claims that it had provided a model of 'how truthful inferences about the external world' could be made. As a model of vision, the *camera obscura* suggested that the apparatus produced a more 'truthful' representation than personal observation. Crary claims that:

> Sensory evidence that depended in any way on the body was rejected in favour of the representation of this mechanical and monocular apparatus, whose authenticity was placed beyond doubt.
>
> (Crary 1994: 26)

He argued that the *camera obscura* represented vision as a mechanical procedure that placed the onus on individuals to judge their own vision against the publicly available 'evidence' produced by the *camera obscura* — limited in scope as this necessarily was. This perpetuated a fundamental misunderstanding about the *monocular* image produced by the *camera obscura*, because viewers fail to appreciate the level of interpretation their *binocular* vision bestows on its flat image. The monocular rhetoric of the *camera obscura* lingers still in the commonsense understanding of audiences as passive receivers of media information — their heads conceived as empty black boxes on which the monocular images of contemporary photographic media are imprinted. The scientific investigation of vision in the nineteenth century demonstrated the unhelpfulness of assuming that perception 'interferes' with the observation of reality. On the contrary, the development of optics demonstrated that it is not possible to observe reality except through the perceptual apparatus of the human body. In the same way, cultural studies of audiences have ensured that we now understand that people's experiences and lives are not incidental to their interpretation of media information, but are dynamically integrated with it.

Crary's work prompts us to reconsider how much of the discussion of 'the active audience', discussed at length in this and following chapters, is informed by the 'monocular' assumption that the media text is an object that can be correctly or incorrectly understood. We are reminded that mediated engagement with the world is not a transparent process. Audiences exist as individual people with 'interior' lives, patterned psychologically, physiologically and culturally by the flow of events and experiences they encounter. That 'interior' patterning influences the sense they make of the world around them. The ideal of an accurate match between the real and perceived worlds is an impossible one. It fails to take adequate account of the role of the observer in creating the world observed. But there are many different ways that the role of the observer can be influenced by mind, body and experience.

A somewhat different approach to the embeddedness of the human body in the process of viewing media images has emerged in the writing of contemporary film theorists committed to examining the deployment of *affect*-inducing imagery in feature films (see, for example, Carroll 1996; Plantinga and Smith 1999). They argue that while textual interpretation makes an important contribution to the study of film, it can inadvertently obscure the physicality of audience response. Where the emphasis on text and ideology in cultural studies in the 1980s minimized the importance of the physical as opposed to the interpretative work of the audience, these researchers set out to redress the privileging of interpretation by exploring the evolutionary basis of affect responses. Plantinga (1999), for example, has argued that film engages not just the mind, but also the body and the senses, especially in its use of facial expression to arouse audience affect. Affect is physiological. It is triggered by the sight of other human faces and by the sound of human and animal cries. The affect theorists explore how the represented face provokes mimicry of on-screen expression that, in turn, generates affect responses in the viewer. Plantinga therefore argues that audience engagements with film should be understood as being as physical as they are intellectual.

Engaging bodies: more physical dimensions of audience activity

A similar idea about the physicality of the interface between human bodies and the media is evident in Leppert's (1995) investigation of the nature of musical experience. Leppert's historical analysis of the class and gender divisions of labour in music-making made extensive use of data from paintings and drawings from the seventeenth to the nineteenth centuries. The images on which he based his argument depicted people listening to music or performing it. He traced the impact of musical 'sonority' — the physical impact of sound on the body — through its visual representation in art. While the study of listening audiences was not his primary purpose, Leppert's analysis reinforced an approach to understanding audiences that affirmed the whole-body nature of the listening experience. For Leppert, what it meant to listen to music in the past is deduced from an analysis of the ways the body offers itself as a canvas on which the impact of sound can be traced, and then recorded using a visual medium — in this case the painting, drawing or sketch.

Leppert's emphasis on sonority, on the impact of sound on the body, contrasts interestingly with Butsch's (2000) exploration of changes in the ways people act while *in audience* with theatrical and audio-visual performances. Butsch studied the changing nature of audiences in the United States from 1750 to 1990, and his analysis allows us to contrast the lack of physical restraint among theatre audiences in the past with the studied restraint of contemporary theatre audiences today, and with the radically individualized media engagements with broadcast media. He states, for example, that, 'Nineteenth-century audiences were, and were expected to be, very active' in accordance with a tradition of audience activity that had persisted from Elizabethan times and that:

> In Elizabethan theatres, courtiers and gallants treated theatre as their court where they could measure their importance by the attention they received. Fops sat on stage, interrupted performances, and even on occasion grabbed an actress. All of this annoyed the plebeian pit, who shouted, 'Away with them.' But pittites were hardly meek. They too ate, smoked, drank, socialised, and engaged in repartee with actors. Restoration theatre was more expensive and exclusive. Still, merchants and professional men, civil servants and their wives, and the critics (poets, writers, and competing playwrights) sat in the pit and squabbled, teased the women who sold oranges, baited the fops on stage, and wandered from pit to gallery and back. Nobility continued to sit on stage and in boxes, treating the theatre as a place to chat, play cards, argue and even occasionally duel.
>
> (Butsch 2000: 4)

Butsch draws attention to just how dramatically audiences have changed — in terms of where people can *be* audiences, how they engage with performers, with the work performed and with other members of the audience, and in terms of the extent to which their thinking about the mediated materials they encounter is open to public discussion and debate. His work provides an important complement to the exploration of the activities of contemporary audiences, and exemplifies how audience bodies are presupposed by the media in viewing, listening, reading and other audience activities. Taking a similarly long view of history, Anderson's (1991) explanation of how the introduction of print capitalism created conditions that facilitated the emergence of the nation state shows that the management of mass audiences can be seen today to act as protection for the maintenance of national sovereignty.

Print capitalism and imagined community

Anderson (1991) investigated the ways industrialization of communication media precipitate changes in the relationships between people and media that have unexpected repercussions. His argument is that newspaper reading in the nineteenth century fostered a political consciousness that enabled people to place themselves in imagined community with others, on the basis of recognition of shared interests in the achievement of economic, political, legal and scientific goals. The capacity to imagine one's personal interests as widely shared within a given territory by a given community of individuals contributed to the establishment of levels of political activism needed to effect the social changes required for the formation of the nation state. In a sense, Anderson's position challenges those who see the masses as being oppressed by the media, because it documents a period when well-placed sections of society were mobilized, energized and focused by the media. Communication media empowered readers to use that mobilization to consolidate their economic, political and legal interests.

In the case of the development of the European nation states, Anderson points out that reading publics for print products were made up of the literate, the mercantile classes and some sections of the aristocracy. The reading publics therefore consolidated the knowledge, wealth and political power of some (but not all) influential sections of society. He suggests that the 'reading publics' were produced by a combination of capitalist production and print technology, and that this combination changed the composition of the pre-existing knowledge and language hierarchies. Anderson cites 'language fatality' as a sign of this change, and as a significant factor in the establishment of the nation state because it contributed to a shake-up of the power structure. Where manuscript knowledge had been 'scarce and arcane lore', Anderson argues that print knowledge 'lived by reproducibility and dissemination' (1991: 37). Print production therefore precipitated a knowledge revolution that allowed new participants access to discourses of power and authority. Publishing in a vernacular language, rather than in an ecclesiastical and administrative language like Latin, made it possible for groups excluded from political and administrative power to pursue previously unimaginable political aspirations.

> The coalition between Protestantism and print-capitalism, exploiting cheap popular editions, quickly created large new reading publics — not least among merchants and women, who typically knew little or no Latin — and simultaneously mobilised them for politico-religious purposes.
>
> (Anderson 1991: 40)

Anderson identified three ways in which print-languages laid a foundation for the development of 'nation' consciousness. First, print-languages addressed a constituency below the elite languages but above the vernaculars of the common folk. This meant that the older elites and the aspirant classes were on an equal 'knowledge' footing. Second, print-languages gave a permanence or fixity to language by stabilizing spelling and grammar conventions. The materiality of the printed form allowed ideas to be more carefully analysed, and to be mulled over at leisure and in private. Third, print-languages brought change to the political status quo by privileging groups whose languages enjoyed print status. Spoken languages that were not, or could not, be printed gradually came to be considered 'vulgar' or 'sub-standard'. Because publishing was one of the earlier forms of capitalist enterprise, print-languages were linked to the expansion of capitalism, and to the opportunities it offered for access to economic activity.

Most importantly, print-languages created language monopolies that marginalized non-speakers at the same time that they created new alliances among reading publics. Anderson points out that the linguistic diversity and politically defined hierarchy among language groups that characterized monarchical realms gave way under print capitalism to consciousness of membership in 'imagined communities'. Imagined community allowed language groups and reading publics to combine in previously unimagined ways, and to organize collective action to ensure that their newly recognized common political and economic interests were secured.

Print capitalism was therefore a catalyst for change. Not only were print commodities made available to many more people, but those newly admitted to the ranks of the reading public were able to find ways to ensure that their ideas were also published (even if this meant using pseudonyms or noms-de-plume) and so read by others. The relative ease of participation in the print economy created a dramatic shift in the contemporary knowledge economy and in political consciousness.

Anderson's historical research teaches us the importance of looking at the bigger audience and media picture. Periods of rapid and dramatic communication change may produce media effects more dramatic than appetites for screen violence or so-called addiction to computer games might suggest. Yet we can only begin to appreciate the bigger picture when we recognize that audience formations (masses, fans, clubs, enthusiasts) are just as important a basis for audience research as individuals. Anderson's analysis draws attention to the significance of both mediatization and industrialization of cultural production. It documents the potential for socio-cultural change that is packaged, often unnoticed, alongside the media commodity. He recognizes that media have the capacity to dramatically alter our appreciation of time through the ways stories are told and information sequenced. And perhaps most importantly, he catalogues the pervasiveness of print capitalism as it rearranged the power and language structures that had previously held sway. The similarities between the impact of print-capitalism and the experiences of audiences in contemporary cyber-culture are unmistakable. This theme is taken up again in Chapter 7, because audiences are again searching for 'a new way of linking fraternity, power and time meaningfully together' (Anderson 1991: 36), but this time in the context of the information revolution.

Broadcasting and audience research

According to Butsch (2000), the introduction of broadcasting played a pivotal role in changing the 'collective dimension of public audiences, dispersing them to their homes'. This change took place very quickly. Radio was introduced in the 1920s and within ten years over half the homes in the USA had radio sets (Butsch 2000: 173). However, the rapid diffusion of radio amplified concerns about the potential use of mass media by foreign states for propaganda and persuasion purposes. The immense cost of introducing radio, in the USA at least, posed a funding challenge that was solved there by commercializing the sector. Smulyan (1994) has documented the political struggle that resulted in the decision that radio should be funded by advertising in the USA, even though many listeners were annoyed enough by programmes being interrupted to write letters of complaint to the stations.

The commercialization of radio in the USA had far-reaching consequences. Almost immediately it established a need for audience measurement, because advertisers and programme sponsors needed to know how many people were listening to justify their advertising expenditure. The first audience research tradition to develop, therefore, was ratings research (Beville 1988; see also Chapter 3). Early audience measurement research provided a service that allowed the broadcasting industries to manage audiences by adjusting the types of programmes funded to attract the largest numbers of listeners. The rating of radio programmes became the rationale for making decisions about which programmes to fund, how much should be allocated for programme production, and how much to pay everyone involved (from the executives to the performers and the cleaners). From a research perspective, ratings analysis was the first application of quantitative methods to audience research. From an investment perspective, ratings research made radio a more secure financial proposition. As we demonstrate in the next chapter, once the ratings system was established, it in effect transformed audiences into commodities. Because advertisers are attracted to the relative loyalty of audiences to their preferred programming, advertisers are able to decide how to target audiences with their advertisements. But audience loyalty also encouraged the development of strategies that would ensure standardization of production (Neuman 1991).

Broadcasting and the question of propaganda

Some recent historical studies draw attention to rather different aspects of industrialization that contributed to the displacement of the 'reading publics' of print capitalism by the mass audiences of broadcasting. Mattelart (2000), for example, characterizes the industrialization of communication in modernity by its emphasis on networking and circulation, on the development of standards (that is broadcasting standards, production standards, time standards, engineering standards), and on the impact of increased international communication on the initial development of an international consciousness. While the communication networks initially followed colonial ties, they had been transformed into geo-politically strategic information flows during World War 1, when the presses had been used to distribute propaganda to the enemy and to manipulate public opinion at home. Mattelart comments that:

> In both belligerent camps, the role of propaganda in the outcome of the war was such that it acquired a reputation of omnipotence. The apologetic discourse of the advertisers and political scientists who founded American sociology of the media transposed this wartime experience into peace-time. The idea developed that democracy could no longer do without modern techniques of 'invisible control of society at large,' both within the boundaries of the nation-state and beyond.
>
> (Mattelart 2000: 37)

Mattelart explicitly links the institutionalization of this strategic model of information and audience management to the influence of Walter Lippmann

(1922) and Harold Lasswell (1927), whose work, in somewhat different ways, provided examples of the transfer of the research agendas of military strategy to the commercial and educational spheres. Lippmann used his wartime experiences as the basis for the development of a theory of public opinion in relation to international peace, while Lasswell played a seminal role in the establishment of American sociology and wrote about the use of propaganda in wartime.

The earliest social research about media audiences therefore had its origin in wartime insecurity and paranoia, and was strongly influenced by concerns about national security. It sought to assist social administration rather than to question it. Working initially in the aftermath of the war, Merton (1968) had started to research media audiences when the impact of business and government on the research agendas of the day was intense. He described how market and government demands shaped the categories and concepts chosen for the analysis of media audiences by American social scientists. In his words:

> The purpose of a research helps determine its categories and concepts. The categories of audience measurement have accordingly been primarily those of income stratification (a kind of datum obviously important to those ultimately concerned with selling and marketing their commodities), sex, age, and education (obviously important for those seeking to learn the advertising outlets most appropriate for reaching special groups).
>
> (Merton 1968: 505)

Merton described his media research, by comparison, as a 'species of that genus of research which is concerned with the interplay between social structure and communications' (Merton 1968: 493), and as research that attempted to resist the continuing push towards 'campaign' (or propaganda) research. It is possible, therefore, to discern in his work both the influence of research demands emanating from government and industry interests, and an attempt to rationalize these with the theoretical sophistication of international academic social theory.

Crothers (1987: 86) has explained that Merton's sociology posited that institutional patterns shape the alternatives for social action available to individuals, and that individual actions invite response from others in terms of their beliefs about the social institution. This affects the individual's experience of the institution and then feeds back into the ways the institution is understood. For example, marriage is a social institution that generates certain social patterns for how individuals should or could act as married or unmarried couples or individuals. The ways that particular individuals act in relation to the institution of marriage (for example by deciding to marry, not to marry, to commit adultery or not, to divorce or to stay together) bring a range of reactions (perhaps condemnation, approval, physical attack — depending on the behaviour) from others. The nature of people's experiences in relation to the institution of marriage then feeds back into the operation of the institution and the patterns of social action it offers.

Merton's investigations into the media follow this pattern. The media are seen as a social institution that provides certain opportunities for engagement with media content. Individuals engage in media activities, but the nature of their engagement also provides important feedback on the state of the media as a social institution. While studies of audience size and composition, the central concern of advertisers and governments alike, had quickly taken a lead and focused audience research on audience measurement and composition, researchers like Merton and his colleagues were among the first to identify that empirical research about media audiences offered an insight into how social relations might be facilitated by the media in the broadcast era. His media research singled out processes of affiliation and the maintenance of group unity as they were played out in people's engagements with the media.

In his collaboration with Paul Lazarsfeld, Herta Herzog and other researchers at Columbia University in the 1940s, Merton helped shift the emphasis in audience research away from propaganda and onto a similar but strategically different agenda, that of 'content and response' analysis. Merton's interest in *anomie* (the experience of lack of direction resulting from social alienation), a concept he had adopted for use in the American context from Emile Durkheim (Crothers 1987: 34), left its mark in his audience research, in its commitment to explaining the affiliative dimensions of media use as a functionally meaningful and rewarding activity. He was interested in how the media make it bearable to live in a highly competitive, achievement-oriented, mass society. His work reflected an ongoing commitment to exploring *gesellschaft* in contemporary society. While unapologetically pragmatic and user-centred, determinedly functionalist, and committed to the development of social science by the quantification of research data and findings, his research is a kind of 'new world' search for class formations that are not inherited as a birthright, but cohere through self-selection as social formations. This model of affiliation is evident today in the studies of fan and internet communities (see Chapters 6 and 7 of this work).

Audiences and propaganda events

In 1949 Merton (1968: 570) had researched the effectiveness of using mass media for purposes of propaganda and persuasion. The goal had been to explain when propaganda and persuasion work, and when they don't. To this end, Merton first analysed the propaganda and then asked the research participants to discuss it. 'Content analysis' and 'response analysis' of published or broadcast messages were systematically compared. Merton and his colleagues used content and response analysis to pinpoint the communication problems inherent in the structure of the media message. This involved judging how well the sender's intentions had been expressed by comparing it with how well the information was understood. For 'response-analysis' Merton advocated the use of focused interviews (see Morrison 1998 — reprinted in Nightingale and Ross 2003). On the basis of his content and response analysis, Merton identified a communication effect he called 'the boomerang effect'. The 'boomerang effect' occurs when peoples' responses to propaganda are 'wholly unanticipated'. It was used to pinpoint the errors of judgement senders make in constructing media messages, and it depended on a process called 'deviant case analysis' that involved paying particular attention to the unexpected responses people made to the media content.

Merton described four types of boomerang effect: The first type of boomerang effect can occur when people do not have the background knowledge to understand the technical language used or the references made in the propaganda material. In this situation, Merton claimed listeners are likely to respond to propaganda initially with impatience, then disbelief and finally distrust. The second type of boomerang effect occurs when the audience is 'psychologically heterogeneous'; when there is no consistency of 'states of mind on a given issue'. This makes it extremely difficult to integrate diverse interests or particular references within the message. The third boomerang effect occurs when the propaganda is structurally flawed because 'different themes in the same piece of propaganda [work] at cross-purposes'. While more easily corrected, this effect predisposes people to come to unintended conclusions because they cannot reconcile the components of the message into a meaningful whole. And finally the fourth type of boomerang effect occurs when parts of the audience are familiar with, or have first-hand experience of, the issue at hand. These people 'consult their own experience' in deciding how to respond to the message, and Merton claimed that respondents reject it out of hand if it fails to recognize the authenticity of their experience (see Merton 1968: 571–7).

In the description of the boomerang effect, Merton's use of the term 'effects' is very different from contemporary usage of the word in media studies. The 'effects' identified by Merton's team at Columbia University were produced by the interaction of media materials and participant interpretations, and interestingly, they were not 'behaviours' so much as misunderstandings. The reason for the misinterpretation was attributed to faults in the message construction, and not to cultural differences among research participants. Merton understood the audience response to media messages as the means by which belonging or affiliation with the broader social process could be expressed. Industrialization distances people from each other, and intensifies competitiveness, individualism and a preoccupation with achievement. In this context people seek affiliation with others in ways that make sense in terms of personal interests and meaning agendas. It is therefore not so surprising that, following their collaboration with Merton, Katz and Lazarsfeld (1965/1955) focused on the ways people use the media to create personal knowledge specializations that attract others to them.

Personal influence and communication flows

In the introduction to their book, *Personal Influence: The Part Played by People in the Flow of Mass Communication*, Katz and Lazarsfeld (1955/1964) drew attention to a polarity in (then) contemporary views about the mass media. They claimed that at that time, most people thought of the mass media either as evidence of the dawn of a new era in democracy, or alternatively as the means by which people were likely to be stripped of their capacity for independent thought and action. Whichever view people held, Katz and Lazarsfeld explained, the same understanding of the *process* of mass communication was assumed to operate:

> Their image, first of all, was of an atomistic mass of millions of readers, listeners and moviegoers prepared to receive the Message; and secondly, they pictured every Message as a direct and powerful stimulus to action, which would elicit immediate response. In short, the media of communication were looked upon as a new kind of unifying force — a simple kind of nervous system — reaching out to every eye and ear, in a society characterized by an amorphous social organization and a paucity of interpersonal relations.
>
> (Katz and Lazarsfeld 1965/1955: 16)

This, they argued, was the context that produced the traditional divisions (or specializations) in media research that by then characterized the field: audience study, content analysis, and effects analysis. Since word usage changes over time, it seems worth noting the distinction they made between effects analysis and audience study. In the 1950s, the term 'audience study' referred to the work now performed by audience measurement services: definition of the size and composition of audiences in particular reception fields, and to the various types of quantitative analysis this information permits. Their use of the term, 'effects analysis', by contrast, seems to change in the course of the research. In the earlier chapters of their book they link effects to intervening variables, but in the later sections they shift decisively to a causal effects position, arguing that since influence is linked to exposure, opinion leaders are themselves likely to be more influenced than others.

The approach initially taken to the study of personal influence was to investigate an **intervening variable** in the interaction between the mass media and the masses. They identified four intervening variables they considered particularly pertinent for media studies: exposure; medium; content; and 'attitudes and predispositions' of audience members. Noting that media studies research (then) addressed only one question (viz. 'what can the media do?'), they had lamented that most attention had been devoted to the investigation of what they called media *campaigns*, 'Campaigns to influence votes, to sell soap, to reduce prejudice' (Katz and Lazarsfeld 1965/1955: 19). They felt that the focus of media research had been placed too firmly on how to devise media messages that would influence people, or persuade them to change their minds. Such an approach closed off research possibilities prematurely, and unnecessarily limited the research agenda available to the social scientist. In this context, the study of *intervening variables* offered a way to open up the assumptions covered over by the 'media-and-the-masses' focus of other contemporary work.

Overall, Katz and Lazarsfeld's research documented the ways patterns of engagement with the media could be used to identify people to whom others turn for advice. They described this process as a 'two step flow' — where opinion leaders in particular spheres (public affairs, movies, fashion, and so on) access media information which is then sought and acted on by others in their networks of associates and in their communities. The surprise finding of the research was that the *influentials* were less likely to be community leaders than *specialists* in particular fields where media knowledge gave them an advantage. Their expertise in engaging meaningfully with the media marked them as possessing specialist knowledge about the types of information the media provide, and how to put it to good use in everyday life. *Influentials* spent a lot of time using the media, and had developed the capacity to integrate their media-derived experience in their daily lives. The *personal influence* research marked a deepening of focus on audience participants and their activities. Katz and Lazarsfeld used terms like 'discovering the people' to explain their attempt to reposition studies of audience by looking beyond the 'exposure' mind-set. They sought to uncover the hidden processes that govern the working of a mass audience they assumed to be culturally homogeneous. In this respect they approached American society as a cultural whole, where position and status was sought and won in diverse fields of influence.

By centring their research on an intervening variable, Katz and Lazarsfeld drew attention (as Merton and Lazarsfeld had done earlier) to the fact that things happen when people are *in audience with* the media. The problem is that the things that happen are intangible, experienced as thoughts, fleeting impressions or emotions. They occur almost imperceptibly, as friends ask what you thought of a certain film or whether the latest fashions are worth following. In this sense, media events are difficult to pin down. According to Merton (1967) this is precisely the sort of problem the concept of the *intervening variable*, first formulated by Durkheim (1930), was designed to address. Durkheim had suggested that, 'It is necessary . . . to substitute for the internal fact which escapes us an external fact that symbolises it and to study the former through the latter' (cited in Merton 1967: 146).

Now audience is a classic example of just such a happening. An event occurs but its full significance cannot be directly observed. The accounts people give of what happened to them while they were in audience provide a representation (but not a full account) of the event. By focusing on personal attitudes and predispositions, Katz and Lazarsfeld had sought to expose the interiorized dimensions of the audience event for analysis. They offered a rationale for the later focus on heavy and light media exposure and the hypotheses about its social and cultural effects (Gerbner and Gross 1976), and for the more psychology-driven research into motivations for viewing that characterizes the **uses and gratifications** approach. However, in its insistence on the importance of audience activities, the functionalist approach had reduced the attention paid to production processes and to the analysis of media content. And it remained administrative in its orientation. Like studies of audience measurement and composition, it naturalized the perspective of the network manager, the advertising executive and government policy-maker.

The pragmatism of functionalism versus the communality of cultural action

The 1970s marked the period of the first stage of transition from industrial society to the Information Age. Information richness provided the conditions for an unprecedented global mobilization of people, money, technology, ideas and media (Appadurai 1997: 33), and this in turn had a dramatic impact on the sense of cultural unity that had characterized understandings of the nation state since the late eighteenth century.

As indigenous and marginalized groups began to stake their claims to cultural territory and access to national broadcasting opportunities, the assumption that it was benign to assume that technocrats, administrators and business managers were capable of providing a one-size-fits-all media service came in for heavy criticism. In audience research this confrontation presented itself in the critique of the functionalist approach for its lack of a theory of popular culture (Nightingale 2003). The debate was also about audience activity. Where the functionalist approaches were shifting towards individual psychological explanations of media activity, the cultural approaches were demanding recognition of the cultural dimensions of media engagement.

The 'uses and gratifications' approach presented itself as the flowering of functionalism in audience research (Blumler and Katz 1974), yet turned away from the social theory that had underpinned Merton's early application of European theories to media research. Instead it promoted an individualistic understanding of mass communication.

So what exactly was the 'uses and gratifications' approach, and why was it so widely respected before the 'cultural revolution' in audience research (Nightingale 2003)? 'Uses and gratifications' investigated the socio-psychological motivations for the information-seeking activity of audiences. Blumler and Katz (1974), the chief protagonists of the 'uses and gratifications' approach, considered their work to be a development of earlier functionalist research in media studies that sought to match media content with audience response. They presented 'uses and gratifications' as the third phase in a long-term functionalist media research initiative. In their view, the first phase had demonstrated, 'The "feel" and quality of audience attachment to mass communication in its own right' (Blumler and Katz 1974: 13). The second phase had pioneered the application of quantitative analysis in audience research, and established that, 'The tendencies for audience members to seek certain satisfactions from media content could be measured and deployed in quantitative analysis' (1974: 13). And 'uses and gratifications', the third phase, demonstrated that the individual media choices of audiences could be statistically analysed to demonstrate the social functions performed by the media. They describe the approach as being:

> Concerned with (1) the social and psychological origins of (2) needs, which generate (3) expectations of (4) the mass media or other sources, which lead to (5) differential patterns of media exposure (or engagement in other activities), resulting in (6) need gratifications and (7) other consequences, perhaps mostly unintended ones.
>
> (1974: 20)

The 'uses and gratifications' approach shifted attention away from the media and from media content, and focused directly on the role of the audience, stressing the use of media to satisfy social and psychological needs. In a complete break with the earlier functionalist traditions, the interest in the mass media, as a social institution, was discarded as a 'more or less "elitist"' concern, and audiences were positioned centre stage as the controllers of media effects.

One of the most attractive features of the 'uses and gratifications' approach is the plausibility of its project. It sounds like an account anyone might offer of their viewing practices, yet it has been almost completely abandoned today because of its low explanatory power. The problem is that both social and psychological needs are context specific, but 'uses and gratifications' offers only an individualistic explanation of audience behaviour. 'Uses and gratifications' was most successful in explaining media use in extreme situations, like war, natural disasters or elections, when otherwise diverse communities are united in their 'need' for specific information. Peled and Katz (1974: 66), for example, investigated the viewer expectations generated during the Yom Kippur war of October 1973, discovering that:

> Television was seen as the primary medium for relief of tension. Action adventure programs served as agents of catharsis, distracting attention from real-life tensions by focusing on fictional tension. Television programs on Israeli and Jewish themes gratified the demand for a heightened feeling of social solidarity.

But even in this research the war figured as little more than a setting for individual viewing, rather than as a context that patterns the meaning of media information.

In a very different type of 'uses and gratifications' project, Greenberg (1974) investigated which young people sought particular types of gratification from their television viewing. He found eight clusters of reasons for media choices by young people. These included a) to pass time; b) to forget; c) to learn about things; d) to learn about myself; e) for arousal; f) for relaxation; g) for companionship; and h) as a habit (Greenberg 1974: 72–3). A questionnaire was then devised and completed by classroom groups of children of various ages. Whilst the detail of Greenberg's findings cannot be adequately represented here, six of the eight gratifications identified as significant in the pre-test were also rated as 'significant' by the questionnaire's respondents: learning, habit, arousal, companionship, relaxation and to forget. In presenting his summary, however, Greenberg commented on the circularity of the 'uses and gratifications' approach:

> Skirted entirely in this type of study is the question of whether the data referred to are motivations sought, gratifications received, or combinations of these. Surely what a child derives from television may well include some portion of what he sought, else he would turn elsewhere for these gratifications, but the specific extent to which this is the case remains unexamined.
>
> (1974: 89)

An undoubted drawback in the 'uses and gratifications' approach was the assumption that mass communication is no more than need gratification, and that media effects are demonstrated by people's ability to indicate that their needs have been gratified.

But focusing on the shortcoming of its method obscures the central important achievement of the approach. In the 1970s it had become common in much **left criticism** of the media and in media effects research to describe the mass audience as passive, existing simply to soak up the ceaseless flow of popular programming (Neuman 1991). The 'uses and gratifications' approach was the first to champion the cause of 'the active audience'. It shifted the emphasis from what the media do to people, and placed the issue of what people do with the media firmly on the research agenda. Instead of focusing on the ways human bodies, needs and motivations are co-opted by the media, however, 'uses and gratifications' perpetuated the cyborg myth of human supremacy, expressed through the ideology of individualism. In other words, the 'uses and gratifications' approach implied that audiences were unaffected by the industrialization of culture. This omission became the space that emerging research teams would decide to interrogate. By ignoring the fact that the media are an industry, 'uses and gratifications' left the door open for a challenge from researchers with a better-developed sense of the cultural significance of the political economy of the media.

For some popular culture theorists of the mid-1970s (for example, Carey and Krieling 1974), 'uses and gratifications' research was a debasement rather than an enhancement of the functionalist approach. It crossed the line from sociologically grounded investigations that Merton and others had used to link media research to the work of social theorists like Max Weber, Emile Durkheim, Karl Mannheim and Talcott Parsons (see Crothers 1987), to an individualist social psychology preoccupied with motivations, needs and gratifications. The 'uses and gratifications' approach played down the connection of media research to social theory, and positioned itself in the field of social psychology, where the study of motivation had long been a central concern.

The shortcomings of 'uses and gratifications' motivated researchers, particularly those in the United Kingdom, to frame their approaches to audience research within different theory traditions. Their work reflected the centrality of issues of class and subculture in British social research. The two British approaches discussed in this section are the **political economy approach** (for example, Halloran et al. 1970), and the **culture theory approach** (Hall 1980 — reprinted in Nightingale and Ross 2003). Because the British research was premised on the existence of differences within the cultural totality it was better placed to articulate with the cultural complexity of the Information Age. In the USA the **naturalistic research paradigm** (Lindlof 1987; Lull 1990) had also challenged the narrowness of the 'uses and gratifications' focus on needs and gratifications. The naturalistic research paradigm drew on symbolic interactionism, seeking the political in the personal by showing media engagements to be 'rule governed' (Lull 1990), but remained unable to articulate a convincing connection with the emerging context of cultural diversity in the Information Age. All drew back from the individualist orientation that had surfaced in 'uses and gratifications'.

Emerging approaches in the 1970s proposed instead that audience activity should be researched using phenomenological or ethnographic methods rather than quantitative methods, and that audiences should be researched as communities or cultures. The British approaches situated audiences within an overarching theory of popular culture that would permit critical analysis of the media and media content (Nightingale 1996: 43–53). The British preference for using urban ethnographies for the study of audiences and other subculture formations (Hebdige 1979) meant that they were well placed to promote a different understanding of audiences that saw them as performers of culture rather than as passive receivers of information services. The presence of a textual dimension in the cultural approach aligned it with changes then taking place in literary theory (Tompkins 1980; Fish 1980), and to studies in art and literary theory, drawing in particular on the British culturalist traditions and on the European structuralisms (Levi-Strauss 1978; Althusser 1971).

Audiences, professional practice and political process

As noted earlier, the coordinated study of media content and audience response had characterized the work of Merton and Lazarsfeld, and it was to this earlier model that researchers of the late 1960s and early 1970s returned. By the late 1960s, the interest in intervening variables had all but disappeared, and mixed-method research of this type had been replaced by specialist research areas devoted to the investigation of media politics, media production processes and media content analysis. Audience research was marginalized (see, for example, the media agenda laid out in Curran, Gurevitch and Woollacott 1971). At this point, British researchers interested in the study of media industries and the sociology of the professions (Elliott 1972) were questioning the political and economic control exercised over mass audiences. They brought to audience research a more sophisticated class-based interrogation of broadcast culture, and used it to evaluate both journalism practice and audience interpretation. The result (see Halloran et al. 1970) was media research that attracted considerable international attention at the time because it tracked the processes of news production alongside the gradual transformation of a public event into a broadcast news item, and finally as a topic of conversation among viewers. Halloran, Elliott and Murdock were committed to the development of, 'a comprehensive strategy which would include the study of the mass media as social institutions and of mass communication as a social process, both within the wider social system' (18). The research team therefore chose to examine the news-making process and the media content it produced, followed by a hurriedly put together study of viewer reactions to the reporting. The decision to investigate the coverage of a large anti-Vietnam War rally linked the media process to the wider (international) political context. The aim was to elucidate the role the media plays in contemporary politics.

The *Demonstrations and Communication* (Halloran et al. 1970) research demonstrated some fundamental differences from media research practices prevailing at the time. First, the focus was on a public event of considerable political interest. Second, the politics of the newsroom, where decisions were made as to what should be broadcast and how, played an important role in the research. The reportage was examined and viewer reactions to the media reports were not assumed to be 'gratifications' or to be psychologically based, but to reflect the ways the media coverage predisposed audience reactions to the news items. The researchers stated that they wanted to investigate the consequences 'for general knowledge and for social and political attitudes' of agenda setting and news coverage, and to examine reactions to the representation of violence and aggression in a news context (238). In other words, the media event was seen as an integral component of British political life, and news production, news content and viewer reactions were all treated as equally important contributing elements in the making of the real-world event as a media event. Perhaps the most important difference from prevailing research was that mass communication was not seen as the actions of the media on the masses. Rather the media and the masses were seen as dimensions of an overarching political process.

Because this research was hastily pulled together, the audience component was not as carefully planned nor as meticulously executed as research in the functionalist tradition. The plan had been to explore audience reactions as political process, so participants were sought from groups likely to hold very different views about the demonstration and its political importance. The groups chosen for inclusion were the police, students, and 'neutrals' — people 'selected at random from lists of adults attending classes at two university extra-mural centres' (Halloran et al. 1970: 241). All participants were asked to watch the news bulletins on the day of the demonstration, and to complete a questionnaire. In addition, discussion groups were organized to view the news as a group and to discuss the coverage. The researchers showed that all the research participants were likely to accept the news reportage as appropriate since they had no grounds on which to dispute the claims made. In general, though, the police held more conservative values and described themselves as less interested in politics than the neutrals and students. The student groups were less conformist than the neutrals and the police. The lack of critical comment from all groups was noted, and the extent to which the shared news values of all media contributed to this complacency was questioned. While the research participants freely used their own experiences to evaluate the general political situation, this critical perspective did not extend to the news coverage itself.

This project marked the beginning of a series of new interventions in audience research. The strength of its grounding in social theory made it possible for media sociologists and others to imagine how media research might be done differently, and how audience research might be a necessary component of such a development. The focus on class and media representation was extended to studies of racist practices by media professionals (Hartman and Husband 1974), and to the impact of such practices on ethnic identity. This study was the forerunner of contemporary research (see Chapters 6 and 7) that explores the place of media in the lives of exile and diaspora communities (Ross 1996; Gillespie 2000; Husband 2000; Sreberny 2000).

Mediatization and cultural worlds

Earlier, we noted that media technologies engage audiences because their design interfaces with, and amplifies, sensory dimensions of the human body. The 'body-sensitivity' of media illustrates the radical reconceptualization of cultural production, and the role of audiences in it, that preoccupied cultural researchers from the 1970s to the 1990s. The field of cultural research was radically reoriented by the underlying socio-cultural changes then taking place in the approaches to the industrial production of communication services and cultural works. Raymond Williams (1974) noticed that commercialization of the media and its *flow* technology dramatically lessened the importance attributed to any one text, and privileged the continuous supply of cultural material over the quality of cultural work. Williams's (1974) insight adds weight to Kellerman's (2000) observation that by the early 1970s, the preconditions for the information revolution were already in place. Kellerman (2000: 538) argues that information and knowledge were replacing 'labour and possibly also capital as leading production factors'. This change in the basis of economic production was accelerated by the privatization and *laissez-faire* ideology of capitalism, the information practices demanded by the Cold War, and the mass audience demand for 'constant and rich transmission of written and oral information' (539).

While communication media are body-sensitive at the level of the individual human, these observations suggest that, at the level of mass audiences also, the macro-dimensions of mediatization depend on communal forms of body sensitivity. At the very least these are likely to be linked to the differential availability of media consumers over the time-space of a whole day or a whole week. But the recognition that product flows rather than individual works are what the media produces points us in a different direction, forcing us to recognize the significance of textual flows rather than of particular texts. The context of reception shifts to centre stage where audiences play a greater role in defining the cultural significance of individual texts and of texts in general (Williams 1974). So, nowadays we talk about going to the movies, rather than going to see a particular film, and we talk about watching television rather than selecting individual programmes. We wait with baited breath for the release of the next film in the *Harry Potter* oeuvre, *The Lord of the Rings* or the *Matrix* trilogies. This *flow* logic also holds for radio and the internet. Flow treats texts as interchangeable and interruptible, rather than as unique, complete and irreplaceable. A cultural production system that operates on a flow logic adopts its own characteristic techniques to interpolate audiences.

The concept of 'flow' has philosophical ramifications linked to theories of time and space that we cannot deal with in this book. Instead, we reflect initially only on how the concept has been used by Williams in order to suggest some reasons why the issue of audience activity became a matter for cultural analysis rather than simply media management in the 1970s and 1980s. When Williams described the flow of an evening's entertainment on television, he approached it from the perspective of the problems flow poses for textual analysis. He was puzzled, when viewing television during a visit to the USA, by the difficulty of pinning down the television text for analysis, by the degree of textual rupture given the choice between channels, and by the way advertisements interrupted the rhythm of the text. Williams described his experience in the following way:

> Nothing is at all reported fully, though time had been made for the theft of a barn in a distant state. Yet the flow of hurried items establishes a sense of the world: of surprising and miscellaneous events coming in, tumbling over each other from all sides. The events are caught as they fly, with a minimal and conventional interpretative tag. The most ordered messages, with a planned use of sight and sound, are the recorded commercials, which clearly operate in the same communicative dimension. Voices are used in both news and commercials to catch passing attention.
>
> (Williams 1974: 116)

On the basis of his observation of American television, Williams concluded that the televisual text was better understood as 'an evening's viewing', and he engaged in some speculation as to how such a 'text' might be read. But the broader conclusions he drew indicated his early recognition that the flow of television promoted a complete change in the nature of cultural value in that it replaced communal sensibility with consumer demand:

> This general trend, towards an increasing variability and miscellaneity of public communications, is evidently part of a whole social experience. It has profound connections with the growth and development of greater physical and social mobility, in conditions both of cultural expansion and of consumer rather than community cultural organization. Yet until the coming of broadcasting the normal expectation was still of a discrete event or of a succession of discrete events. People took a book or a pamphlet or a newspaper, went out to a play or a concert or a meeting or a match, with a single predominant expectation and attitude. The social relationships set up in these various cultural events were specific and in some degree temporary.
>
> (Williams 1974: 88)

The flow of television added a new dimension to the deployment of information, in Williams's view one that broke with previous patterns of engagement with texts. But his cultural perspective also appreciated that such a reorganization brought with it profound changes in cultural practices by mass audiences. Williams's analysis of broadcasting therefore showed that a cultural account of popular culture would of necessity include a radically different type of analysis of audiences than was possible using the approaches developed for functionalist social science in the USA. His work was, in many ways, a stimulus for the development of cultural approaches to the study of audiences (Nightingale 1996).

Encoding and decoding: the cultural patterning of audience activity

The *encoding/decoding* approach (Hall 1980) extended the political initiative started by Halloran, Elliott and Murdock (1974), but expressed itself more explicitly as an attack on the hegemonic position of American positivist research and pursued a cultural agenda. Where the 'uses and gratifications' approach was based on an understanding of audiences as individuals, the 'encoding/decoding' approach considered audiences to be culturally formed and situated, significant as formations rather than as individuals. Hall (1980) envisaged the encoding/decoding project as an initiative that was capable of demonstrating how *hegemony* operates through popular culture. The encoding/decoding model proposed that audiences actively contribute to the political process by the ways they deal with media meanings — by accepting, negotiating or rejecting the ideas advocated by the media. The activity of accepting, rejecting or negotiating was thought of less as the activity of individuals, and more as activity through which culture in general, and the particular cultural location of the respondent in particular, was expressed. Mass communication was seen as 'a structure produced and sustained through the articulation of linked but distinctive moments — production, circulation, distribution/ consumption, reproduction' (Hall 1980: 28). Hall argued that the advantage of this approach was, first, that it could offer an account of how the media are an integrated component of the social order and as such actively maintain the existing power structure; and second, that by understanding mass communication as a 'passage of forms' (28) where the story being told changes as it is reworked by subsequent groups of cultural workers, the discursive process by which culture operates would be revealed. The meaning of the programme or cultural work was theorized as incomplete until the audience had both consumed and reproduced it in a way that makes sense within the contexts of everyday life.

The encoding/decoding approach lessened the importance attached to any one text (for example, the television programme or the advertisement) as the bearer of cultural meaning, and made it clear that communication does not occur just because a TV programme or an advertisement has been made. It also demonstrated that while messages could privilege the likelihood of certain interpretations in a given audience, they did not have the power to determine interpretation. The message could not dictate what meanings it would be called on to generate by its next user. Interpretation was understood to depend on the generosity of the audience who make time to engage with it and 'reproduce' it in the contexts of their everyday worlds.

The encoding/decoding approach proposed that the dominating power of the media could be demonstrated by investigating discourses and meanings at the 'moments' when power was exercised, rather than by pursuing a preoccupation with the individual needs or motivations of individual audience participants, or a political economic analysis of the structures and processes at work in media industries — though these were of course recognized as relevant and important. The activity of the audience was redefined in two ways — it was conceived as interpretive rather than psychological and as political rather than personal. When Hall (1980: 135) referred to 'selective perception', it was in the context of a discussion of where to begin to define a different research practice for the cultural approach. He argued that, 'Selective perception is almost never as selective, random or privatised as the concept suggests', and advocated looking for the patterns of response that reveal the political impact of media discourses.

One of the more interesting aspects of the encoding/decoding model is its emphasis on 'discourse' over the participants in the event. Superficially, the approach may appear to repeat the simple coupling of message and audience interpretation pioneered by Merton (1968). For example, one of the first studies based on the encoding/decoding model presented a textual analysis of the evening news magazine programme, *Nationwide* (Brunsdon and Morley 1978). That research was complemented by research with audiences for the same programme (Morley 1980). Morley interviewed groups of people from various walks of life after they had viewed an episode of *Nationwide*, and noted how they discussed the items included in the programme. He then mapped the responses in terms of the political stance taken, showing that responses were politically patterned. The two components of the *Nationwide* project did not, however, dovetail particularly well. For example, it was not possible to clearly demonstrate the impact of the programme's rhetorical features in the audience talk about the programme. Instead, the research outcomes suggested that the socio-cultural situation of viewers was strongly implicated in the meanings they created about the programme. In other words, the meaning structures involved in 'decoding' proved more useful for explaining the cultural positioning of the viewers, in terms of class and proximity to socio-cultural power, than of showing how the media contributed to such understandings.

The encoding/decoding approach encouraged researchers to investigate audience talk more rigorously than had previously been the case, and also to investigate the communities where talk is both produced and 'normalized'. This change represented an important new direction for audience research. Instead of investigating individuals, researchers began to focus on other sorts of audience groups and communities, particularly marginalized or disadvantaged groups. For example, youth subcultures and ethnic communities, who utilize media materials in characteristic ways and/or create media materials that express their socio-cultural location and their experiences of the dominant culture, became and remain the focus of ethnographic documentation (see Hebdige 1979; Gray 1987; Buckingham 1993). Second, dispersed communities of viewers, listeners and readers, people who share sets of interests based on the contribution particular media materials make to their sense of identity (like fans), were and continue to be investigated (Hobson 1982; Jenkins 1992a; Markham 1998; Baym 2000). Community groups and groups with special media needs (like children, people with disabilities), especially groups that share both socio-cultural location and interests in media materials, have also been the focus of yet more interest (Buckingham 1993; Ross 2001). Somewhat unfortunately, however, the community focus of the cultural approach has sidelined the investigation of mass audiences by focusing only on the operations of cultural power in marginal, hybrid and other 'exotic' audience groups and activities. This has blunted the overall political edge of cultural research as a means to influence cultural policy.

Globalization, mediatization and industrialization

In the quotation with which we began this chapter, Raymond Williams drew attention to how the introduction of television had prompted examination of the ways it combined and changed earlier media forms. The introduction of interactive media in the late twentieth century has had a similar impact on the questions we ask about contemporary media and the changes new media seem to be bringing about. This change has generated an unprecedented level of interest in audiences — in when people are audiences, what they do as audiences, what types of communal or cultural ties pattern their engagements with media and cultural texts and how media presuppose and predict the human proclivities of audiences.

In the 30 years since Williams wrote, academics investigating audiences have challenged the opposition he postulated between consumerism and community by mounting a determined effort to show the persistence of community in the experience of consumer culture (see Chapter 6). This research has helped us to recognize that people frequently create 'community-like' structures (fan clubs, associations, subscription services) to make their access to and enjoyment of mediated entertainment and information more comfortable and less alienating. But the fixation with community has deflected attention from the challenge, inherent in Williams's observation, that theorization of consumption and its links with 'the growth and development of greater physical and social mobility' might prove equally important for understanding the relationship between media and audiences.

In this chapter we have reflected on how mediatization itself, and the industrialization of media production and distribution that flows from it, have both generated concern about audiences and provided the problems audience researchers seek to solve. In particular we have seen that the problematics that frame audience research oscillate between celebration of the benefits of new media and the dread of undue dependence on them. Today, the digitalization, computerization and mobilization of telephony generates almost daily press speculation that the mobile phone is fragmenting the computer — miniaturizing, mobilizing and fragmenting its interactive capacity across a diverse array of new digital media that bind people into the consumerist capitalism of contemporary democracy. Such changes, unfolding now, echo the reverberations felt at the introduction of television, but also challenge the 'information and entertainment' logic that has until recently defined the television industry. Making media more mobile, extending the range of media we engage with in the course of doing other things, weaves human bodies into new audience phenomena for which we seek precedents from our cultural history. For audiences, the introduction of interactive media has brought with it unprecedented opportunities for engaging more actively with both new and old media. Connectivity and networking put a different, and more active, spin on discussion about what audiences *do*, and this in turn challenges us to reconsider both the foundational audience activities — viewing, listening and reading — and the ways the social and cultural meaning of these activities has changed over the years.

In important senses, industrialization of media production in the nineteenth and early twentieth centuries was linked to nationalism and nationalist imaginings (Anderson 1991). Audience research had its beginnings in the wartime threat to security of the nations so formed. In recent years, however, the cultural hegemony of the state has been strongly challenged by globalization. The 'rise of the network society' (Castells 1996) has meant that the impact of globalization has been felt throughout the world. Transnational companies (for example Microsoft, MacDonalds, Sony) and international organizations (for example the United Nations, international aid organizations, and countless others), shift their spheres of operations and displace the checks and balances that national governments had earlier developed to protect the social security, human rights and cultural interests of their citizens.

Empowered by new information technologies, the process of globalization has dispersed ethnic and cultural communities geographically, but allowed them to maintain and expand as networks of influence with worldwide reach (Castells 1998). Access to a media presence is essential for the maintenance of such community. This is why Castells has argued that, 'Cultural battles are the power battles of the information age' (1998: 348). Clearly cultural approaches to the study of media audiences are essential in such a context. The nature of the appropriation of cultural power through the establishment of global audience formations is addressed today by the focus in ethnographic approaches to audience research which stress the communication rights and communicative relevance of diaspora audiences (Naficy 1993; Gillespie 2000).

From an audience perspective, the effects of globalization can be seen in the spread of global media networks and the cultural transformation of audiences from mass viewing and listening publics to interactive networks of affiliations and personal interest. Globalization has intensified research interest in the ways marginalized communities position themselves vis-à-vis mainstream media production, and in the protective action available to traditional and indigenous cultures (Jakubowicz 2001; Meadows 2002). The ethnic diversity of contemporary global culture provides character and identity templates that give meaning to, and enhance pleasure in, engagement with global culture. But while global culture has created space for greater diversity of cultural expression, it has also increased the rate of cultural change and of assimilation of cultural difference (Naficy 1993). And it is by no means certain that cultural research alone will prove sufficient for solving the problems encountered by audience formations in the future.

Further reading

Anderson, B. (1983, 1991) *Imagined Communities: Reflections on the Origin and Spread of Nationalism*, revised edn. London and New York: Verso.

Merton, R.K. ([1949] 1979) Patterns of influence: a study of interpersonal influence and of communications behaviour in a local community, in P.F. Lazarsfeld and F.N. Stanton (eds) *Communications Research: 1948–1949*. New York: Harper & Brothers.

Merton, R.K. (1968) *Social Theory and Social Structure*, enlarged edn. New York: The Free Press/London: Collier Macmillan.

Morrison, D.E. (1999) *Defining Violence: The Search for Understanding*. Luton: University of Luton Press.

Nightingale, V. (1996) *Studying Audiences: The Shock of the Real*. London and New York: Routledge.

AUDIENCE COMMODITIES AND AUDIENCE ACTIVISM

Whereas the key to the children's market used to be the products, the branding and the marketing, tomorrow's winners will be those that first find ways to make children true stakeholders of the company and so part of the company's destiny. Tomorrow's winners are those that realise that they need children to reach children.

(Antorini 2003: 212)

Media industries are not immune from the impact of social and cultural change. The increasing complexity of the media environment affects all stakeholders in the media, including audiences. A recent book by Lindstrom and Seybold, *Brandchild* (2003), from which the above quotation is taken, envisages a future where consumer identities are so integrated with product branding that cultural identities that lie outside the sphere of consumption will be of secondary importance in the development of personal identity. It demonstrates the closeness of the relationship imagined between customers and services promoted by the new customer focus in marketing. This new focus blurs the distinction between commercial and social science research and advocates the mediatization of all aspects of cultural life. Whether it is appropriate or not, commercial research undertaken to make marketing more successful is increasingly presented as social science and/or cultural research. This is the case in Lindstrom and Seybold's book, and it also characterizes the positioning of ratings research by Webster et al. (2000).

This chapter explores the relationship between broadcasting and ratings analysis, and introduces the key terms used in ratings practice, before examining a range of perspectives that have been used to criticize ratings and the impact of ratings on the system of mass communication. It returns to the question, introduced by Meehan (1984), of whether ratings research is social science or an industry service. It identifies and analyses the underlying assumptions of the industry service model of audience research, before looking at some of the unexpected ways the imagination and sometimes desperation of particular audience communities has motivated them to an audience activism. Such activism allows them to present stories, ways of thinking and cultural histories that are fundamental to their personal (identity) survival, but which are neglected in mainstream media's programming.

As the repercussions of media convergence change the power balances between broadcasting and user-pays media, more and more audience activities are being mediatized and subjected to commercial control. The withdrawal of arts funding by governments has added to this shift from public patronage to commercial development and exploitation of arts audiences. This chapter looks at what this shift might imply for audiences.

Ratings and broadcasting

Audience measurement is a type of audience research that documents the size and composition of media audiences. It allows patterns of audience activity to be tracked over time and it generates the type of data that permits comparison of audience behaviour from one medium to another. An industry-based research service, audience measurement generates information that is essential to the operation of media industries. Information about audience size and composition is, after all, the basis on which programming and pricing decisions are made. Webster et al. (2000) note that audience measurement is widely used by a range of organizations, companies and government authorities to determine not only what is broadcast, but also what opportunities for engagement with media are offered to whom. Advertisers use audience measurement data to plan media campaigns and then to evaluate them. Broadcasting companies use audience measurement to plan broadcasting schedules, to guide decision-making about programming and to evaluate their performance. Governments, government authorities, media organizations and financial planners use audience measurement to develop broadcasting policy, allocate broadcasting licences and to determine the commercial value of media companies and other media properties. This dependence on, and preference for, ratings is questioned in this section, as we examine the relationship between broadcasting and ratings and consider the justification of claims that ratings provide an adequate account of audience behaviour.

Beville (1988) has described ratings, the measure that records the percentage of a population that watched or listened to a particular programme, as the centrepiece of the broadcaster-audience communication system, because, 'Ratings with their feedback element are the nerve system that largely controls what is broadcast' (Beville 1988: ix). Webster et al. (2000: 1) consider the ratings system to be, 'indispensable to the media's interest in building audiences and to society's interest in understanding mass media industries'. They describe ratings analysis as commercial audience research, and situate it alongside the social and cultural audience research traditions, rather than in the field of marketing. There are several reasons why, at face value, this characterization may appear appropriate. The information generated by ratings analysis is as much about the media as it is about people and their consumption of media commodities. The underlying assumptions of ratings assume the occurrence of a media event: in particular it is recognized that the generation of audience exposure to particular media products depends on structural dimensions of mass communication (the licensing to broadcast to particular populations, the regional restrictions on operations of the media, and so on) as much as on individual choices about which media equipment to buy and whether or not to turn it on. Ratings analysis draws attention to aspects of audience engagement with media that are, in general, considered peripheral in cultural approaches, but central for the day-to-day operation of the mass media.

The ratings approach, therefore, represents one extreme in the field of audience research — an extreme Webster et al. (2000) characterize as:

- *Applied* — in the sense that it sets out to provide answers to specific questions, like 'how many people watched the programmes we broadcast last night?' or 'what percentage of the people who watched the programme were women aged 18 to 35?' In this sense it is pragmatic rather than 'theoretical' research.
- *Administrative* — ratings analysis contributes directly to the decisions broadcasters make as to how to operate as a business (what types of programmes to buy, when to schedule them, what pricing policy should be adopted for selling advertising spots, and so on). Ratings analysis helps broadcasting companies operate more efficiently, and in this sense it is not *critical* of the media — rather it is part of the communication system.
- *Quantitative* — ratings analysis relies on sampling procedures, and on adding up instances of audience behaviour described as '*exposure*' (discussed below). Qualitative information about audiences is outside its scope.
- *Syndicated* — ratings analysis is used to generate reports that are offered for sale to companies and individuals involved in the media industries.

It is not designed to solve social or cultural problems, but to deliver immediately usable information to the industry.

For these authors, ratings analysis is important because it is how the commercial audience research sector operates. Their work alerts us to the fact that for many in the broadcasting and advertising industries, and in the field of government policy, audience research is synonymous with syndicated commercial audience research services. The fact that ratings analysis exists to serve the needs of industry creates suspicion in the minds of researchers who are committed to theoretically informed, critical research that draws on qualitative data and that asks questions about audiences that question the system of mass communication and whose social, cultural, political and economic interests it serves (Ang 1991; Meehan 1993; Nightingale 1993).

Key concepts in ratings analysis

Whether or not we agree with Webster et al.'s (2000) account of their value, ratings are clearly important in terms of the basic media knowledge required to understand what media services, products and texts are produced and distributed, and how audience interests are taken into account (or not) in making those decisions. The data recorded and the statistical analysis of that data have produced some of the key terminology (for example *rating*, *share*, *frequency* and *reach*) used by media industries and by the press to evaluate the performance of broadcasters and to assess the popularity of particular programmes, to set the price for advertising spots and to indicate how many times an advertisement should be repeated during an evening's viewing.

The ratings approach is based on techniques developed for counting and statistically analysing a single audience behaviour, referred to in the media industries as 'exposure'. Sissors and Bumba state that:

> Industry leaders have chosen a measurement of media audiences-exposure-that is less than perfect, but that can differentiate media vehicles on the basis of their audience sizes.
>
> (1996: 69)

They define *exposure* by the simple phrase, 'Open eyes facing a medium' (1996: 467–8). In an advertising-driven media environment, media industries can be understood as existing to generate exposures. In this sense, audience exposures are the commodity at the heart of broadcasting. Exposure is, in effect, the only *commodity* produced by the broadcasting industries. All other products of broadcasting (the programmes, the newscasts, the personalities, the advertisements) are *services* designed to generate audience exposures. From this industry perspective, exposures are counted and analysed in ways that allow them to be pre-sold to advertisers and others. The capacity to predict, and therefore to pre-sell, audience exposures provides the cash flow for commercial broadcasting. And the capacity to predict audience exposures for particular media vehicles is based on another mass-audience behaviour: the loyalty demonstrated by the inclination to view additional episodes of programmes enjoyed.

The broadcasting companies, in turn, finance the production of ratings reports. Probably the best-known commercial audience research services are offered by AGB Media Services and Nielsen Research, the main providers of ratings and other media research in the USA and many other countries throughout the world, but the internet has provided the means for many new companies to enter the market in audience measurement services. For broadcasting research, the broadcasters operating in a given region each contribute funding for the production of their syndicated service. They set up or subscribe to a ratings service that provides the sort of data they need, but that can be seen as impartial. Impartiality is important. Without it advertisers and others who buy media services could not be sure that the ratings reported were accurate and reliable. In addition, advertisers, production companies, and government agencies are able to buy their own customized reports about ratings directly from the research companies.

Key measures used in ratings analysis

Audience measurement and ratings research use two types of analysis — *gross* and *cumulative* analysis of the recorded exposure data. *Gross* measures record audience size and include *ratings*, *share* and *gross ratings point* (GRP). Cumulative measures count up exposures over time, and include audience *reach* and *frequency*, *cumes* and *audience duplication*. These concepts are the basic conceptual equipment needed for a rudimentary understanding of audience measurement (Webster et al. 2000: 159).

Gross measures of audiences

Webster et al. (2000) describe the 'gross measures' of audience exposures as 'snapshots' of the population, and they consolidate this photography analogy by referring to audience viewing as 'exposure'. Counting exposures can be thought of as rather like taking 'snapshots' of audience button pushing, and extrapolating general pictures of programme and channel selection from that data. Exposure data is used repeatedly in diverse combinations to generate the type of information advertisers or broadcasters need for media planning and programme scheduling. Contemporary metering technologies have made the measurement of exposures on a minute-by-minute basis (if desired) a reality, and statistical analysis of the recorded data is reused for a variety of purposes.

The most publicized measure of audience size is the *rating*. Ratings are based on counting up how many people are *exposed* to the programme. Measures are taken at quarter hour intervals for the duration of a given programme. It is not uncommon for commentators to talk about the ratings 'peaking' at a given figure, thus indicating the highest number of viewers the programme attracted at any one point in time. Webster and Lichty (1991: 255) define *rating* as 'the percentage of persons or households tuned to a station or programme out of the total market population'. Taken alone, a rating makes no sense — it is just a number. It becomes meaningful only in comparison with other numbers — particularly the ratings for other programmes. Now, at a given point in time it may be that only 50 per cent of people are watching TV. If a programme broadcast at this time received a rating of 10, this would mean that 10 per cent of the total sample population were watching that programme; 40 per cent of the sample were watching something else; and the other 50 per cent were not watching TV at all. The rating indicates the percentage of the sample who were watching the programme. On the basis of the *rating* it is possible to calculate a *projection* of how many people altogether watched the programme. When we see ratings reported in the newspaper as hundreds of thousands or millions of viewers, this is a projection of the actual number of people who watched the programme, based on the exposures recorded for the sample.

The concept, *share*, has been generated to talk more easily about the relative size of audiences. It is based on only the people who are viewing at a particular point in time. In the hypothetical example above, 50 per cent of the total population are viewing and we know that 10 per cent are tuned to our target programme. The calculation for *share* is based on the total of the 50 per cent who are tuned in (the households using television), and so our target programme has attracted one fifth of the viewing audience — or a 20 per cent *share*. *Share* is an important concept because the size of the viewing audience changes so much over the day. Small audiences during the day gradually grow larger as people return from work, dwindling again as people go to bed. It is therefore to be expected that some programmes with very small ratings may attract a very high share of the audience, if the overall size of the viewing audience is small.

A third audience measurement which appears to be of particular interest to advertisers (and almost no one else), is the *gross rating point* (GRP). The GRP is 'the gross impressions of an advertising schedule expressed as a percentage of the population' (Webster and Lichty 1991: 250). The GRP records the number of times a particular advertisement, or series of advertisements, was seen. It does this by summing up the ratings for the programmes broadcast at the times the particular advertisement was scheduled. As Webster et al. (2000) indicate, the problem with GRPs is that they are not able to distinguish repeated viewing by one person from single viewing by many people. Nevertheless, the GRP provides an indication of how many people in a population are likely to have seen a particular advertisement.

These three concepts, *rating*, *share* and *GRP*, are all described as *gross* measures because they count up the numbers of viewers (exposures) for programmes, channels, or advertisements. As Webster et al. (2000) suggest, they are like photographs. They are snapshots taken at the time of exposure. They record past behaviours. For this reason they are not necessarily a good indication of what the audience will watch next. Ratings experts have therefore developed another type of analysis based on exposures that records past viewing patterns and provides the basis for predicting future viewing patterns. This type of analysis is called cumulative analysis.

Cumulative analysis

Cumulative analysis involves tracking audiences over certain periods of time, and on the basis of that tracking, making predictions of future viewing. The key concepts in cumulative analysis are *reach*, *frequency*, *audience duplication*, and the *cume* itself. The term cume is short for 'cumulative audience'. Webster and Lichty (1991: 248) define it as, 'the size of the total unduplicated audience for a station over some specified period of time'. This definition draws our attention to the fact that cumulative measures sift out the carry-over or 'duplicated' audience from the new viewers tuning in. They add the new viewers to the carry forward totals. The cumulative audience is then the total of the people who tuned in for at least some time during the period for which the cume is being calculated.

Audience duplication is the term used to discuss the likelihood of the same people turning up in the audience of another programme. It 'describes the extent to which the audience for one programme or station are also in the audience for another programme or station' (Webster et al. 2000: 236). The term is used in discussion of audience loyalty and is fundamental to establishing programme, channel or advertisement *reach* and *frequency*. The concept *reach* refers to the number of people in a population who see the advertisement, programme or channel at least once in a given period of time. *Frequency* refers to the number of times each person reached is likely to have seen a particular advertisement, programme or channel. Reach and frequency are often used together to provide a sense of the depth of penetration of channels or messages within the population. For example, a broadcaster may argue that a given advertisement has a reach of 80 per cent and a frequency of 5, meaning that 8 people of every 10 could have seen the advert an average of 5 times over a given ratings period. Reach and frequency allow advertisers and others to judge how frequently they need to repeat their ads, and in which time slots, in order to make sure that the people they want to see their adverts do so.

Reach and frequency measures are also used by channels, including publicly funded ones, to demonstrate the cultural importance of their operations. In countries where publicly funded broadcasting is a small component of the broadcasting mix, publicly funded channels are charged with a responsibility for enhancing the diversity of programme choices available. Where commercial channels aim to attract as broad a reach and as high a frequency as possible, public channels often face structurally ambiguous expectations from the governments that fund them and from the general public. They are expected to rate well, but not to compete actively with the commercials; to provide diversity and yet still to compete; to develop a small but loyal audience and yet to provide something for everyone. In other words, it is expected that many different people will watch the public broadcaster a little, and a few people will watch the public broadcaster a lot. In terms of reach and frequency they are expected to achieve high reach with low frequency at the same time that they achieve a low reach with high frequency. This is a scheduling impossibility. Of course, commercial channels argue that since their reach is so broad and their frequency so high, public broadcasting is completely unnecessary, with the result that there is very little diversity programmed into the broadcasting system until many more channels are competing for audiences (as has occurred since the introduction of cable and digital TV).

Sampling

Before *exposure* data can be collected, people willing to take part in the research must be located. Not just anyone will do, however, because the ratings companies must be certain that the people chosen for inclusion in the research, as a group, are representative of the total population. All audience research is based on *sampling* — the process whereby some people are chosen to represent the whole population. Ratings surveys may be local, regional or national. The idea is that the people in a given geographic area, or people with particular characteristics, are identified as the target population, and then a subset of that population is chosen as the sample population. It is important that the sample chosen is representative of the target population, otherwise the research data will not be reliable. In ratings research two types of sampling are often combined: *multi-stage cluster sampling* and *stratified sampling*. Obviously some rules apply to how samples are chosen to minimize bias and sampling error.

Multi-stage cluster sampling (see Webster et al. 2000: 102) involves several stages of listing and sampling. It is a sampling procedure that involves listing all the counties in the nation first, then selecting a random sample from the total; second, all census tracts in the chosen counties are listed and random samples of census tracts chosen; third, all city blocks in the selected census tracts are listed, and a random sample of city blocks are chosen. Researchers will then go to the chosen city blocks, to randomly selected households, to locate people to take part in the research. However each stage included in the sampling allows a little more sampling error to creep in, so considerable care is taken to decide on how many sampling stages need to be included.

Because multi-stage cluster sampling is based on a geographic spread of the population, it may not be possible to avoid the problem that too many of the same sort of people (for example too many singles or too many children) may end up in the sample. A second type of sampling is often combined with multi-stage cluster sampling to minimize this problem. The second type of sampling is called *stratified sampling*, and it again involves listing and sampling — this time for characteristics like age, sex, income level, ethnicity — information recorded in national databases which provide the guidelines for sample stratification. This information provides the researchers with knowledge as to what proportion of people with particular characteristics they need to recruit so that the sample matches the national profile as closely as possible.

Combining these two sampling strategies helps to minimize sampling error for syndicated research services, but it is such a complex and expensive process that once it has been set up, the operators tend to want to make use of the sample for some time. As a result, most television ratings services establish research panels, which are used for a number of years before panel members are replaced. Panels are one of the reasons ratings research is criticized since, over time, the household composition and demographic status of panel members can change dramatically — people get older, members leave the house or new members arrive (Meehan 1993). The desire to maintain a panel for as long as possible has been affected by the introduction of expensive metering technologies like *people meters*. So the service providers face the difficulty of keeping the panels for as long as possible while trying to avoid the introduction of sampling error by attrition.

Sometimes events outside the control of the ratings service provider can jeopardize the reliability of the sample. For example, if a channel decided to cover a story on ratings, this might prove of disproportionate interest to the panel members, attracting more of the panel to watch the programme than would otherwise have done so because of their personal involvement in the ratings process. Such acts can even be undertaken as a cynical attempt to alter the outcomes for a ratings period, and to disadvantage other broadcasters. In effect it is a case of the broadcaster directly targeting the panel members. Given Meehan's (1991) concerns about the targeting of the 'consumerist caste' by the ratings system, this type of act may point to the possibility of endemic bias in the panel system.

Critique of ratings

While the importance of ratings analysis for media industries cannot be disputed, the impact on society and culture of a system of broadcasting driven by ratings has been strongly criticized. This debate took on international significance in the early 1980s when Smythe (1981) argued strongly that advertising-supported broadcasting treated audiences as though they were commodities. Smythe argued that while people might feel they were being entertained by broadcasting, the reality was quite different. He suggested that audiences were in fact bought and sold on the basis of their viewing habits and their capacity for participation in the sphere of consumption.

A few years later, Meehan (1984) suggested that, as a form of communication between people and broadcasters, the ratings system is a technology of domination, and that, unfortunately, its significance has been largely overlooked by studies in political economy of the media. Hartley (1987) criticized the propensity for channel executives and others to patronize audiences, and as a result, to assume a low level of interest in quality television production. This point is echoed in Neuman's (1991) analysis of the economics and politics of programming. In a discussion of 'the economics of common denominators', Neuman demonstrates that the forces of competition operating in the mass broadcasting context create imperatives for channels to programme for majority taste at the expense of minority interests. He concludes that:

> If one thinks about the likely career benefits to broadcasting executives, one can imagine that the pressure is consistently in the direction of making optimistic forecasts about winning large portions of the mass audience, rather than retreating from a possible position of industry leadership to serve smaller minority audience tastes.
>
> (Neuman 1991: 155)

The broadcasting context

Broadcasting distributes information from an industry centre (TV channel; radio station) to a local periphery (people's earphones, homes, cars, workplaces, or clubs). It seeks ears to listen and eyes to see, rather than individuals, groups, subcultures or communities. If people have access to the infrastructure for broadcasting, they can join the audience. The logic of mass broadcasting assumes a mass distribution system capable of reaching those eyes and ears. Broadcasters produce and distribute media materials using transmission systems they either own or lease from governments, in accordance with national communications policies for the regulation of broadcasting. Such regulation differs markedly from one national context to another, between the extremes of total commercial control on the one hand, and total government control on the other. Broadcasters therefore produce and distribute information. They manage broadcasting technologies, production, and the distribution systems that operate through the media, and this managerial control places them at an advantage, vis-à-vis audiences, when it comes to making decisions about what type of information will be broadcast and how that information should be packaged. As managers of the broadcasting system, they are always in the stronger position when it comes to organizing the terms of their contact with audiences.

Audiences, by contrast, are dispersed. Most people never discover the extent of the interests they share with others in broadcast materials. Of those who do, a few form clubs and associations to share the pleasure of particular texts, to help each other find out more about favourite programmes, or to lobby for changes to broadcasting or broadcast information. Fans, as will be demonstrated in Chapters 5 and 6, are excellent examples of audience formations that organize communally to enhance their enjoyment of favourite media texts. They develop associations based on their interests in particular texts, and have been documented to use their combined power to change production or broadcaster decisions that threaten those texts (Hobson 1982; Jenkins 2002).

Audience power in the broadcasting context

In general, mass audiences have been characterized as helpless in the context of broadcasting, but this is not, strictly speaking, a particularly useful way to think about the problem. Generally speaking, audiences have a range of powers at their disposal that, at least hypothetically, should make it possible for them to take an active role in mass broadcasting. Even if, currently, such powers are dissipated by a system of broadcasting and audience feedback that, at best, subdues and, at worst, effectively silences audience activism, it is important to understand that the potential for a more active audience intervention in broadcasting does exist. The sources of power available to people *as audiences* are linked to people's simultaneous participation in three interlocking spheres of activity: in **the public sphere**, in consumption, and in the media sphere. It goes without saying that power is not equally distributed in these spheres of activity, and this is reflected in the ways that some allegiances and associations result in particular socio-cultural groups being better served by broadcasting than others.

By virtue of their humanity, nationality, ethnicity, citizenship or other right-bestowing affiliation in the public sphere, audiences are able to lobby the broadcasters, governments, advertisers and others to intervene in broadcasting. Later in this chapter we consider examples of audience activism where marginalized communities have created opportunities for the production of media programming that suits their communal needs. Since mainstream audiences, however, are dispersed they are often slow to take advantage of such rights unless or until they devise the means to organize such lobbying action. People are, however, increasingly using their power as private citizens to undertake litigation directed at the impact of mass broadcasting on their lives. Such action is usually directed at advertisers or manufacturers after people have experienced harm as a result of information released through the media. To date, litigation has mostly been associated with the use of advertised products like cigarettes or fast food. Sometimes litigation is mounted on the basis of the ways actions or people are represented in advertisements, for example dangerous driving in motor vehicle advertisements, sexist representation of women, or racist representation of particular cultural groups.

The second source of audience power lies in people's consumption activities — as we will see, the more people spend, the more power their needs and wants command in the broadcasting system. The link between the market, advertising and broadcasting is sensitive to people's consumption activities. This sensitivity is heightened by the ratings system. If broadcast advertising did not produce increased sales for advertised products, then commercial broadcasting would be unable to continue. The value advertisers attach to having their advertisements broadcast at times when the consumers they seek are likely to be viewing is the reason why commercial broadcasting exists.

Meehan (1993: 206–7) has argued that the commercial broadcasting system has had unintended consequences, in that it has been set up around the interests of the better-educated middle classes, whom she describes as the *consumerist caste*. As a result, the ratings system does not provide programming for the public so much as for the consumerist caste. She claims that the educated middle classes with comparatively large disposable incomes were, and remain, the 'quality audiences' the syndicated measurement services were designed to identify. Much of the evidence provided by Beville (1988) and by Webster et al. (2000) confirm this privileging of the consumerist caste, since in the early years of broadcasting it was more wealthy listeners who first had access to radio and television sets, whose literacy and self-discipline was sufficiently developed to easily comply with diary and survey completion requirements. The better educated were also more likely to be sufficiently interested to cooperate with the self and family monitoring required to complete ratings diary entries, which rapidly becomes boring and repetitious. The power associated with consumption is therefore reflected in the design of ratings — particularly in the data selected (exposures and demographics, psychographics and geographics) and the recording arrangements required.

There is a second level at which consumption endows some audiences with an unequal share of broadcasting power. Because advertisers want their products advertised to people who are willing and able to buy them, practices like *audience targeting, niche advertising* and *audience segmentation* have developed. In recent years these practices have sought increasingly close association between product and programme or favourite characters. Synergies and correspondences between programme and viewers, the products advertised, and characters and plots are carefully fostered. Ratings are kept high by sticking with proven formulas. In recent years adverts that feature actors from the sponsored programme have been screened during the programme, and alternately actors from the adverts make guest appearances, in role, in the programmes. The difference between advertisement and programme is minimized in a way that suggests the ubiquity of the product — that it is best because most people use it. Turow (1997) has argued that the practice of audience segmentation has increased social inequality by desensitizing people to the needs and interests of others as a result of seeing only consumerist versions of social and cultural life on TV. Clearly, more attention is paid to the production of programmes that will attract viewers who are also likely consumers of advertised products. People's level of participation in the consumerist caste provides an indication of the satisfaction they will experience as broadcast audiences.

The third source of audience power, and the most carefully monitored, is the power inherent in people's activities *as audiences*. In mass broadcasting, people's power stems from the fact that broadcasters need them to keep watching or listening. Audiences are the reason broadcasting companies exist — no audiences, no broadcasters! The availability of people as potential audiences can be seen as a commercial opportunity — as it has been wherever the media are commercially funded, so broadcasters use programming to attract audiences, particularly the audiences sought by their advertisers and sponsors.

Broadcasters therefore offer a broadcasting *service* to audiences, and they sell access to audience *exposures* to advertisers. In this way audiences are simultaneously consumers of broadcasting services and commodities sold to advertisers. Ratings analysis is the process that transforms audience exposures into the statistical reports and profiles that will convince advertisers to buy audience exposures. It is a form of value-adding that enhances the raw material of audience exposures, making them saleable commodities. It is also the feedback system that guides the network in scheduling programmes so that the audiences advertisers want to see their adverts are tuned to the designated programmes. In this sense ratings analysis assists the regulation and management of broadcast audiences.

In this context, issues of audience agency need to be disentangled from audience power. Most audience research, outside audience measurement, has focused on audience agency (see Chapter 6) — the personal power people exert when making sense of broadcast media materials and integrating them into their self-understanding or life-worlds. Studies of audience agency focus on what people do with media materials. Tuning in is one small and rather insignificant expression of audience agency. Yet ratings research transforms it into the justification for a system of audience regulation.

Exposure as audience engagement

In the final analysis, the simple twist of the wrist (or push of the button) of people switching their sets on and off or tuning from station to station provides the single most important piece of information about audience behaviour.

(Beville 1988: xii)

A critique of ratings would not be complete without commenting on the strangeness of the assumption that *exposure* is the most significant audience behaviour. Advocates of the ratings system (Beville 1988; Webster et al. 2000) accept switching on/ switching off as an adequate account of audience agency. This assumption circumvents attempts to set a wider agenda for the discussion of audience issues in contexts like information services, advertising and audience policy development. We have identified six grounds for concern about the use of 'exposure' as, in effect, a measure of audience agency.

a) *Exposure* is the only information registered and recorded as data for ratings. In their model of audience behaviour, Webster et al. (2000: 181) outline the structural and individual constraints that affect audience behaviour. They explain that from an industry point of view, the only significant audience behaviours are tuning in, staying tuned, channel changing, and turning off. All these behaviours are recorded as just the one behaviour, *exposure*. Accordingly, there is room for concern that projections based on the patterns of exposure to media inform the 'long-term development of technologies, programming services and strategies' that are used in mass communication, and that in turn influence the 'long-term cultivation of tastes, expectations and habits' (Webster et al. 2000: 181). The ratings system accepts as 'given', or as inevitable, that control over broadcasting is held by broadcasters and can be used as and how the broadcaster wishes. While this view may reflect the ways the broadcasting industry understands itself, it should be noted at this point that other commentators on the USA communications industry, for example Neuman (1991), have offered more complex and critical evaluations of the power of broadcasters. This illusion of control is possible only because such a narrow definition of audience engagement and agency is adopted and because it is not more often questioned by media researchers.

b) *Exposure* is an audience behaviour — the behaviour of tuning in to a broadcast programme. To achieve the abstract measurements desired for statistical analysis of mass audiences, everything about audience that is not directly relevant to this act is stripped away. Focusing on exposure produces a view of audience engagement evacuated of socio-cultural meaning, in a process whereby exposure behaviour is transformed from being but *one* dimension of an audience event into the *only* sign of an audience commodity. Fundamentally it does not matter to the broadcasters and advertisers whether a particular programme is interesting to its audience or not — all that matters is that they are tuning in to it, that the programme rates better than the others available at the same time, and that advertisers are prepared to pay for advertising space. It is assumed that this can be achieved by clever scheduling rather than by better audience research (Neuman 1991). By basing the ratings system on exposures, all the difficult and disputable issues involved in the complex action of being an audience are conveniently bundled into a basket labelled 'irrelevant'.

c) *Exposure*, as a sign of audience activity, indicates little about people's media likes and dislikes — though perhaps it could if exposure data were combined with audience/text studies. It is impossible for information based on exposures to provide feedback on the social or cultural meaning of the choices people make when viewing television. At best, exposures may provide data that allows post hoc speculation about the reasons why people acted the way they did, but in a system that cannot differentiate between free viewing (watching programmes because you want to) and forced viewing (watching programmes chosen by someone else — a situation described in Gray (1987) and Morley (1986) and noted in many audience ethnographies), the jingoistic suggestion that 'audiences get the media they deserve' simply does not make sense.

d) *Exposure*, as an audience behaviour, involves a choice between limited options. To some extent this is inevitable given the nature of free-to-air broadcasting, but the limited choice situation has allowed broadcasters to assume that audiences would not be discriminating if they had other options available. Fortunately, perhaps, the introduction of new technologies of trans-mission (optic fibre, satellite, data casting and so on), and the tendency for people to have more than one television set in the home, is making it possible for people to select media materials on the basis of personal interest more than was possible in the past, though Neuman (1991) has warned that the competitive nature of broadcasting will continue to favour mass-audience interests.

e) *Exposure* — when considered the centrepiece of the audience event — leads to other dimensions of the audience/media event being disregarded. In Chapter 1, we noted five dimensions of the audience/media event: the people and the nature of their affiliations, the diversity of audience activities, the nature of the media materials with which people engage, the nature of media time-spaces different technologies create, and the media power relations that structure media industries and set the parameters for audience action. As noted in Chapter 2, the early audience researchers thought of exposure as but one of the intervening variables in mass communication. In ratings analysis, however, exposure is taken to *be* the audience event, and in this respect, the acceptance of its relevance leads to an extreme and abstract rendering of media events, that focuses attention on *tuning in* at the expense of a bigger 'media and audiences' picture that might allow audience interests in information to be more closely scrutinized. Among other outcomes, this protects the media from having to seriously evaluate the quality of their programming.

From a pragmatic industry perspective, abstraction provides a standardized measure of audience activity. By ignoring most of the differences between viewers and disregarding reasons for viewing, quite diverse acts of audience can be treated as examples of the same thing — being tuned in. Audience exposure is beyond dispute if the reasons for the exposure are defined as irrelevant. Either people tuned in or they did not. There are no grey areas, and provided those who use the information generated agree that the instruments used to measure audiences are sufficiently accurate and properly recorded, disputes as to the validity and reliability of the measures can be avoided. Neuman (1991: 153–7) has demonstrated how the competitive nature of the media, the restrictions of the numbers of broadcasters permitted by law to operate in a given market, and the size of the audiences served, ensure that a mass-audience focus will continue to dominate new programme development. This is because, crudely speaking, more advertising revenue is obtained from mass-audiences than from catering to specialist interests.

f) *Exposure*, as used in ratings analysis then, covers up the very differences that, if they were taken into account, would provide the basis on which better programming and better broadcasting services could be developed. Scheduling for the highest rating means that some audience participants are not served well by the broadcasting system. Add to this the preferential treatment offered to the 'consumerist caste' (Meehan 1993), and the groups likely to experience dissatisfaction with free to air broadcasting become obvious — the intelligentsia, the poor, older people, children.

Neuman (1991) has provided a helpful analysis of how marketing theory can shed light on the reasons why, even when more media carriers (magazines, TV, radio, press, HD TV, games consoles, the internet) are available, the programming on offer remains oriented to the mainstream mass-audience. Basically, since broadcasters always seek the highest rating in a particular time slot, they will aim to schedule programmes that are only a little more attractive to more people than their opposition, rather than try to outstrip the competition. Speaking hypothetically, if a given media market sustains three free to air channels, each would aim to attract one third of the available audience. This may seem counter-intuitive to people who imagine that a broadcaster would want to dominate the market by aiming for a 100 per cent rating. However, apart from very rare occasions like a celebrity wedding or the World Cup soccer finals licensed to one channel only, aiming for 100 per cent ratings is short-sighted. In a three-station market, each station will be most viable (and equally attractive to advertisers) if they are each able to regularly attract about a third of the available audience. When a second-ranking station decides to challenge the top-rating station, it will do so only by diverting audiences away from both the top-ranking and the lowest-ranking stations. However, offering a programme that is radically different from programming that already rates well is more risky than offering something only marginally different from programmes already rating strongly in a given time slot. The risk is that the existing core audience may shift in the opposite direction to that desired. Neuman has noted that:

> The promotional hurdle imparts a conservative influence, tilting programming decisions away from one-shot programs in general, and risky gambles on unfamiliar formulas and new faces in particular.
>
> (1991: 151)

As a result, unconventional programmes are often scheduled at times that are inconvenient for the viewers most likely to enjoy them. The task of providing programming that is innovative or looks to expand viewer interests beyond the comfort zone falls to publicly funded broadcasters (like the British Broadcasting

Corporation or the Australian Broadcasting Corporation) and to broadcasting services set up for this purpose (like the US Public Broadcasting Service, Britain's Channel Four and Australia's Special Broadcasting Service). From the perspective of the mainstream broadcasters, this has the added advantage of transferring some research and development costs to the public sector, or to private companies or individuals whose work is bought by the public sector. Successful public sector programmes can later be purchased for broadcast by the free to air channels.

The implications of statistical thinking

Webster et al. (2000) justify the ratings focus on *exposure* by pointing to the analytical difference between broad patterns of mass-audience behaviour and particularized and localized accounts of niche-audience activities. They acknowledge that mass-audience statistics are unable to account for particular instances of audience choice. They use this distinction to justify the preference for statistical analysis:

> This science of predicting mass behaviour and audience characteristics has been called statistical thinking. It was developed in the eighteenth century by, among others, insurance underwriters. Consider for example, the problem of life insurance. It is almost impossible to predict when any one person will die. But if the researcher aggregates large numbers, it's not hard to estimate how many people are likely to expire in the coming year.
>
> (Webster et al. 2000: 8)

This comment draws our attention to the history of statistical analysis and its use in social administration and urban planning, since this 'statistical thinking' is by no means just a matter of preferring quantitative methods over qualitative analysis. While the origins of statistical thinking may be traced to the eighteenth century and the beginnings of social administration, the particular type of statistical practice found in ratings analysis is more closely linked to at least three mid-twentieth-century movements:

- behaviourism in psychology;
- the 'disciplinary technologies of "philanthropic" Fordism and the Keynsian welfare state' that were associated with 'the rise of new social movements aimed at achieving greater social justice in the city' (Soja 2000: 98); and
- political behaviouralism and its application to public opinion polling in political science (Cook 1978).

The reduction of audience response to a measurable action like *exposure* mirrors the approach to stimulus-response behaviourism advocated by Skinner in the 1950s, which proposed that all psychological behaviour could be studied by analysing behavioural responses and refusing to have your thinking messed up by unmeasurable phenomena like feelings and opinions (Skinner 1973).

The fixation with what might be called collective consumption was a component of the social movements that endorsed egalitarianism in the 1960s — particularly in urban planning and renewal programmes. In this context, statistical analysis could provide evidence of the scope and depth of social problems and assist with the planning and costing of improvements. In the context of broadcasting, though, the statistical approach has worked to cover up ordinary people's interests, as individuals and as communities, and to privilege an amorphous notion of the public (in this case 'the silent majority'). The commercial use of ratings allows exploitation of people's viewing time rather than an improvement in the broadcasting services.

Because of the close parallels between ratings analysis and public opinion polling, the criticisms of the use of statistical thinking in political science in the 1960s and 1970s offer some interesting perspectives on the application of statistical thinking to contemporary audience research. Cook (1978: 101), for example, suggested that statistical thinking in 'political behaviouralism' (his terminology) emphasized *analysis* rather than *substance*, *general patterns* rather than *particular or individual* action, and *explanatory* rather than *ethical* attitudes. Webster et al. (2000) put forward an argument for the superiority of research committed to *analysis*, *general patterns* and *explanation* to situate ratings analysis as audience research.

In Cook's view, the proclaimed neutrality of 'political behaviouralism', as it applied to public opinion polling, was actually a form of conservatism. He proposed that this reductionist conservatism consolidates the status quo, circumvents the development of critical evaluation of political situations, contexts or policies, and devalues the complexity and importance of the political behaviours it measures. The so-called value-free terminology used in political polling 'describes voters *as if* the most that can be expected of them is what we rightly expect in the case of ill informed and prejudiced voters' (Cook 1978: 107). His criticism echoes the dilemma ratings analysis has posed for other approaches to audience research. The reliance within the broadcasting industry on ratings severely compromises the options for other audience or media research agendas and undermines the recognition of the value and relevance of other types of audience research, particularly research concerned with identity and cultural value (see Chapters 4 and 5). Hartley (1987) expressed just this concern when he explained how the ratings system encourages industry personnel to talk about audiences as though they are childlike and unable to think for themselves.

Overall, the emphasis on exposure in ratings analysis, advertising and media planning fails to take into account that what is excluded at the moment of the initial transformation of a complex human activity (*engagement* with media) into a standardized measurable behaviour (*exposure*); this may be important for understanding the larger patterns and meanings of media consumption in contemporary society too. In particular, by reifying a mundane act, *exposure*, as *the* sign of audience, the importance of other audience action and agency is under-valued. By claiming that ratings analysis *is* audience research, Webster et al. (2000) situate audience measurement as the dominant approach to audience research and assume that the audience questions pursued by other media researchers mirror their own. They are in good company by doing so, however, since the marketing approach that informs the understanding of more and more information service sectors is based on this assumption.

This affirms Meehan's (1984), admittedly minority and academic, view that ratings analysis is fundamentally not social science research, but a commercial service designed to provide specific types of information, for which broadcasters and advertisers are willing to pay. Rather than present ratings analysis as a story of progress and enhancement of social science practice, Meehan proposed that increasing collusion between broadcasters and advertisers constructed, in turn, a relationship between broadcasters and audiences that normalized broadcaster control. Meehan considers the industry use of ratings to be a hegemonic practice that protects the interests of dominant economic groups by allowing the industry to position critical analysis of the media outside the sphere of its normal operations.

The commodity audience

The information about ratings and their use, outlined above, has shown us how audience behaviours are transformed into measurable statistics that allow audiences to be traded as commodities by the broadcasting industries. The systems of audience measurement and public opinion polling, devised in the first half of the twentieth century, pioneered a system of continuous audience monitoring using representative population sampling. In the 1990s, the applicability of these systems outside the broadcasting environment expanded dramatically because of digitization and the development of computer programs designed specifically to process the data on entertainment exposures and to track audience movements from programme to product, from channel to supermarket, medium to shopping mall.

During the 1960s and 1970s, banks and marketing companies had begun a similar tracking of commercial transactions, based on records of credit purchases. For example, the use of bank and credit cards makes it possible to track credit and *eftpos* (electronic funds transfer — point of sale) transactions in much the same way that *audience exposures* are tracked for broadcasting. In the internet environment, these two data sources — product purchase records and entertainment choice records, have converged, and the systems of analysis based on audience/customer choices has expanded dramatically. In the internet context, being an audience attracts a cost as the free-to-air mass-audience scope of the broadcast media is replaced by a user-pays system.

In this context data mining is increasingly used in conjunction with transaction tracking to enable commercial operators to be even more discriminating about whom to contact with product information and special deals. Honeywill and Byth (2001), for example, advocate more finely tuned **discriminant analysis** to allow distinctions to be made between relevant audience segments and likely prospects. The 'prospect' is identified on the basis of past purchase transactions, and then tempted to buy with inducements like special offers, loyalty deals, free gifts and other preferred client 'opportunities'.

Clearly the structure of broadcasting is showing the impact of changes linked to the information society, since this type of discrimination in the global e-commerce environment is a good example of the disjuncture Castells has described 'between the market logic of global networks of capital flows and the human experience of workers' lives' (Castells 1998: 346). The development of new services for online audiences are based on statistical analysis of the frequency and duration of site visits and the average number of purchases of online products a consumer is likely to make before shifting on to a new supplier or a new enthusiasm, but the reasons why one person begins and ends their use of an online service, and the personal meaning to the audience/ consumer of the information gained while the customer/service provider relationship remained active, is not investigated. The division between industry research and socio-cultural research remains unchanged.

As consumer activities gather momentum online, and as media convergence dissolves the distinctions between media that had characterized their delivery of information to audiences, the use of information about audiences/consumers by the commercial sector draws to our attention the increasing importance of the consumption activities of audiences on the one hand, and to the mediatization of activities that were previously not thought of as audience activities, on the other. For example, many research activities that were previously carried out in libraries, museums and archives are now available online, packaged as media commodities, supported by links to product tie-ins and merchandising that allow the immediate purchase of new materials to enhance the data-gathering activity. These are audience activities that are not entertainment but information-based.

For example, the commercial opportunities available in B-2-B (business to business) and B-2-C (business to customer) transactions have encouraged a significant investment in the acquisition, development and deployment of online databases, that are in turn marketed as new information services. It is interesting to note, in this context, that over the last ten years, the language of marketing has pioneered metaphors like **data mining** and **information warehousing**, to describe the development of audience/consumer research methodologies for internet marketing — **customer relationship marketing** (CRM) and *mass customization*. Mass customization is a powerful variant of the ratings system that creates a sales environment where mass audiences can be individually addressed. It involves 'mining' e-commerce transaction records and using them as the basis for designing the relationship between manufacturer or service provider and audiences/customers. Honeywill and Byth (2001: 161) describe this process as 'relationship architecture'. In the e-commerce context, the distinction between audience and consumer collapses, and is transformed into the *customer relationship* (see Gronroos 1994) or the *mass customization strategy*.

The process of *mass customization* is based on the idea that the economics of information, in particular the 'universal trade-off between richness and reach' can be redefined in the e-commerce context. It is a variation of the link between *reach* (how many people see an advertisement or programme) and *frequency* (how many times the advert is seen by the people reached) introduced earlier in this chapter. Evans and Wurster explain these terms in the following way:

> 'Richness' means the quality of information, as defined by the user: accuracy, bandwidth, currency, customisation, interactivity, relevance, security and so forth. The precise meaning of richness varies from one context to another, but in any one context, it is generally clear what the word means. 'Reach' means the number of people who participate in the sharing of that information.
>
> (2000: 23)

Here, a concept about quality, *richness*, has been added to the rhetoric for the management of audiences. Richness refers to both the value audiences attach to the information service, and to the commercial value of information about the audience. Evans and Wurster (2000) identify six aspects of information that contribute to its 'richness'.

- *Bandwidth* is used to distinguish between narrowband ('stock quotes') and broadband ('film') information.

- *Customization* refers to the specificity of the communication — the directness with which it addresses the interests of the audience.
- *Interactivity* refers to the mode of address used — considering the trade-off between monologue and dialogue, for example.
- *Reliability* refers, in this context, to the credibility of the participants in the interactions. It contrasts 'a small group of trusted individuals' with a 'large group of strangers'.
- *Security*, in this context, is a way of referring to the judgements made about how widely particular information should be disseminated.
- *Currency* refers to the length of time information has been in circulation.

(Evans and Wurster 2000: 25)

Evans and Wurster claim that the traditional relationship between the richness and reach of information held that the more people who were addressed by a message, the less rich its information could be, and vice versa. So a television advertisement could have massive reach but would be low in richness, because it cannot provide detailed information about the product (low richness for the audience), and it will be seen by many viewers who are not considered prospects by the advertiser or marketer (low richness for the marketer). Evans and Wurster suggest that in the e-commerce context this relationship has been replaced because e-commerce operates on a global scale (high reach) but is interactive in nature (offering a richness of communication for both audience and marketer). As they put it, 'Digital networks are now making it possible for a very large number of people to exchange very rich information' (Evans and Wurster 2000: 29).

This relationship appears to offer benefits to both audience/consumers and to commercial operators, but it depends heavily on the willingness of audiences to disclose large amounts of 'rich, comprehensive, and perhaps intimate data' about themselves. It also depends on technical and informational inequalities between consumer and commercial operator, since 'consumers cannot know what financial arrangements underlie the information and recommendations that are presented to them' (Evans and Wurster 2000: 155). They note that the audience/consumer is less able to conserve anonymity, prevent reselling of personal information, avoid SPAM, protect themselves against false information and avoid being manipulated by sellers who are 'armed with the latest in discriminant analysis' (154–5).

As a basis for deciding which information is provided to whom, discriminant analysis and mass customization may be experienced by audiences as ruthless, or as heartless if people become aware of the ways they are being grouped and classified, or that they are discriminated against in the offering of special privileges. Mass customization and discriminant analysis remain, in this sense, examples of Pierre Levy's (1997) **molar technologies** in that they still treat people as 'masses' and they work on principles of mediatization that draw on 'immobilization, reproduction, decontextualization, and distribution of messages' (Levy 1997: 41). Such administrative approaches to 'customer' management create divisions among those participating in media events, and in this respect their positioning of the online audience misses out on the benefits of the internet as an environment for the sharing of 'collective intelligence' (Levy 1997: 41).

The creative industries are another site where the media marketing treatment is applied to the management of consumer activities. Here, however, the process is called 'audience development', and its aim is to ensure that government funding for the arts is supported by a broader cross-section of the general public than would occur in other circumstances. The idea is that audience tastes are surveyed as the basis of planning by arts institutions, and used as a guide to develop exhibitions and performances that will be strongly supported by potential product users.

Barban, Cristol and Kopec (1987) identified two alternative approaches to matching target markets (the people an advertiser wants to reach) and vehicle audiences (the people who make up the audience following of a particular programme or product): the *demographic* approach and the *product-usage* approach. Audience development is based on the *product-usage* approach.

The *product usage* approach starts by profiling users of products or services already available. The profile of the product users then becomes the basis for locating additional products or services, perhaps in synergistic fields, that attract people who share similar demographics to the current service users. The product user demographics are matched, first, to the demographics of media vehicle audiences (age, gender, income, education, and so on) and second to the demographics of heavy, medium, light or non-users of the medium. The aim is to develop a media strategy that offers precise placement of advertising, where the target market cannot miss the advert, but which does not waste money by advertising to people who will not be interested in the product. This means that the advertiser is looking for particular types of audience vehicles for advert placement, but also that the audience is continuously segmented and differentiated in a search for the qualities sought by particular marketers. In audience development the aim is to attract new people to the audience for arts products (exhibitions, performances, seminars) by promoting synergies across diverse arts contexts. The *demographic approach*, by contrast, involves deciding on the preferred demographics of potential users for a product or service and seeking out vehicle audiences that provide a high proportion of people with those demographics. It is well suited to brand advertising and the broadcasting environment, but does not lend itself so readily to arts audience development because it is less powerful as a means for locating audience synergies.

The application of market research approaches to arts audience development has created mistrust and widespread misgiving among arts industry workers. As O'Regan has noted:

> Marketing and market research directly challenge the value and sig-
> nificance of an organisations's own understanding of its audience — often
> a source of great pride. They introduce a layer of external expertise inter-
> vening in what many arts administrators see as their organic relations with
> their audience. They entail a perspective that the audience is never wrong,
> leading to research programs which start from 'where people are at' rather
> than where the sector thinks 'they should be'. They give rise to new sorts
> of expertise needing to be accommodated by cultural organisations. Some
> claim it has shifted the power within cultural organisations, as market
> research and audience development initiatives challenge the primacy of
> creativity in the production process. Turning the arts into 'just another
> business', and adopting the objectifying language of consumers, markets
> and the like, can be a profoundly alienating experience for artists and
> cultural workers.
>
> (2002: 129)

The problem is that audience development uses the same profiling of user engagement with audience vehicles (art objects in this case) as the mass media. The same behaviourist approach to research is taken. The same preference for recording actions rather than experiences or opinions pervades the approach. The inherent disregard for exploration of the intensity of arts/media events signals a lack of preparedness to accept the cultural significance of artists, art works and arts events that characterize popular culture production. The intrusion of marketing into the arts context suggests that a deep-seated realignment of distinctions between high art and the popular arts may be occurring, as the art object becomes yet another entertainment vehicle, and arts patrons become yet another audience to be commodified.

The active audience

Despite the increasing and relentless commodification of audiences by the entertainment and information industries, individuals and groups do exercise power in a variety of ways, not just as fans who produce their own cultural artefacts (see Chapter 6) or produce their own websites and news stories (see Chapter 7), but also as producers of media outputs which have broad distribution and reach. In some situations, local audiences have taken the provision of the type of media they want to experience into their own hands. Naficy (1993), for example, has documented how Iranian exiles in Los Angeles produced periodicals and radio broadcasts, sponsored newscasts and TV programmes, rented airtime and sold advertising space during their broadcasts. Access to broadcast materials that represented the culture left behind were considered essential for the survival and mental health of the exiles. Naficy has suggested that the state of being in exile heightens the desire for the autonomous construction of being different, and independent media production can work towards achieving such desires.

Using media to actively construct difference bears testimony to the fact that media are an important mechanism for learning about the world. They give materiality to stories that would otherwise exist only as reminiscences and family folklore. Experiencing one's cultural heritage in the media gives an authority to the story that takes it beyond the personal and into the historical-social. Naficy notes that, in the case of the Iranian exiles in Los Angeles, the popular culture they produced in exile assisted the development of a grounded sense of self from which an engagement with mainstream American culture could be negotiated.

Paradoxically the production of exilic popular culture also helped some 'exiles' to reduce their dependence on their 'home' culture by more clearly designating their class and social position in the adopted culture:

> Exilic popular culture and television are instrumental in the survival of uprooted Iranians. They constructed a cohesive semiotic and discursive space for exilic communitas and an exilic economy, but their commercially driven nature served ultimately to recuperate their resistive and counter-hegemonic spin, turning them chiefly into social agencies of assimilation.
>
> (Naficy 1993: 192)

While the production of exilic popular culture may prove a transitional phase in the assimilation of an immigrant community, Naficy's analysis points to the fact that identity groups, even when dispersed within the audience, may cultivate shared interests, define agendas for the production of particular media events, produce the required media materials, and identify exhibition strategies to secure participation in the global *mediascape*.

The term *mediascape* was first used by Appadurai (1997: 35), who suggested that, 'the complexity of the current global economy has to do with certain fundamental disjunctures between economy, culture, and politics'. For Appadurai, contemporary society is fundamentally disjunctive because, in the global capitalist system, social organization is based on flows of ideas (*ideoscape*), media (*mediascape*), money (*financescape*), people (*ethnoscape*) and technology (*technoscape*). He calls these the five dimensions of global culture 'flows' and argues that they operate in a quasi-independent manner. For example, he suggests that mediascapes, 'Provide ... large and complex repertoires of images, narratives and ethnoscapes to viewers throughout the world, in which the world of commodities and the world of news and politics are profoundly mixed' (1997: 35). To become part of the mediascape, news-worthy events are processed as media information, in ways that make them fit the rationality of the media (as opposed to the *lived*) world. As a result, Appadurai assumes that people engage with the real world through the **proto-narratives** the media provide in order to make the realities of their daily lives fit the media's aphoristic account of the world, rather than the other way round. In this sense, the *mediascape* demonstrates not just that culture is now 'information-based', but that in fact it is 'information dominated' (Kellerman 2000).

Appadurai believed that the flow of contemporary media teaches people to engage with information in characteristic ways — and predominantly as a commodity — and that this development would lead from a world in which the media report and record, to one where the media agenda and worldview dominates the information landscape. Similarly, Castells (1998: 336) has argued that the emergence of the information society has its origins in more funda-mental changes than just the development of information technologies and growth in the production and distribution of information. The social, economic and cultural changes that have taken place over the last 40 years, he claims, have their historical origins in 'three *independent* processes: the information tech-nology revolution; the economic crisis of both capitalism and statism, and their subsequent restructuring; and the blooming of cultural social movements, such as libertarianism, human rights, feminism, and environmentalism' (1998: 336).

One reaction to the increasing life differences between information producers and generic labour, and the lack of recognition within the information society of people who are marginalized or ignored because they are no longer (or have never been) able to contribute productively to the information economy, is the pursuit of a more activist engagement in the *mediascape*. This involves finding a way of becoming part of the *mediascape* rather than of being left outside it. Engaging with the *mediascape* therefore is obviously a survival strategy for cultural audiences who wish to secure their cultural heritage and its narratives as part of the global cultural pattern. Castells has argued that:

> Cultural battles are the power battles of the Information Age. They are primarily fought in and by the media, but the media are not the power holders. Power, as the capacity to impose behaviour, lies in the networks of

information exchange and symbol manipulation, which relate social actors, institutions, and cultural movements, through icons, spokespersons, and intellectual amplifiers.

(Castells 1998: 348)

One way in which less powerful actors can gain part of the cultural terrain is through negotiating the meaning of mainstream media products. Gillespie (2000), for example, has pointed to disjunctures between global media and local experience in her ethnographic research among British Asian youth in London. She noted that coming to terms with their 'limited' representation in mainstream media led to a devaluation of British/Asian identity, and fostered instead a 'desire for new kinds of transnational and Diaspora identities' (2000: 165). The disaffection with British/Asian identity precipitated more intense identification and involvement with transnational issues like consumerism, feminism, environmentalism, and human rights, alongside Diaspora identifications and connections. These *Diaspora* identifications and connections included viewing everything from Bollywood blockbusters to home videos that maintain family connections, exchange family information and allow family members to engage in video tourism. Gillespie suggests that the consumption of both global and 'local' media contributes to the development and maintenance of split identities as young British/Asians continuously switch between global affiliations, home culture orientations and local traditions.

The media initiatives of indigenous and ethnic minority communities in the 1980s and 1990s were important steps in the development of independently owned and controlled alternative media industries throughout the world. Their activities included production, distribution of imported videos, CDs, magazines and other entertainment from the home culture, support for ethnic radio and community TV and subscribing to specialist broadcasting. Importantly, alternative media industries are largely made possible by the tireless and unpaid labour of numerous enthusiasts and amateur presenters. The range and quality of work undertaken by local communities who are determined to contribute their voices to the mediascape parallels the work of fans and audiences on the internet. Engaging with flows of media product by contributing work and time has strengthened communal information networks associated with the discovery and enjoyment of the media materials. Based on recognition of the centrality of media in the operation of contemporary society (its 'information-based' nature), ethnic and indigenous communities have initiated strategies for taking control of their representation in both mainstream and local contexts.

Conclusion

Earlier in this chapter, we noted that Meehan (1984) had expressed concern at the possibility that ratings might become the only system of communication between broadcasters and audiences. We have seen that ratings analysis treats the audience event as an abstract and measurable behaviour: *exposure*. The ratings system has worked well for broadcasters, in that it has kept audiences viewing (if not satisfied), advertisers paying and broadcasters in control of the mass communication system for more than 75 years. It is perhaps ironic therefore, that advertising practices, informed by ratings and other market research data, appear to be making changes to broadcasting inevitable. The interests of advertisers and the emerging competition with the internet, a medium that simultaneously engages, entertains and sells, are shifting the balance of power, not just in broadcasting but in the entertainment industries in general. It is clear that in broadcasting, manufacturers will play a more informed and active role in their relationships with audience/consumers, but the situation for arts manufacturers (artists and musicians) remains unclear. The type of competitive environment promoted by the application of marketing principles is not well-suited to the production of excellence. Rather, as we have seen, it benefits mainstream production and middle-brow culture at the expense of the type of commitment to excellence that traditionally has been the cornerstone of the arts industries. Yet it seems that the mantra of the 'consumer relationship' is being chanted and is challenging the commitment to audience cultures that has held sway in audience research for the past 20 years (see Chapters 6 and 7 especially).

In this chapter we have seen how ratings analysis and audience development define the audience/media event in terms of one audience behaviour: *exposure*. While ratings analysis may present itself as the most influential form of audience research, its claims seem tenuous. Current developments in customer relationship marketing are adding new audience management tools to the commercial research context, with the management of consumers based on analysis of complex data banks. These developments challenge media researchers to look again at what is happening in this field.

While the shortcomings of these approaches are considerable, as we have shown, they cannot alter the fact that ratings and other audience measurement services receive massive support from broadcasting industries, governments and public authorities. A clear articulation of the shortcomings of the marketing approaches by media researchers is needed to ensure that audiences are convinced of the value of lobbying for change, and of the importance of audience activism — not just as a service to particular audience communities but as a source of difference in the communication system.

Further reading

Meehan, E. (1993) Heads of household and ladies of the house: gender, genre and broadcast ratings, 1929–1990, in W.S. Solomon and R.W. McChesney (eds) *Ruthless Criticism: New Perspectives in U.S. Communication History*. Minneapolis and London: University of Minnesota Press.

Neuman, W.R. (1991) *The Future of the Mass Audience*. Cambridge: Cambridge University Press.

Webster, J.G., Phalen, P.F. and Lichty, L.W. (2000) *Ratings Analysis: The Theory and Practice of Audience Research*, 2nd edn. Mahwah, New Jersey and London: Lawrence Erlbaum and Associates.

4 | CAUSE AND EFFECT: THEORIES IN FLUX

Many opinion polls show wide public concern for limiting 'violence' on television and film. Yet the same people, when asked, have much greater trouble naming the films and programs which they think have too much. My proposal is that we need to research *how different segments of the public develop their category 'media violence', and what they mean by it.*
(Martin Barker 1997: 43, original emphasis)

Introduction

This chapter is concerned with mapping the trajectory of 'effects' research, from the early days of mass communication research which was concerned with identifying the ways in which media subtly influence the behaviour of their consumers — the **media dupe** — to more recent work which looks at the relationship between, say, playing violent video games and juvenile delinquency in 'real' life. Importantly, it considers the contemporary debates which continue to provoke some researchers to insist on the dangers of media effect and others to insist just as strongly that no relationship between watching and doing exists. It argues that, despite decades of work in which researchers have tried to demonstrate the cause-effect relationship, it has never actually been possible to isolate out the specific influence of media from other factors, including individual pathology, on human behaviour. This doesn't mean that policy has not been formulated as if such a relation *does* exist, however, such has been the desire to find someone or something to blame for antisocial and dangerous behaviour. Many contemporary researchers, however, have been keen to rehabilitate mass media as a benign or at least neutral influence in society, so the cause-effect conundrum is set to run and run.

Sliding on the ice

All research into audiences is, to a greater or lesser extent, about effect, about how and in what ways (including if at all) the consumers of media messages react and relate to their content. But the particular interest of 'effects' researchers has been to identify specific behaviours resulting from watching, listening and reading specific kinds of mediated material. There is a common understanding (see, for example, Abercrombie and Longhurst 1998) that audience research has developed chronologically through successive phases which are usually characterized as: effects, uses/gratifications, encoding/decoding and a somewhat ambivalent contemporary environment which positions media influence anywhere along the all–nothing continuum (see Chapter 2). However, much current and recent interest tends towards viewing the audience member as autonomous and interactive, especially in the context of information communication technologies (ICTs), as self-knowing and self-aware about the potential blandishments of the media machine, easily able to cut through the propaganda and take from the media whatever is useful and meaningful.

Much current research focuses on what audiences *do* with media, how we work with and through the material we consume because of the **polysemy** of the text, that is, the way in which messages are open to many interpretations. About how we interpret the 'message' in the context of our experiential understanding of social life. Nonetheless, there continues to be concern raised about the relationship between, say, watching TV programmes or playing video games and then acting out the action in real life. So, in some, quite serious ways, media researchers' interests in situating the audience as fully conscious and media literate is in direct contrast to an increase in public and political anxiety about media influence, especially in relation to violence in popular media (see later for an elaboration of this point). Thus, although there is a certain logic about suggesting a linear progression of research methods as researchers became more sophisticated in their understanding of the relationships between audiences and texts, contemporary theory continues to be fractured by the debate about effect, and contemporary studies continue to try and identify cause-effect relationships (or their total absence!) between consuming media and subsequent behaviour in the 'real' world.

Interestingly, one of the key differences between early studies (for example, Lasswell's work on propaganda during World War 1 (1927)), and more contemporary accounts in the twenty-first century, is the locus and intent of production bias and control. Much early work was specifically oriented towards unmasking the propagandist potential of media to dupe the masses and the ways in which political elites used the media for their own sly purposes. In other words, the bias was from the powerful to the masses, where the public were brainwashed into being docile and unquestioning wage slaves, playing into notions of power, culture and ideology — **hegemony** — and the media's role in their circulation. Whilst there is a clear Marxist ideology at play in such a construction of the politics-media nexus, concerns about propaganda and interference by our political leaders are regularly invoked at times of war. For example, the war correspondent Eve-Ann Prentice (2003) talks explicitly about the news embargoes forced on journalists covering conflict in the Gulf War in the 1990s as well as more contemporary news management strictures that came into play in the war on Iraq (2003). She argues that news organizations wanting to send their journalists into conflict zones had to agree to abide by government protocols relating to exactly what was allowed to be broadcast or published. Whilst there are obvious concerns about security in times of war, Prentice argues that the degree of restriction is far in excess of what could conceivably be considered as sensitive information, suggesting instead that government influence over news management is rather a strategy of control and deliberate obfuscation. It is scarcely surprising, then, that it tends to be governments who are more concerned about the effect of 'affect' than much of the public, setting up numerous watchdog quangos and committees to police the media. The question to ask, then, is are we any nearer reaching a conclusion about the cause-effect conundrum now than we were 50 years ago, or are we actually asking the wrong question?

A potted history of effects theories

In a very useful summary of historical shifts in effects research, McQuail (1994: 328–32) describes four phases which have developed over time in response to changing social environments, each building incrementally on what has gone before, including both incorporating and challenging the 'old' order. This is not to suggest that theory necessarily progresses in a neat and orderly fashion, since it is as likely to be cyclical as linear. But it is to indicate that there are key moments in the development of a field, which can be understood in the context of an organizing framework for understanding social phenomena.

1st phase — media as all-powerful
This research phase spans the turn of the twentieth century to the 1930s and the assumptions during that early period were that the mass media were highly

influential and operated as modes of persuasion, if not control, in a one-way direction, from the economic and political elites to 'the people'. However, this phase was more inferential and ideological than empirically driven, resting on the popularity of certain media forms and an assumption that the audiences for those messages were generally naïve and susceptible to covert propaganda.

2nd phase — challenge to the all-powerful media model

The move towards empirically oriented studies began as a challenge to the earlier theoretical ideas about media and effect and developed a more sophisticated research agenda which looked at differences in media format, genre and content (see, for example, Blumer 1933). Much research in this period, from around the 1930s up to the late 1950s, looked at the media's potential to influence voters (through political campaigns — see Chapter 3), at the effects of certain narratives on deviant behaviours (for example the moral panics constructed in the media around juvenile delinquency — see Cohen 1972) and at the media as sources of information. What became clear in many of the studies of this period were the number of variables which needed to be factored into analyses, including personal characteristics, but also the kinds of exposure to other sources of information. This phase ended with a strong sense of the media's place in any number of influences, suggesting that the media did, probably, have some impact but they were only one *part* of a pre-existing social, economic and political structure in which individuals function. By thinking of the media as part of a larger picture, it then becomes difficult to isolate the precise influence of the media away from other possible sources.

3rd phase — powerful media revisited

However, as with any theory, no sooner is it written than someone wants to challenge its veracity, and so it was with the 'no-effect' model. By the 1960s, researchers were questioning the basis on which claims of no-effect had been made and began to seek out ways in which to demonstrate effect (see Lang and Lang 1981). But this time, the tools for analysis had moved on from a simple stimulus-response model which could measure immediate effect, which characterized the 1st phase, to ones which sought to identify longer-term effects, subtle shifts in understanding, diverse contexts and motivations for attending to media outputs. This phase also saw an interest in the more structural aspects of media production such as journalistic practice, media ownership and wider questions of political economy, as well as looking at less visible notions such as ideology. Crucially, the development of television in this era prompted a renewed interest in the power of media persuasion (Elliot 1972). A particular and popular theory which emerged during this time was Gerbner's **cultivation analysis** theory which explored the relationships between audience exposure to TV (especially those of heavy 'users') and their beliefs and behaviours, specifically to identify the 'acculturation' effect of TV on viewers (Gerbner

1967). Importantly, Gerbner insisted that it was the *cumulative* effect of watching hours, days, weeks, months and years of TV which 'cultivated' the effect, not simply watching a few violent TV shows or hearing periodic outbursts of swearing.

4th phase — negotiating media meaning

This latest (but perhaps not last!) phase, which began in the late 1970s and early 1980s, has been characterized by an interest in the ways in which media messages are constructed and offered up to audiences for their consumption and how audiences either accept the (dominant) ways in which texts are *encoded*, or reject them or negotiate them (see Chapter 2 for an elaboration of the encoding/decoding model). In other words, audience research began to focus on an examination of what audiences did *with* media, rather than what media did *to* audiences, emphasizing agency rather than passivity. Studies such as Morley's (1980) work on the *Nationwide* programme and Hobson's (1982) work on *Crossroads* made clear that there were many different ways in which audiences understood and interpreted media texts. Moreover, what also became clear was that audiences used media texts in a variety of ways — as ways in which to 'practice' other ways of being or as the basis for workplace discussions. In other words, media consumption had a utility over and above the immediate consumption of a particular programme or news item. This phase also saw the further development of alternative methodological practices, moving away from quantitative approaches towards more nuanced understandings of audiences' lived experiences, necessitating a more qualitative approach which would enable the personal meaning-making process and belief structures to be teased out (see Hall 1980; Morley 1980). These new methodologies included strategies such as observing how families watch TV and looking at who has control of the remote. McQuail argues that what this phase contributes to our understanding of effects is that there are two broad imperatives: one is that the media 'construct social formations and history itself by framing images of reality (in fiction as well as news) in a predictable and patterned way; and second, that people in audiences construct for themselves their own view of social reality and their place in it, in interaction with the symbolic constructions offered by the media' (McQuail 1994: 331). Thus the influence of the media will vary along the continuum of all–nothing, depending on where we, as individual consumers, are situated along that line in terms of our own relationship to the message, our experience, our background and our beliefs.

Whilst McQuail (1994) offers a useful way into understanding shifts in audience effect theory, his is by no means the only model available. Perse (2001), for example, argues that looking at the *types* rather than the *extent* of effect is a different way of thinking about the phenomenon, although she makes the point that such models can provide only partial explanations of the highly complex process of *affect*. For Perse (2001: 51), then, there are four models of effect, which she describes as: direct, conditional, cumulative and cognitive-transactional:

Direct effects — these are generally short-term and testable and assume a passive audience unable to challenge 'hidden' media messages or an audience unconscious of the impact of media content on their behaviour (see later discussion on violence and affect).
Conditional effects — these are effects which are contingent on the pre-dispositions, personal attributes and belief systems of individual audience members and allow the audience active agency to decide which aspects of a given media text they are willing to accept.
Cumulative effects — this model suggests that despite the potential for individual negotiation and decision to consume some but not other messages, the media is saturated with certain kinds of message where repetition of theme subverts conscious agency.
Cognitive-transactional effects — this model sees media effects as the consequence of individual cognitive responses towards media content and uses the concept of 'priming' to suggest that audiences are primed to watch, remember and thus potentially be influenced by, certain kinds of content rather than others. The transactional aspect of the model refers to the fact that both media content *and* audience characteristics are important in understanding media effect.

Whilst Perse presents an interesting analysis of media effect, the relationship of her typology to more familiar renditions of media effect is not substantially different except for her insistence on understanding effect through the combined lens of both content and audience profile, which is powerfully persuasive. Most studies tend to look either at content or at audience, so a model which combines both these elements can provide, in principle, a much more comprehensive analysis. Yet other contemporary researchers are moving beyond (or perhaps alongside) the orthodoxy of identifying audience effect as constituting either passive incorporation or active resistance by constructing a new paradigm, that of spectacle/performance. Some proponents of this new audience-think, such as Abercrombie and Longhurst (1998), believe that 'the audience' should be set free from the confines of medium and genre. Instead, the 'every-dayness' of being an audience member and thus witnessing a variety of performances (that is via consuming TV, newspapers, films, radio shows and so on) should be understood more intuitively and holistically in terms of our/their forms of identity with the entire **mediascape** which has become our ordinary, media-saturated world. Methodologically, Abercrombie and Longhurst are arguing for a research paradigm which is essentially ethnographic and which takes a much more comprehensive approach to the notion of audience and effect than has been attempted hitherto.

Of course, new theory about media influence (and the lack thereof) is developing all the time, but what remains clear is that many people, advertisers and politicians among them, *do* believe that the media have an influence so that the argument is less about *if* and more about *how much*. And as Carey (1988) points out, mass media are an easy target to blame in times of significant social shifts or developments of new social phenomena, although the extent to which the media construct those social shifts or simply report on their progress continues to be a primary point of research contention.

But at crucial times in history, the media *are* influential in informing publics about the progress of, say, a war or other armed conflict, as we said earlier, but it is the extent to which the media construct and therefore influence what becomes 'the agenda' which is important (but difficult) to map. Exploring the ways in which news media are mobilized by politicians, and identifying news media's agenda-setting strategies, are topics set out in Chapter 5 and are not therefore elaborated again here. But we can say that most media scholars would cede *some* effect to mass media, but the point here is that the media have effects simply by their existence: suggesting they have *power*, on the other hand, suggests an effect which is altogether more deliberate than just 'being there'. Having discussed some of the broad theoretical developments in research on audience and media effect, we now turn to a consideration of one of the key thematics which has dominated the 'effects' agenda for decades, that is, viewing violence.

Violent affect

The way in which media such as newspapers and television deal with and treat issues of crime and violence has been an abiding preoccupation for media researchers, principally because of the potential for copycat behaviour by audiences, especially children (Schlesinger 1991; Paik and Comstock 1994; Wilson et al. 1997). Two of the earliest studies were carried out in the mid-1950s by Head (1954) and Smythe (1954), both of which argued that acts of violence were three times as frequent in programmes aimed at children than in mainstream programming. Other similar studies followed throughout the subsequent decades with repeated attempts to map patterns and trends in the *volume*, if not the actual *impact*, of TV violence. Whilst early researchers shied away from an overly prescriptive definition of what a violent act actually comprised for counting purposes, the scholar whose body of work on 'counting' violence has become part of the accepted canon in the area — George Gerbner (see *cultivation analysis*) — defined it thus:

> . . . the overt expression of physical force against self or other, compelling action against one's will on pain of being hurt or killed, or actually hurting or killing. The expression of injurious or lethal force had to be credible and real in the symbolic terms of the drama. Humorous and even farcical violence can be credible and real, even if it has a presumable comic effect.
>
> (Gerbner 1972: 31)

Gerbner's work and that of other US colleagues throughout the 1980s and 1990s (for example, Gerbner et al. 1995; Cole 1996) suggests that the trend at the close of the twentieth century was a decreasing amount of violence, in simple volume terms, on terrestrial TV but an increase in volume across non-terrestrial programming. Whilst the precise reasons for this apparent pattern are not immediately apparent, US-produced programmes appear to be significantly ahead in their violence quotient when compared with the output of other industrialized countries (see Takeuchi et al. 1995). In a UCLA study of home video rental content, researchers found that in the monitoring period 1995–97, more than 50 per cent of rentals had so much violence that concern would have been raised if any of them had been broadcast uncut on prime-time TV (UCLA Center for Communication Policy 1998).

The problem with the incidence of media violence is that it is completely contradicted by the statistical evidence; even in the USA, crime rates are going down rather than up (Bureau of Justice Statistics 1998). The point is, why does the volume of violent material on television matter? Why are we interested in measuring it and mapping its contours? Well, obviously, it is because there is a belief that there is some kind of cause and effect relationship going on, between watching violence and 'doing' violence, between a viewer consuming violent TV programmes and then perpetrating violent acts against real people in real life. It is odd, then, that the early studies of TV violence were almost entirely oriented towards *content*, counting specific acts across the television landscape, identifying which genres or media were most culpable in their displays of tele-visual aggression and which genres were performing better or worse over time, rather than investigating viewer response and therefore *affect*.

> Public convictions that violent media content contributes to violence in society are supported by anecdotal reports of criminals' media use, naïve beliefs in the connections between crime rates and media violence, media reports of 'copycat' crime and the publicized reports of some highly visible research.
>
> (Perse 2001: 199)

The cause and effect relation was often implicit in such studies but was rarely 'tested' for its strength with real audiences or even by mapping trends in the volume of TV violence against trends in the volume of real-life violence. Perhaps part of this reluctance to seriously engage with the potentiality of 'real' affect has been an acknowledgement that TV violence is not the same as the real thing which happens messily inside people's lives (Fiske and Hartley 1978; Lichter et al. 1994).

> The violence and terror we see on television bear little or no relationship to their actual occurrence . . . television violence is an overkill of 'happy violence' — swift, cool, effective, without tragic consequences and in other ways divorced from real life and crime statistics.
>
> (Gerbner 1995: 71, 73)

Most acts of domestic violence, for example, are perpetrated against women by men they know, and stranger rape is substantially less frequent than rape by a husband, partner or boyfriend. More than twenty years ago, it was estimated that between three and four million American women were battered by their partners (Stark et al. 1981) and global predictions more than a decade ago were that two-thirds of all married women would be battered at some time in their married lives (Stout 1991). In the UK, in 2001–02, one in four women experienced domestic violence (British Crime Survey for England and Wales 2002). Domestic violence accounted for 25 per cent of all violent crime and one third of all murders in 2002 (Tweedale 2003): also in that year there were 635,000 reported incidents of domestic violence in England and Wales and women were the victims in 81 per cent of cases (Gorna 2003).

Other crime facts which run counter to common-sense myths are that murder is not the most common crime, that black people are much more likely to be victims than perpetrators and that older people are much less likely to be assaulted on the street than young people. This is the actuality of crime trends, but television shows us exactly the reverse of these facts because TV-land is about excitement and drama with neatly closed ends: only rarely are we offered glimpses of the real impact of violence on people's real lives and relationships.

To unpack this a little and focus on the media's portrayal of crimes against women, Myers (1997) argues that one of the ways in which the media simplify what are very complex issues is in their persistent use of two contradictory frames: Madonna and whore. In this schema, women are either innocent victims of male lust and violence or guilty of incitement by their own behaviour and conduct. The repetitive use of these two central motifs or what Myers (1997: 9) describes as the 'male supremacist ideology' produces a powerful social lesson. Women are warned through these reporting mechanisms about the limits of 'acceptable' female behaviour and the likely outcome (rape/ murder) of their behavioural transgression. This setting up of a binary opposition of good girl/bad girl finds resonance with feminist notions of patriarchy and the supposed 'place' of women in society (Soothill and Walby 1991; Benedict 1992; Meyers 1994).

What such an analysis offers is a critique of the media's tendency to pathologize male rapists as monsters (and therefore not like 'us'), by showing that most rapists are actually the *partners* of their victims or at the very least are known to them. The archetypal rapist is not the sinister man in the shadows but the bloke washing his car. But perhaps the media's proclivities towards sensationalizing violence is precisely because the reality of case reporting is so ordinary. The perpetrators of real violence are the guys (mostly) in the pub and the men in the office and the blokes reading stories to their children, but this reality is both too mundane for TV to portray in actuality and, just as importantly, too close to home for most journalists to acknowledge. Thus, out of those twin impulses comes a way of writing, reading and viewing violence which downplays its terrifying ordinariness — and thus limits the very real lessons it could provide to potential victims — by inflating its deviance.

But in any case, as is clear from the more nuanced accounts of viewer reaction and interpretation laid out by Stuart Hall in his seminal work on **encoding/decoding** (Hall 1980), it is no longer tenable to assume an identical response to a given message by its various consumers. Thus arguments relating to the effects of exposure of violent images on audiences cannot credibly make claims which culminate in a verdict of collective harm (Gunter 1985). This is absolutely *not* to say that there can be *no* link between watching and doing violence, but rather to suggest that the strength of that relationship is extremely hard to pin down and disentangle from all the other contributing factors which influence behaviour, such as an individual's character, background, life experiences, lifestyle, friendships, pathological profile, exposure to and enjoyment of other cultural influences and so on.

It is interesting then, to note how public *belief* in the existence of precisely such a direct cause and effect relationship, despite the conspicuous lack of hard or even soft evidence, has been able to mobilize support for legislation to restrict the volume of violent material on television, in the USA and elsewhere. Whilst it has not been possible to single out media violence as the only or even necessarily the major contributor to the incidence of violence and aggression in real life, it is likely to be one factor. Donnerstein et al. (1994) have usefully summarized what they consider to be the primary attributes of violent media content which are most likely to be linked with aggressive behaviour that is, where media violence is:

- rewarded, not punished;
- justified;
- resonant with aspects of everyday life;
- motivated by harmful intent;
- realistic;
- arousing.

and where the perpetrator of violent behaviour:

- is similar to the viewer;
- can provoke identification with the viewer.

The utility of thinking about violent media as a set of characteristics as suggested by Donnerstein et al. is neatly encapsulated in the findings from recent National Television Violence Studies (see Wilson et al. 1997, 1998) which suggested that viewers perceiving *justification* for an act of aggression had an impact on subsequent violent behaviour. Thus watching 'justified' violence appeared to give 'permission' to viewers to be aggressive themselves, whereas watching unjustified acts may have the opposite effect. In work with children and violent TV, Krcmar and Cooke (2001) argue that age (and therefore the range of experiences on which viewers have to draw) has a significant impact on ideas about the rightness or wrongness of violent behaviour. Young children are more likely to see unpunished aggressive acts as being 'better' than punished acts, whereas older children are more likely to see provoked acts of violence as more acceptable than unprovoked ones. In an experimental study with 10–12-year-old children in the USA, images which showed an armed criminal being killed (that is, attracting negative consequences for violent action) were a stronger inhibitor to imitative behaviour than scenes where the armed perpetrator 'got away with it' (Bernhardt et al. 2001).

Successive opinion polls have shown that a majority of Americans believe that the influence of television on the incidence of crime is either important or critical (US Department of Justice 1994: 222; cited in Fowles 1999: 13). Such third-person effects (Davison 1983; McLeod et al. 2001), that is believing that something affects *other* people, but *not* oneself, are particularly strong is this contested area of effect, and Hoffner et al. (2001) show that audiences believe *they* are much less influenced by violent images than *other* people. Similarly, Duck and Mullin (1995) found that viewers rejected being influenced by negative content (oriented towards violence, sexism and racism) whilst accepting their own openness to 'good' content, for example, public service announcements. Conversely, they believed other people *were* influenced more by 'bad' content than they were. The existence of such beliefs — that other people are easily duped but I am not — have been identified across any number of studies focusing on any number of topics and demonstrate the strong desire that we have to believe in ourselves as autonomous and discriminating human beings.

Giving evidence at one of a series of congressional hearings in the USA between 1988 and 1994, on the topic of violent media material, George Gerbner (1993: 65) testified that 'our homes are drenched with carefully and expertly choreographed brutality such as the world has never seen and does not occur in any other industrial country'. In that same year, there were nine bills before Congress attempting to reduce broadcast violence. Both Bob Dole and Bill Clinton included the issue in their campaign agenda, Clinton going so far as to suggest that there should be a 'V' (violence) chip installed in all new TV sets so that parents could restrict children's access to 'unsuitable' material. The V-chip was intended to operate in the same way as filters do on computers, by recognizing and censoring programs with specific words and terms in their titles (or web address in the case of computers).

Interestingly, some people believe that media violence has a stronger copycat potential than real violence. For example, after the shootings at Columbine High School in Denven on 20 April 1999, the 106th Congress decided to take no action concerning the availability of guns but agreed to continue their plans to restrict access to violent media content, principally reinvigorating the 'V' chip idea, this time specifying its installation in all new TV sets with screens of 13 inches or wider (cited in Perse 2001: 197). The appalling events at Columbine, where 19 children and teachers were killed, was reported by most media as the tragic 'consequences' of two adolescent killers' obsession with violent video games. The following headline makes clear who 'society' blames: 'School massacre families to sue creators of violent games' (*The Independent*, 7 June 1999: 3). Such a response mirrors that provoked by the killing of a 2-year-old child, James Bulger, by two adolescent boys who were also reported to have been fascinated with violent material. In that instance, the film *Childs Play 3* was linked directly with the killing.

The brutal death of James Bulger in 1998 prompted the Home Office to pursue yet more research into the impact of violent media, culminating in a study which, not surprisingly, *did* suggest such a link, although it had to stop short of making the link directly causal. The headline, though, is somewhat less scrupulous: 'Film violence link to teenage crime: new twist to video nasty debate — 'vulnerable' young people may be influenced by screen killings' (*The Guardian*, 8 January 1998). The salient words here are 'vulnerable' and 'may', both of which are contestable and controversial. But we do need to understand that concern with viewers' propensity to unthinkingly imitate media violence or be depraved or corrupted by it, is nothing new and efforts to prevent violent media content in books, magazines and newspapers have been ongoing since at least the late nineteenth century (Saunders 1996).

Now, as then, one of the principal arguments *against* restricting and further regulating media content is that of freedom of speech (Gunter 2002), often linked with exhortations that consumers have the power to switch off or not read or listen to offensive material. In a recent, industry-funded project into effect, the researchers insist that it is misleading to point the finger of guilt at all broadcasters for portraying excessive violence since the worst excesses were mostly seen on pay-per-view channels or at times when children were unlikely to be watching (Gunter 2003). Whilst it is tempting to simply dismiss such research as mere industry propaganda, the differentiation between different parts of the industry does need to be acknowledged.

In any case, the efficacy of strategies to limit vulnerable viewers' (such as children) access to violent material in response to concerns expressed by society and government are hard to assess. The criteria for classifying films, for example, are persistently challenged by the industry and on the grounds that members of the classification board are out of touch with reality and with public understandings of taste, decency and what is 'acceptable' material for different aged audiences. A recent study found that the effectiveness of V-chip technology is severely limited by the industry's reluctance to label programmes in ways which accurately reflect their adult/violence/sexual content (Kunkel et al. 2002).

Violence as (kidz)play

The continuing debate around copycat violence is often complicated by the contradictory nature of research findings in the areas, so that for every study showing a cause-effect relation, another suggests the opposite conclusions, thus producing an entirely inconclusive evidence base. This is not least because the different foci, context, sample-base, age cohort and exposure times in different studies has resulted in substantially different analyses and interpretation. It is therefore highly problematic to try and develop either comparative perspectives or to reach credible conclusions. Just as many researchers believe there *is* a relationship between violent-content video games and aggression (Irwin and Gross 1995; Ballard and Lineberger 1999) as believe the opposite (Cooper and Mackie 1986; Graybill et al. 1985; Scott 1995). Even reviewers of the literature cannot agree on the existence or not of causal effect (Dill and Dill 1998; Griffiths 1999), although some, like Freedman (2002) uncompromisingly assert that there is *no* scientific evidence to suggest effect. He argues that the fact that violent video games have proliferated at the same time as violent crime has decreased makes it improbable that one causes the other, since the effect appears to work in the 'wrong' direction.

Part of the rationale of so much research focusing on children's viewing and doing behaviour is the notion of their increased vulnerability to 'inappropriate' media material and the concomitant desire to protect their innocent eyes from harmful images (Buckingham 1993), resulting in political and moral responses such as the development of the 'V' chip, discussed above. Concern has been continuously raised about the harmful effects of TV on impressionable children, ranging from the rather benign impact of suppressing their intellectual development (through the mindless activity of watching mindless TV) to the more contentious suggestion that watching violent acts (on TV, in games, on video or at the cinema) provokes violent behaviour in real life. In between are anxieties about children being exposed to adult problems too early and the subsequent effects on their psychological health, that children will be encouraged to take up delinquent lifestyles or become sexually promiscuous (Cohen 1972; Pearson 1983) or that children can be desensitized to violence and become incapable of distinguishing between fantasy and reality, good and evil.

But most empirically based work demonstrates the complex and sophisticated ways in which even quite young people think about and interpret potentially harmful messages. In Nightingale et al.'s (2000) study of young (under 16 years of age) people, for example, they found that three distinct considerations were salient to children's discussion of 'vulnerable' viewers: personal characteristics (age and gender); fantasy/realistic content; and belief that events could really happen to them. Importantly, as with older (mainstream) viewers, young people also displayed significant *third-person effects*, discounting personal susceptibility but acknowledging that 'other' people, especially children younger than themselves, *could* be affected (see Buckingham 1996): the principal 'harm' was being made to feel scared or insecure by horror movies and by news programmes.

Video games have been especially targeted as the focus of much audience-based research relating to children and affect, largely because of their popularity, the sociable context of interaction (that is, often with other children) and the fact that they can be experienced with a VCR and are therefore more accessible than games requiring computer facilities. The violent content of video games has prompted concern about affect for more than ten years and as recently as 2000, the mayor of Indianapolis spearheaded a campaign to ban children under 18 years old from playing violent video games unless accompanied by an adult (cited in Sherry 2001: 410). Whilst links are often made between watching violence on TV and playing violent video games, that is, that the impact on the audience is more or less the same, there are very specific differences between the two modes which require more sensitive analyses, such as the relative importance of agency, concentration and realism (Dominick 1984).

Playing video games requires a high degree of active concentration, is competitive and physically demanding, the content is often highly abstract and the violence often has the same fantasy quality as cartoons. Given that any number of studies of TV and film influence suggest that violent reactions amongst audiences are correlated to the degree of realism and believability contained in the story (see Atkin 1983), the affect of violence in games is likely to be qualitatively different precisely because of the game genre. There are three principal theories which attempt to explain how watching and using violent material (through interactive game playing) leads to aggressive behaviour, all of which are taken from social psychology, which are broadly:

- social learning;
- arousal;
- priming.

The first of these, social learning theory, is by far the most frequently cited affect model, which suggests that behaviour is learned by imitating those activities which are highly rewarded. In the case of video games, the high density absorption of players/audiences coupled with identification with game characters encourages an 'acting out' of those strategies which are especially rewarded: inevitably, such actions are those which feature fighting and overcoming 'the enemy' (Irwin and Gross 1995). The arousal affect (see Zillmann 1988), in the specific context of using aggressive media content, suggests that the stimulus of aggressive play activates and then accelerates a pre-existing tendency to aggression amongst those audiences who already possess that particular characteristic or predisposition (Brody 1977; Ballard and Lineberger 1999). Priming is similar to arousal except that a pre-existing tendency to aggression does not need to be present in order for the player to be primed to transfer aggressive thoughts into aggressive actions (Jo and Berkowitz 1994).

In Europe, growing concerns about violent video games eventually produced a legislative response: that from April 2003, all computer games sold in the European Union must carry a specific classification, as with films, which relates to the age of the player which the regulators deem appropriate to use the material (Ahmed 2003). Thus games with no violent content or sex will be rated 3+, rising through 8+, 12+, 16+ and 18+. In Britain, computer games which are so violent that they fall outside this classification system will be regulated by the British Board of Film Classification and could be banned. Whilst the fine for selling a banned game is currently (2003) unlimited, the profits to be made in an industry which is estimated to be worth around £4 billion may well encourage some producers to take the risk.

It should be noted here that there is a competing theory which suggests that watching violent material has a cathartic effect, a theory which probably originated with Feshbach (1955) several decades ago, who argued that aggressive feelings can be harmlessly discharged by watching the fictional enactment of violence — see the following section. However, the **catharsis** theory is not widely supported, although periodically, a study will emerge which once again places it at the centre of the debate (for example, Fowles 1999).

Is violence so bad, really?

Such has been the force of the anti-violent TV lobby, that very few commentators have suggested more complex (let alone 'positive' readings of the relationship between viewing and doing violence, although there have been a growing number of voices urging caution over the past ten years (see Cumberbatch and Howitt 1989; Gunter 1994; Gauntlett 1995, 1998), even as others now routinely assert the link as being unarguably true, despite the gaping evidential lack, such as: 'There is no longer doubt that television violence is causally related to negative behaviours such as increases in aggression' (Krcmar and Greene 1999: 30).

Most researchers now rehearse more modest claims for the cause-effect relation, but one very outspoken dissident voice has been that of Jib Fowles who, for more than 15 years, has insisted that violence on television, especially programmes aimed at or watched by children and young people, have effects which are cathartic rather than anti-social. For Fowles (1999), consuming violence enables (principally young) viewers to release tension and animosity and to use violent images, including cartoons as an 'antidote' to the real world. To be sure, his is one of the few voices to be raised in 'support' of TV violence, and the title of his latest book — *The Case For Television Violence* (1999) — suggests that his support does not merely comprise a *lack* of condemnation or even an insistence on complexity, but is a much more *proactive* endorsement of the benefits of TV violence. To bolster his principal argument of violence as a public 'good', he finds numerous examples of TV programmes which have been falsely accused of provoking children to carry out abhorrent and sometimes fatal acts of violence. These actions are undertaken by young people, say the critics, as imitative behaviours of their favourite characters or particular storylines in popular shows, but Fowles triumphantly reveals how particular shows have been exonerated, if sometimes considerably post-hoc, from performing this function.

Choosing an example from the 1970s, the film *Born Innocent* (1974), in which a young girl is raped by four other girls using a wooden tool, was cited as the trigger for a similar kind of assault carried out by a group of girls just days after the film was broadcast on TV. However, the legal case which was brought by the mother of the victim against NBC (the broadcaster who aired the film) was dropped after it was revealed that the ringleader had not watched the film. Another example Fowles cites is from 1993, when a five-year-old boy set fire to his family's trailer home in Ohio, killing his two-year-old sister. His mother blamed the *Beavis and Butt-head* show for inciting the child to set fires, but reporters investigating the tragedy found not only that the boy's trailer home was not hooked up to cable — and that he could not therefore have been a regular viewer — but that the trailer park itself was not wired for cable.

The point that Fowles is trying to make is that the adult public is keen to condemn TV for its routinized portrayal of violence and programmes get scapegoated for their provocative material when in fact, 'the total number of antisocial acts directly attributable to television entertainment antics must be minuscule' (Fowles 1999: 3). He also points to the abiding contradiction which is the cause-effect conundrum relating to TV violence: whilst individuals believe that there is too much violence on TV and that exposure does have an impact on violence in society, so they simultaneously get their daily fix of TV mayhem as if they are not also part of the problem. For Fowles, this contradictory behaviour can best be understood by way of an individual's need to 'act out' aggressively (in an aggressive world), but within the safe confines of the TV set, a desire which is encouraged by the wider community:

> Societies need to tame the maliciousness of their populaces in the interest of their own well-being, and symbolic displays of video violence is a late-twentieth century response to that perpetual requirement. Without harm to himself or herself or others, the voluntary violence viewer steeps himself or herself in phantasms of vile play, derring-do, and deterrence, and emerges in an improved state of mind.
>
> (1999; 119)

Whilst this *could* be a plausible thesis, it suffers from exactly the same flaw which Fowles criticizes in much other research into TV effect, that is, he provides no empirical evidence other than his own experiential beliefs and textual interpretation. Moreover, by using terms such as 'phantasm' and 'derring-do', which are terms more commonly associated with fantasy and adventure, Fowles renders tame, benign and ultimately harmless any number of extremely violent programmes, films and games. This is not to argue that such material *is* in fact dangerous, but Fowles simply *saying* it is harmless on the grounds of his own theory and *not* on the grounds of compelling empirical evidence is just as contentious.

As importantly, Fowles' theory makes no distinction between women and men viewers of violent media (and what they 'do' with the material) which is, in itself, surprising, given that much of the concern about imitative behaviour has been and is still focused on the proclivities of boys and men rather than girls and young women. For example, in Koukounas and McCabe's (2001) experimental work with women and men viewers of violent film material, they found that men tended to experience positive feelings, were entertained and curious, whereas women were more likely to experience boredom, disgust and anger. But the search for effect must also be sensitive to the type of 'violent' material being used. For example, studies focused on determining men's reaction to (and subsequent behaviour from) watching pornographic or sexually explicit material with a violent component produce entirely inconsistent findings on effect.

Fisher and Grenier (1994) suggest that contradictory findings in the literature can be partially explained by the use of different methodologies. Their own experimental study with men in which they attempted to create the conditions which would produce effects from watching violent pornography found no such effect. Davies (1997) also argues that men's exposure to high or low levels of pornographic material was unrelated to their attitudes towards women generally and violence against women in particular. On the other hand, Bauserman (1998) found that the *tone* of sexually explicit material (that is, whether it was 'egalitarian', sexist or aggressive) was a key feature of men's affect, and Bogaert et al. (1999) suggest that men's IQ influences the ways in which they are 'affected' by watching pornography in relation to subsequent behaviours towards women, that is, the higher the IQ the less likely were men to be (negatively) affected by viewing that kind of material.

But what about women and violence? Annette Hill wants to rescue violent media from the grip of analyses which position enjoyment of violence as gendered (male-focused) psychopathology and set out to investigate what made women into fans of what she terms 'new brutalist' (2001: 146) films. She argues that women's interest and pleasure in films such as Quentin Tarrantino's *Pulp Fiction* and *Reservoir Dogs* is as much about the innovative structure, complex and sophisticated narrativization and ability to surprise as it is about the violent content, which is simply part of the package. What she also discovered was that women enjoyed confounding the 'social' expectations of gendered repulsion but also testing their own boundaries, daring themselves to watch and then finding that watching could be thrilling as well as revolting, for example:

> *Reservoir Dogs* I found entertaining because it was completely different to anything I've seen before and quite exciting for all that but at the same time

quite disturbing and horrific. So it was the entertainment side but it was also the other side which isn't what I'd call entertaining . . .

(anon. woman film-goer, cited in Hill 2001: 145)

Returning to the catharsis thesis proposed by Fowles (1999), the theory has a few other proponents. Comstock et al. (1978) together with Scheff and Scheele (1980) have also argued that watching violent media can lead to overt behaviour catharsis, whereby viewers can safely 'act out' an emotional response which neutralizes negative affect. In an attempt to more precisely identify the motivations for watching violent material and the subsequent pleasures derived, Krcmar and Greene (1999) worked with young people between the ages of 11 and 25 to identify the salience of watching violent material in relation to sensation-seeking behaviour in real life. They found that individuals who like to take real risks in the real world are less likely to be interested in watching television, violent or otherwise, as they see themselves as doers rather than watchers.

On the other hand, those individuals who were attracted to illegal or socially sanctioned activities, but who didn't actually engage in them, were more likely to watch violent-content material, especially realistic crime series and contact sports. In other words, genuine thrill-seekers want to experience the authentic buzz whereas the less adventurous wannabes will content themselves with the vicarious pleasures of second-hand (mediated) sensation. Such a view is not inconsistent with Fowles' (1999) notion of TV as catharsis, since it appears that young people can 'act out' danger without needing to actually experience it. In contrast, Hagell and Newburn's (1994) work with teenagers found *no* substantial differences in viewing preferences for violent TV and films, between juvenile offenders and non-offenders, once again demonstrating the unrelenting contradictions to be found in the body of work on effect.

The effect/affect conundrum

What we hope we have shown in this chapter is the endurance and tenacity with which proponents and detractors of 'effect' continue to argue about the cause-effect relation within mass media research. However, despite the clear lack of demonstrable and verifiable evidence that a cause and effect relationship *does* exist between the sender and the receiver, supporters of the 'negative effect' thesis will often make very firm statements about causality. In several US studies published very recently, all make clear that the (high) volume of violent material on TV across all genres and channels, has dangerous consequences for society in terms of imitative behaviours, especially amongst children, and an increasing sense of social menace and fear (see Smith and Boyson 2002; Smith et al. 2002; Wilson et al. 2002). But all these studies focus exclusively on programme *content*, not on *audience perceptions*, so their strong statements on the cause-effect relation can only actually be speculative and derived from their own private beliefs and concerns. Despite this limitation, though, these researchers are still able to claim that, 'In spite of the lively debates [about the impact of TV] that still occur . . . social science research that has accumulated over 40 years reveals quite clearly that television violence *can* contribute to aggressive behaviour in viewers' (Smith et al. 2002: 84, emphasis added). The use of the word 'can' here both renders the statement completely empty but is also small enough for the reader to miss if she is already predisposed towards believing a positive association.

But *no* such incontrovertible evidence actually exists, and Vine (1997: 126), amongst others, wants to question the casual ease with which many media researchers confidently assert its existence. He argues persuasively that what is at issue is not *if* media messages have an effect — they clearly do, however involuntarily — but rather 'which kinds of effect occur [and] how they are brought about — and whether the outcomes are to be properly judged as harmful'. Crucially, he cautions against seeing one element — violent TV content — as the primary (external) causal factor in antisocial or dangerous behaviour when a variety of both exogenous and endogenous effects will also be in play at any one time.

Not only are effects circumscribed by personal characteristics such as age, gender, ethnicity and class — with gender attributes particularly salient — but issues of genre are also important. For example, several studies suggest that broadcasting 'real' violence in the form of news reports of war is far more damaging to psychological health than watching cartoon renditions of aggression (see Cantor 1994). In Firmstone's (2002: 49) review of the literature on viewer attitudes towards violent media content in factual TV, she found a number of characteristics which influence perception:

a) closeness — viewers were more disturbed by violence where they could identify with the victim;
b) certainty — viewers were less likely to be shocked if they knew how the situation would end and understood the context;
c) justice — viewers tolerated high levels of violence if they thought the victim 'deserved it';
d) sufficiency — viewers were disturbed by programmes using excessive violence to make a point.

One outcome of increasing levels of crime and violence on television is an amplification of a climate of fear amongst the public which does *not* reflect any kind of statistical or even experiential reality. Successive studies in the UK, for example, show that the public's fear of crime and of being victims of criminal activity is unrelated to the actual incidence of crime (see annual studies such as the British Crime Survey). But of course, there is the usual chicken and egg situation in play here: are 'real-crime' shows proliferating because of public demand, or are audiences watching these shows because they are on? Either way, there is a morbid fascination about watching such shows, akin to rubber-necking at accident sites.

But the media cannot really be thought of as an undifferentiated mass, since TV must be considered separately from the press, radio from the internet, not just because their messages could be (and often are) different, but because their purposes are as different as their modes of address and reception. Even within the single category of television or print, there are any number of nuanced differences in terms of differential 'affect', between fiction and documentary, between tabloid and broadsheet, between afternoon and midnight, between adults and children. Ironically, it could be that our fear of crime manifests itself in a greater rather than lesser desire to consume crime-related material, especially 'reality-based' and reconstruction-focused series such as *Crimewatch UK* or *America's Most Wanted* (see Gunter 1987). This is because of the paradox inherent in watching such shows, which can simultaneously exacerbate *and* reduce fears for personal safety, as Schlesinger et al. (1992) have demonstrated persuasively in their work. In their study with women viewers, they found that *Crimewatch* reduced some women's fear but increased that of others. Although women thought that the media's reporting of violent acts against women served to encourage them to be more safety-conscious, such reports also raised women's fears about their potential to become victims of crime. Firmstone's work (2002) also showed that women were more anxious about televised violence where they could imagine themselves as the victim, and depictions showing the unequal power that perpetrators have over their 'innocent' victims was particularly distressing for many viewers (see Morrison 1999).

These contradictory findings once again demonstrate the slippery nature of cause and effect arguments but also emphasize the contingent nature of audience reception: we *are* all different and we *do* read the same media differently. So, women watching *Crimewatch* who have had direct experience of crime or violence and perhaps have had dealings with the police are likely to view crime reconstruction programmes and police responses rather differently to others who have not lived through such painful experiences. It is acknowledging this simple fact that makes the aspiration to firmly map the cause-effect trajectory an essentially empty project, doomed to failure. What researchers *can do*, and *have done* successfully, is show precisely the contours of that complex landscape. Perhaps, as Gauntlett (1998) argues, a more fruitful way of thinking about the relationship between media and consumer is to research influences and perceptions rather than effects and behaviour?

In any case, Vine (1997) pushes us to be more sophisticated in our consideration of audience and effect studies, questioning the methods used and the subsequent claims made for direct causation between watching and 'doing' violence or sex or crime. The entirely contradictory nature of research findings from studies that have attempted to identify the existence (or not) of that association continues to confound those who seek to condemn broadcasters for their perceived irresponsibility. Similarly, much research which looks at, say, racist narratives, suggests that racist views which are articulated by a TV character (for example Archie Bunker in *All in the Family*, or Alf Garnett in *'Til Death Us Do Part*) are held up by audiences as giving permission and encouragement for pursuing racist speech and behaviours in real life (see Gray 1995; Ross 1996).

However, as Krcmar and Cooke (2001) point out, many of the studies which look at aspects of moral reasoning and justificatory aggression are experimental in nature, where the researchers define the context in which acts occur and thus place their own value judgement on situations rather than allowing the 'subjects' to bring their own reasoning to bear. Similarly, in Wood et al.'s (1991) review of studies on violent affect, they found that respondents taking part in experimental trials on violence were more aggressive than those who were surveyed in more naturalistic environments. Other commentators have also been critical of effects studies conducted under experimental conditions, arguing that findings from such work have no generalizability to real behaviours in the real world (Freedman 1984; McGuire 1986) precisely because of their unreal settings. Part of the reason why so many studies are situated within the experimental paradigm is the high costs of qualitative audience research but, as Barker (1998) pertinently argues, tightly controlled and highly segmented audience studies can tell us little about the media's impact on the wider 'we' audience in the wider 'our' world.

Conclusion

In the end, though, the persuasive abilities of research findings will depend on the extent to which findings (for or against) resonate with particular audiences for such results. As Brody (1977) discovered 25 years ago, studies which are entirely contemporaneous — in his case, the American Commission into the Causes and Prevention of Violence and the American Commission on Obscenity and Pornography — can nonetheless produce entirely opposing 'evidence'. The former Commission found that there *was* a link between watching and 'doing' violence and called for a reduction in airtime for such material. The latter Commission found precisely the opposite, arguing that adults would *not* be affected by watching pornography, although there was some anxiety about children being exposed to lewd images. And as Perse (2001) points out, there are significant vested interests involved in buttressing the idea of media's effective affect, not least advertisers and communications advisers who would otherwise be redundant in the face of an acceptance of the 'no effect' thesis.

Media practitioners themselves are often rather ambivalent about the impact of their practice on others, arguing both that they 'only' provide a window on the world (reflector) but also that they have the power to decide the fate of a president (decision-maker). But many audience members, especially those from minority or otherwise disadvantaged communities, believe that how they are represented in and by the media has a direct bearing on how they are treated in the 'real' world. The contentious area of effect/affect continues to provoke heated debate, with supporters and detractors arguing vigorously for their particular position. Perhaps this is a circle that simply cannot be squared, but it won't stop anyone trying to do so.

Further reading

Barker, M. and Petley J. (eds) *Ill Effects: The Media/Violence Debate*, 2nd edn. London and New York: Routledge.

Carter, C.L. and Weaver, C.K. (2003) *Media and Violence*. Buckingham: Open University Press [in this series].

Fowles, J. (1999) *The Case for Television Violence*. Thousand Oaks, London, New Delhi: Sage.

Perse, E. (2001) *Media Effects and Society*. Mahwah, NJ: Lawrence Erlbaum Associates.

Press, A.L. and Cole, E.R. (1999) *Speaking of Abortion: Television and Authority in the Lives of Women*. Chicago: University of Chicago Press.

THE AUDIENCE AS CITIZEN: MEDIA, POLITICS AND DEMOCRACY

5

The production of news is characterized by systemic tensions, such as those between the commercial logic of the news organization and the professional desires of journalists, between the goal of being accurate and truthful and the drive to be first with the news, between personal political preferences and the requirements of objectivity, between the power of sources and the necessity of being critical, and so on.

(Liesbet van Zoonen 1996: 206)

Introduction

This chapter looks at the extent to which the media contribute to a knowledgeable citizenry, focusing on their agenda-setting abilities, the perspectives they allow airtime and the relationships which journalists have with politicians. It moves through a consideration of campaign reporting, including a discussion of political advertising and opinion polls. Finally, it considers the ways in which we, as citizens, can participate more fully in the democratic process, through our involvement in public access broadcasting, as members of citizens' juries and as audiences for political discussion shows. Crucially, we look at the way in which the media can provide opportunities for the citizen audience to exercise their democratic rights in more involving ways than simply voting at the ballot box.

The cynical citizen

Successive studies with citizen audiences have demonstrated an increasing cynicism amongst the electorate, due in no small part to the ways in which the media themselves choose to characterize politicians and the political process more generally. We show our growing disillusionment by our lack of action at the ballot box — in the UK's 2001 general election in June, the turnout was a lamentable 60 per cent, and the highly controversial US elections the year before generated less than 50 per cent. Such turnouts scarcely provide a comprehensive mandate to the incoming government. Many commentators suggest that part of citizens' cynicism is prompted by their lack of real knowledge about how the political system actually works, as if we determinedly keep ourselves ignorant. But, as Thomas Jefferson argued:

> If the public are not enlightened enough to exercise their control [over society] with a wholesome discretion, the remedy is not to take it from them but to inform their discretion.
>
> (Jefferson 1820, cited in Buchanan, 1991: 19)

Of course, providing material with which to educate the public is only the first step (notwithstanding debates about the content of such 'learning'), because the public also need to be interested and motivated enough to access it. Efforts to 'educate' Joanne and Joe Public into a 'proper' understanding of the political process, in its widest sense, can easily be derailed simply by virtue of cynicism and apathy. Perloff (1998) summarizes a series of studies and surveys carried out over a decade in the USA and reveals alarmingly low levels of political knowledge, for example, that in 1987, more than seven years after the Congressional debate on aid to Nicaragua, only one-third of respondents to a survey knew that Nicaragua is in Central America; that in a 1989 survey, less than half the respondents knew which party then had a majority in the Senate (both taken from Delli-Carpini and Keeter 1991); and that in a 1995 survey for the *Washington Post*, nearly half the respondents could not name the (then) Speaker of the House of Representatives — Newt Gingrich (Morin 1996). Part of the British government's response to this lack of knowledge and understanding about the fundamentals of the political process has been to introduce 'citizenship' as a compulsory element of the school curriculum from 2002. It is too early to say whether such education will have an influence on the next generation of voters, but at least they will have a better understanding of the process, even if they still choose not to exercise their democratic rights.

However, some caution does need to be exercised when trying to make general (and usually negative) statements about what Popkin (1991) calls the 'incompetent citizen' literature, since work which tells us what people do *not* know rarely gives equal exposure to those things which people *do* know. Lippmann's (1922) classic work on public opinion still has considerable salience to the contemporary news scene of the early twenty-first century: political opinion is not shaped by direct experience of politics but is rather a consequence of the images which we are given via news accounts of politics. The obvious question to ask, then, is who decides on the content of those news accounts, especially in the over-heated and politically embattled environment of a general election?

Instead of blaming 'the people' for their lack of interest/knowledge, a government which really is genuinely democratic and empowering will seek to 'educate' its citizens through the provision of political knowledge, a concept which is absolutely right for the third millennium where talk of the 'knowledge economy' has become part of the new political rhetoric. If knowledge *is* power, then knowledge about politics should make the exercise of our basic democratic rights — the right to vote — that much more of an informed, and therefore empowering, process. But how do we get that knowledge? Whilst the answer is, for most of us, via mass news media such as television, radio and the press — although increasingly, online news services are becoming more significant players in the game — the question of whether more is actually better remains entirely open. Whilst the media's provision of material for citizens' consumption has grown exponentially over the past 20 years, commencing, arguably with CNN's ground-breaking decision to broadcast news 24–7, followed by the development of cable, satellite and more recently online news and current affairs services, is this explosion about choice or more of the same?[1]

Whilst most politicians are (unsurprisingly) unhappy with what they consider to be the increasingly **tabloid turn** of all news media, from a straight information stance to a more entertainment-oriented genre (see Ross 2002), many academic commentators are similarly worried about this tendency because of its impact on the public's ability to exercise democratic judgement (see Hallin 1994; Negrine 1996; Wheeler 1997). Franklin's coining of the term **newszak** (1997) provides precisely the appropriate flavour to convey what seems to be happening to the news industry, where stories of (apparent) interest *to* the public have largely replaced stories which are *in* the public interest, a subtle but important shift which is not simply semantic but deeply ideological (Keane 1991; Blumler and Gurevitch 1995).

---

[1] For a good discussion of the implications of global media, see Allan (1999) and Barker (1999) in the same series, *Issues in Cultural and Media Studies*.

The media and democratic responsibility

As Bennett (1997) questions, pertinently, the fundamental conundrum to unravel is how a news industry with competing political interests nonetheless manages to construct a political 'world' which is both 'legitimate' across the news landscape and also believable enough to form the baseline for the public's political understanding. The question must be, *who* decides what the news is, what the truth is, which stories to run or discard? Can there indeed be a global consensus on the important issues of the day? In some ways, the consensus idea is considerably enhanced when the forces of global capital provide an explosion of news outlets (Barker 1999). However, the narrow ownership base means that they carry more or less the same perspective and have more or less the same bias in coverage, so what's actually different about content? Rupert Murdoch's *News International* conglomerate provides a powerful and relevant example of precisely such a global enterprise where single ownership determines the (same) political voice, despite the multiplicity of media formats.

Another part of the 'problem' of encouraging an informed citizenry is that the news media's own fascination with sleaze and the ***horse-race*** elements of elections means that their potential to inform the public about the differential policy positions of the competing parties is considerably diminished. In Lichter and Noyes' (1996) study of the 1996 presidential campaign, they found that stories about the 'horse-race' dominated the media coverage they monitored (ABC, CBS and NBC evening news programmes during the 1996 primary season), especially reports of candidates being negative about each other, which most research demonstrates is particularly disliked by the electorate (see also Wertheimer 1997; Ross 2002). When Lichter and Noyes went on to study the political discourse of the candidates themselves, they found that they were not unremittingly negative (as suggested by the media reports) and that instances of positive self-promotion during political commercials out-numbered negative comments against opponents by more than 6:1 (1996: 293).

If 'the people' *are* ill-informed, then the question has be asked, who is to blame? The politicians, for not disseminating their policies well enough or the media for not reporting them often enough? If democracy depends on an informed citizenry and the majority of citizens look to the news media to inform them about the local, regional, national and international context, then clearly the media play an important role in the democratic process, where they are often thought to 'facilitate the public discourse necessary to make the system work' (Miller 1994: 133).

However, despite the apparent lack of real information about the political process, which politicians often lament (the charge of tabloid journalism), the fact remains that most of us, albeit often a small majority, believe we have enough information to make an informed choice at the ballot box. This reality supports the view that even if citizens do not know the precise policy details of different parties, they are nonetheless capable of comprehending the bigger picture, of being what Yankelovich (1991) suggests is 'wise' about the things that matter. In any event, as a number of 'knowledge' studies demonstrate, individuals are notoriously poor at retaining large amounts of information, so that campaigns which focus attention on just a few key issues and explore those in depth are more likely to be remembered than campaigns which take a more scatter-gun approach (Blomquist and Zukin 1997).

It remains a moot point whether the public at large is really so disinterested in big 'P' politics or whether their apparent apathy is simply a response to their belief that that no one is interested in hearing their views, so why should they bother to express them? As Dunleavy et al. (2001) point out, survey data suggest that Britons (at least) were *more* concerned about basic human rights and abuses of government power in 2001 than they were in 1995, suggesting at least a qualification to the mantra that 'things can only get better' (New Labour's campaign slogan). The global campaigns, marches and demonstrations against attacking Iraq in 2003 again testify to the engagement of millions of citizens worldwide who are deeply concerned with fundamental issues such as rights and justice. Such public calls, following on from similar demands for a rational rather than emotional response by the US and British governments to the tragic events of 11 September 2001 (9/11), once again remind political elites that there is considerable public commitment to and engagement with real politics and a concern about acts apparently done in 'our' name but without our mandate. In response to what was widely seen as overt bias and one-sided reporting of the media in the days, weeks and months immediately following 9/11, especially by the US news media, a number of alternative news sites were set up together with the widespread circulation of website addresses to enable different perspectives to be articulated and discussed (see, for example, www.fair.org; www.redpepper.org.uk; www.autonomedia.org; www.zmag.org; www.aclu.org/safeandfree/).

Media and social control

Whilst the news media are with us 24/7, their agenda-setting power becomes of crucial importance at times of crisis (see Chapter 4) but, also, importantly, during a country's general election. It is now commonly understood that the media's impact is less about actively changing values and beliefs (and therefore, say, about turning around the floating voter) than about determining what issues are important for the electorate to know about (Iyengar 1987;

Entman 1989; Ansolabehere et al. 1991; Norris et al. 1999). In particular, studies suggest that news media are seen as mostly *confirming* the views of citizens and reinforcing prejudices, rather than *challenging* assumptions and/or impacting on the election outcome. But are the media more than just framers and agenda-setters? Do they instead operate as an intrinsic part of the apparatus of government, as political actors in their own right, albeit of a non-elected and 'intermediary' variety, as Cook (1998) suggests? In his model, news is regarded as a 'co-production' between news media and government because journalists operate as key participants in the decision- and policy-making. News media as an industry operate as a central political force in government, both by way of the intimate relationship which exists between politics and media — each feeding off the other — but also because of the latter's influence on the electorate.

The culture of the newsroom (Allan 1999) and the way in which news 'works' often means that the reporting and presentation of the political process is less about reportage and more about interpretation, breaking up stories and events into digestible bites and creating a plausible background against which information is provided within a complex relationship-system among politicians, publics and the media. However, our sound bite environment and tendency to switch channels or surf sites with increasing frequency, means that the complexity and background of news stories are rarely described and news instead comprises a series of sharp headlines, with some additional elaboration and explanation provided for those consumers who bother to stay with the report until the end.

But identifying who is enabled and encouraged to access the media, whose voice is heard and whose denied, who is credited as a credible source and who remains invisible, are all pertinent questions to raise in an effort to understand our political world and our potential for democratic participation. The partiality in the selection and presentation of stories and events, of sourcing and citation, produces a view of the world which is as constructed as a soap opera. As the politician and the journalist play out the delicate dance of the 'fool-me-fool-you two-step', each courts the other in an endless bid to 'really' tell it like it is. The inevitable casualty of their display is any kind of reality check which actually provides the public with a clear grasp of the particularity of specific political agendas. *Real* information about *real* policies and priorities often falls into the combat zone between the 'investigative' journalist hunting 'the truth' and the government spokesperson anxious to spin the public the right 'line' and avoid incriminating themselves or their colleagues in sins of omission or commission.

Political advertising and the power of persuasion

Given the routine cry of 'foul!' against the media by political actors, especially during events such as elections, one of the few ways in which political contenders and parties *can* get their messages across without the constant interference of the news media is through political advertising such as party election broadcasts and other kinds of direct, to-camera, public address spots. The proportion of campaign funds dedicated to such activities has grown year on year since the very first televised political advert in 1952 (Jacobson 1992). Advertising accounted for between 60 and 70 per cent of the total campaign budget for the 1992 elections (West 1993). Interestingly, single party election broadcasts during campaigns have experienced a decline in their impact as voters increasingly look to the allegedly more impartial form of political description offered by TV news and current affairs programming (Harrison 1992). Scammell found, for example, that given a choice, viewers vote with their remote controls, '. . .on average one quarter to one third of the *inherited audience* turns off or switches over when a party [election] broadcast comes on' (Scammell 1990; cited in Scammell and Semetko 1995: 19).

But of course, this supposed impartiality is also a mythic 'truth' since journalists now routinely interpret the speech and exhortations of politicians rather than report it straight, much to the wailing disgust of politicians them- selves who continuously reprimand the *lobby hack* for her or his deconstructive rather than journalistic tendencies. However, the power of party election broadcasts should not be underestimated. Scammell warns that despite the turn-off factor, most people will see at least one party election broadcast during the short lifespan of a general election campaign. As such, they '. . . remain the only opportunities for exclusive party control of the airwaves, and they achieve a greater national audience than any other direct party publicity, such as newspaper ads or billboard posters' (1995: 39).

The attack ad

Although research with audiences consistently shows their disapproval of *attack ads* (Lau et al. 1997), these artefacts are still regularly produced by political parties who seem convinced of their utility, despite considerable evidence to the contrary (Hitchon and Chang 1995). These types of political campaigning are exclusively oriented towards attacking the opposition parties rather than promoting the values that the attacking party hold important. Indeed, some researchers argue that despite public antipathy towards their content, attack ads are nonetheless highly efficient in 'moving votes' (Pfau et al. 1992), that is encouraging people to change their voting decision. That political advertising is important has become a 'fact' which has emerged from research on what 'works' in election terms and there is a growing body of evidence to support the view that adverts are an important source of voter information (Scammell 1998). It also seems that the judicious repetition of key messages in ads can have *some* influence on subsequent voter decisions, on the drip-drip principle (Just et al. 1996). Having relatively few key messages — for example the Labour Party's pledge for 'education, education, education' in the 1997 election — seems to help promote a party's 'brand' identity. The proposition that, of all forms of political advertising, it is the *attack ad* which wields the most influence is a little less clear cut, nor do we really know which style of negative advertising has the most impact. Apart from anything else, advertising strategies which work in one country have no guarantee of similar success elsewhere, especially if the political structures are very different, as is the case with the USA and the UK. The UK, for example, doesn't officially allow sponsored political advertising on TV at all, other than the strictly controlled party election broadcasts, although other communication media are used to good and controversial effect, especially billboard advertising.

However, despite very profound differences in what is 'allowed' to be conveyed about political candidates and parties through the media during election campaigns, the last three general elections in Britain have all witnessed an enthusiastic embrace of marketing principles and strategies. The Conservative Party has been especially enamoured of the virtues of negative (attack) advertising, although this latter approach has consistently worked against them as far as voter attitudes are concerned (Scammell and Semetko 1995: Sancho-Aldridge 1997). Perversely, the parties which tend to use attack ads more frequently (Republican, Conservative and other right-of-centre groups) are the very ones which are seen as being most hurt by them. In Lemert et al.'s (1996) study of the 1992 US Presidential elections, they argued that whilst many voters did not appreciate 'attack' ads, no matter who was attacking whom, they worked particularly disastrously for the Republican (Bush) campaign and had done so in 1992 and in the election of 1988:

> Bush was the only candidate whose own attack ads seemed to hurt him and help his Democratic opponent. In contrast, Clinton's attack ads seemed to achieve their purpose of damaging their target's election prospects.
>
> (Lemert et al. 1996: 271)

Political advertising and effect

The lack of real information in political advertising campaigns is one of the most serious issues to emerge from a study of this process, with complaints that ads are more about 'mudslinging' than about real policy differences being almost ubiquitous in research accounts with audiences. Kern and Just's (1997) study looked at the way in which audiences actively 'construct' political candidates in response to the media's coverage and messages about them. Amongst their findings, they suggest that women react more strongly to negative 'attack' advertising and tend to invert the preferred reading by attacking the author of the advert rather than supporting the message. They also found that women and men's gendered social positioning influences the way in which they construct the political persona, and that all voters 'draw heavily on emotional advertising, including negative advertising, in their construction of candidate images' (1997: 111). Going further, Pinkleton et al. (1998) argue that negativity towards media coverage of political campaigns can have the effect of reducing media use amongst consumers and that, in turn, a cynical policy reduces the effectiveness of governments and thus compromises the democratic ideal.

In a study of German politicians and self-presentation, news audiences were shown a series of clips from broadcast interviews and asked to rate the inter-viewees' performance (Schutz 1998). Aggressive behaviours in the form of interrupting questions, deflecting criticism and personal attacks on political opponents were all regarded negatively as displays of aggression and loss of control, whereas cool responses under provocation were regarded very positively. In a global context, this study is interesting since it reverses the roles of politician and interviewer, where the latter is increasingly seen as having the upper hand in what are regarded as public contests of political authority. And it is not just the political 'attack ad' which is largely off-putting to the voters, but the media themselves add to voter hostility by their own persistent negative framing of politics and elections. Liebes and Peri's (1998) work explicitly shows the ways in which the media can undermine the credibility of politicians. First, by making it their business to challenge political rhetoric. Second, by undertaking extended 'disaster marathons' and other melodramatic strategies designed to destabilize serious political debate. Third, by degenerating debate to tabloid levels which again reduces the potency and seriousness of political messages. Barnhurst and Mutz (1997) suggest that the 'social problem' frame articulated via the disaster marathons described above enhances its chances of being reported on as news and enables a greater level of journalistic commen-tary outside the actual event or phenomenon being reported. For example, framing a particular incident, such as a vicious mugging, as part of a wider social problem of, say, youth delinquency. However, such a thesis means that the media are damned if they do and damned if they don't. If they don't include context and background, they are accused of having historical or social amnesia; if they do provide a context, they are accused of scare-mongering. Some kind of truth probably lies somewhere between these two extremes and the trick, for the savvy media consumer, is to work out where that point is, at least for them.

Journalistic self-reflection

When asked, journalists will often identify two primary responsibilities which they say they discharge as professional media workers, which are:

1. providing a channel of news dissemination to the public, delivered as quickly as possible; and
2. to investigate government claims and call politicians to account (adapted from Weaver and Wilhoit 1997).

Clearly this latter is important for our purposes, but there seems to be some equivocation about how journalists actually fulfil this responsibility. Contrary to expectations, the journalists in Weaver and Wilhoit's (1997) study claim that they are not really interested in taking an adversarial approach to politicians. Across different media contexts, print journalists in their study were the ones who wanted to be the most aggressive. Interestingly, journalists refuted the suggestion that they are increasingly taking the role of agenda-setter, and only 4 per cent of Weaver and Wilhoit's sample believed that such a function is *very* important for a journalist to perform.

Through their invitations to particular politicians and particular parties to put their points of view, the media are in an extremely powerful position to determine the relative visibility of political candidates and to rehearse particular arguments of particular parties. Moreover, TV is used much more frequently as the medium of choice in statewide (regional) and national campaigns by political parties than radio or newspapers, for the very good reason of its ubiquity. Goldenberg and Traugott (1987) reported more than a decade ago that more than half of all campaign expenditure in **Senate races** was spent on the production and broadcasting of TV adverts. However, in countries where there is a ban on political 'advertising' during election campaigns, such as Britain, campaign expenditure is focused on different media. During the 1997 British general election, the Conservatives spent £11.1m (39 per cent) on 'outdoor' (poster) advertising compared with £0.5m (1.8 per cent) on party election broadcasts. The figures for Labour were £4.8m (18.7 per cent) and £0.9m (3.5 per cent) (Fisher 2001). In the subsequent election in 2001, Labour, now in government, concentrated an even larger proportion of the budget on posters, '. . .after the party's research suggested that this was the most effective available medium. Around £1 million was spent on each poster campaign, costing around £4m–£5m in total' (Fisher 2001: 696). Whilst the actual monetary difference between 1997 and 2001 had scarcely changed, it should be borne in mind that in 2000, new legislation was brought in to restrict the amount of money that political parties could receive in donations and spend during campaigns.

Politics, media, public and affect

In both Britain and the USA, there is a considerable body of work which has focused on the phenomenon of the general election. Research teams have undertaken both primary research and secondary analysis on the various data sets emerging from successive elections, seeking to explore the relation between media coverage of elections and voter behaviour. In Britain, early work such as that of Butler and Stokes (1974) began a trend in trying to improve our understanding of the electorate's viewing habits during election campaigns. Sanders and Norris (1997) suggest that subsequent studies, whilst closely replicating the initial set of questions posed by Butler and Stokes, have added new ones over time such as attitudes towards bias in news coverage. As society moves on and develops, and as politics and policy shift, public concerns about particular issues also change and researchers must respond to a changing agenda (see, for example, Ansolabehere et al. 1997).

However, whilst researches have shown the complex and sometimes ambivalent attitudes which the public hold towards campaign coverage (Mughan 1996), they have often failed to improve our knowledge about the impact such viewing has on individual voters' positive or negative ratings of parties or, indeed, whether their political preferences were affected in any way at all. Sanders and Norris (1997) thus set out with the specific intention of trying to map the existence (if any) of a cause-and-effect relationship between the tone of political advertising and voter perception of party in their study of campaigning in the 1997 British general election. In designing their study they made two basic assumptions:

- that television news continues to be an important information source; and
- that voters will modify their political preferences and attitudes in response to information they receive about parties.

Linked to this second point are two further working assumptions:

- that although significant shifts in political ideology are only likely to occur after sustained and prolonged exposure to media messages which challenge their beliefs, more limited exposure could produce small but important shifts in perception; and

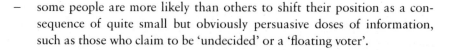

–   some people are more likely than others to shift their position as a con-
    sequence of quite small but obviously persuasive doses of information,
    such as those who claim to be 'undecided' or a 'floating voter'.

What Sanders and Norris found was that exposure to positive party coverage
by the news media provoked a positive response to that party by voters: on the
other hand, exposure to negative coverage provoked contradictory responses.
Importantly, the study also found no evidence of what they term a 'collateral'
effect, that is, negative coverage of one party did not encourage voters to
view other parties more favourably. This suggests that, contrary to some
of the previously discussed US studies which showed attack ads prompting a
sympathetic reading of the party under attack, there was no similar cross-over
impact for British voters.

Looking at the print media's involvement in the same (1997) election and its
impact on voter choice, Burns (1997) argues that the media's much more overt
support for the Labour Party, especially in the tabloid press (with its considerably bigger circulation than the more centrist or centre-left broadsheets)
probably contributed to Labour's success, again giving credence to the suggestion that positive coverage improves voter perception of parties. This is hardly
new news but it does add further weight to the contention that news media *do*
play a part in shaping voter attitudes and that they can materially affect a
party's standing (and ultimate success) by deliberately choosing to frame
parties in positive or negative ways, by their choice of story, their slant, their
perspective and so on. If, as appears to be the case, campaigns continue to be
covered in ways which give the media as much power to control the message
as political parties themselves, then their claim to be able to make or break
politicians (and parties) is still one to take seriously. A good example of this
potential is the case of the media's coverage of women candidates. A growing
body of work shows clearly that women candidates are given less exposure in
the media than their male counterparts and that the ways in which women
politicians in general are portrayed is different to and usually more negative
than news coverage of men (see Kahn and Goldenberg 1991; Norris 1997;
Lovenduski 2001; Ross 2002). There are two possible reasons for this under-
representation: political parties do not volunteer women spokespeople or the
media deliberately ignore their contributions when they do speak. Although it
is not clear which of these two propensities exerts the greater influence, the
outcome is that the public have little idea of what many women politicians
stand for, which could affect their (re)election chances.

Even where individuals actively seek out political information from the
media, they are persistently thwarted by the media's insistence on covering
election *process* issues such as competitor league tables and who is doing the

best character assassination on whom, in preference to elaborating *policy* differences. In the USA, and in other countries like the UK which increasingly emulate US-style politics, the media's persistent framing of elections as a 'horse-race' means that coverage is much more orientated towards the games-*manship* of the principal actors/parties than towards any real engagement with the particular policy or issue positions of candidates (Kiousis 2000). Not surprisingly, most studies of voter perceptions of election coverage produce highly negative results for precisely the reason of style over substance elaborated above (Hart 1987; Patterson 1994; Just et al. 1999). Although Patterson (1994: 28) notes, rather cynically, that the 'United States is the only democracy that organizes its national election around the media', it is not just the USA which is culpable. The veteran BBC news correspondent Nick Jones (1995: 220) makes the relation between politics and media very clear when he says that 'the state of a governing party's relationship with the news media has always been a useful pointer to its chances of electoral survival'.

The ways in which the media have been seen to comprise an active element in political campaigning and, specifically, their role in affecting voting behaviour, have changed over time as the methods of gauging effect have become more sophisticated (Ansolabehere et al. 1997). Initial alarm over the propagandist possibilities offered by a national medium such as television — assuming a passive polity ready to believe any message provided it was slickly packaged — was initially assuaged by early effects studies. These suggested that the media exerted minimal effect on voting behaviour, other than making voters more committed to their pre-selected candidate or party of choice (see Lazarsfeld and Kendall 1948). However, what became clear was that many surveys were insufficiently sensitive as research instruments and opinion polls were often unable to detect the effects of particular 'advertising' strategies. Ansolabehere et al. (1997) suggest that at least two recent theories of political campaigning 'effect' have better explanatory value:

–   the *'resonance' model* posits the view that voters can be persuaded by carefully constructed messages but argues that this is context-specific, depending on pre-existing political preferences and the extent to which political messages conform to voter expectations;
–   the *'competitive' model* comprises a model which acknowledges the inter-relationships between political competitors and the importance of criticism and refutation in the 'game' of political persuasion and vote catching.

Conventional wisdom has had it that newspapers are a superior source of in-depth information during election campaigns compared to broadcast media, especially television. The latter is regarded as providing merely superficial infotainment, whereas newspapers devote considerable space to political stories, including giving background and context and allowing the reader to go through the material at his or her own pace. This folk wisdom has been 'corroborated' by numerous studies which suggest that people who mostly rely on newspapers for information are more likely to score highly on comprehension and recall tests (relating to news content and context) than those who mainly rely on television (see, for example, Robinson and Davis 1990). But the specific medium is not the only variable here, since it may be that media consumers who mostly read newspapers are more literate and highly educated, not (just) that newspapers constitute a better information source (Bennett et al. 1996).

In any case, more recent work on the newspaper/television debate argues that television news can in fact have as much impact on voter understanding as newspapers (see Neuman et al. 1992; Zhao and Chaffee 1995). This is because it is *attention* as much as *exposure* to news which appears to be crucial. Admittedly, viewers have to be sufficiently motivated by a news item to watch it attentively and therefore to actually take in and process the information which is being given out, but that is also the case with newspapers and any other medium.

Of course, different media produce different effects, and numerous studies over the past few years have indicated that print media are more strongly associated with the acquisition and *retention* of political knowledge than television (Becker and Dunwoody 1982; Kennamer 1987; Miller et al. 1988), so that individuals who use 'print media to follow politics rather than solely television or no media are more knowledgeable about politics' (Strate et al. 1994: 168). Part of the distinction between the two media in terms of knowledge- and information-giving is to do with television as a highly visual medium, unsuited to dealing with complex debates but more likely to deal with simple concepts which can be easily represented, such as graphs showing who is doing better than whom in the horse-race. It is ironic, then, that it is television which is seen increasingly as the most important source of information about the world rather than newspapers except, apparently, when it comes to elections. Other studies find that voters' attitudes towards news media coverage of elections were strongly influenced by their level of party identification, so that individuals who were strong supporters of a(ny) party tended to believe that the media were especially biased against 'their' party (Mughan 1996).

Similarly, in an exploration of relations between frequency of media use, media importance, political disaffection and political efficacy, Pinkleton and Austin (2000) report an association between newspaper use and low cynicism, and news magazine use and higher cynicism. They found that the variable of cynicism itself was strongly directed both at the media *and* the message. Interestingly, their study also demonstrated that voters who believe that newspapers are the most important sources of political information were much more sceptical and negative about politics than frequent users of television. Overall, the researchers argue that the most significant variable in their study was *satisfaction* with the media, suggesting that voter dissatisfaction with the media could be a more significant inhibitor of active political participation than hostility towards negative political campaigning. But as Perloff (1998) points out, the newspapers vs. television debate is largely academic, since most people use a mix of sources to meet their information needs, not just traditional outlets such as newspapers, radio and television but also new media such as cable, satellite and the internet. Thus trying to bracket particular media with particular effects is not an especially fruitful research problematic to explore.

Although we now have many more column inches and broadcast minutes devoted to election coverage, what we get from this barrage of information is often less, not more. We are now, in the early twenty-first century, in the absurd and entirely perverse situation where the volume and sources of news material concerning election campaigns has increased exponentially, including the more recent development of 24/7 news channels which are achieving a global reach, while at the same time 'real' information about what candidates actually stand for becomes increasingly elusive. We are turning on its head the truism that the more we know, the less we understand: we understand very well exactly what we don't know and we blame the media, not politicians, for the gaps in our knowledge and for our increasingly cynical approach to politics more generally (Lasorsa 1997; Cappella and Jamieson 1997).

While public confidence in politicians continues its downward trend, the situation is little better when trust in the media industry is explored, since public trust has been in serious decline for at least the past three decades (Patterson 1994; American Society of Newspaper Editors 1998), with newspapers being the focus for particular scepticism (Meyer 1989). A significant element in this public disenchantment is, arguably, the overly negative slant of news in general and political news in particular, especially during election campaigns (Owen 1997; Klotz 1998). In some ways, the persistent interpretative lens through which journalists seem determined to mediate messages from political actors, refracting their efforts to address the polity directly by their casual use of an interrogative style to suggest a hidden agenda if not a downright lie, is part of a wider phenomenon of news as infotainment.

The tabloidizing tendencies of all media are well documented and noted by politicians and polity alike. The news media thus find themselves in rather an awkward place: on the one hand, allegedly (and self-referentially) pandering to the craven appetites of the 'mass' audience but, on the hand, being roundly condemned by that same audience for not providing them/us with straightforward reporting. Is there a happy medium? In his work on what he called 'boomerang' effects, whereby the number of cynical stories and the volume of stories overall are negatively correlated to public confidence in the press, Kiosis (2000) suggests that such effects *do* exist. However, he offers this tentatively, given the limited nature of his sample material, and argues that one way to combat poor public perceptions of news media is for the latter to change their reporting conventions.

One of the important ways in which citizens allegedly 'contribute' to the democratic process, particularly in an election climate, is through their participation in opinion polls, even though their utility and credibility in being able to say anything meaningful is still widely disputed. Lavrakas and Traugott (2000) argue that, in the US context, opinion polling during elections is regarded by the politicians, at least, as a powerful weapon in the elections war. For example, they suggest that anti-Clinton agitators believed that the public opinion polls which consistently supported Clinton were inaccurate, possibly even deliberately so, and much Republican rhetoric was aimed specifically at undermining their credibility and thus their potency to swing votes. Such a spoiling tactic was never likely to succeed, though, since the very public whom the Republicans were seeking to 'educate' was the same one responding to the pollsters. In any case, the importance of polls to the electorate (as opposed to the politicians and the media) is constantly under review (see Lewis 2001), and has been since one of the earliest evaluations of polling data on the public showed good levels of awareness and a generally positive disposition towards their utility (see Goldman 1948).

Polling and effect

But knowledge *about* polls is rather different to *using* poll data to inform one's own voting decisions, and subsequent studies demonstrate rather more ambivalence on the part of voters towards the usefulness of poll information in informing their own decision-making process (Goyder 1986; Roper 1986; Miller 1991; Dran and Hildreth 1995; Nightingale and Ross 2003). There are broadly two hypotheses relating to opinion poll 'effect', namely the bandwagon and the boomerang.

- *the bandwagon thesis* argues that when the public see that one party is ahead of the other(s), some jump on the bandwagon of apparent success, thus ensuring a self-fulfilling prophecy, whilst supporters of the underdog party lose faith and don't turn out;
- *the boomerang effect*, on the other hand, proposes the opposite tendency, that is, that supporters of the stronger party become complacent, and support for the underdog party increases.

Obviously both theses cannot be equally accurate simultaneously and in fact there are no discernible trends which indicate that one is more right than the other (Denver 1989). In any event, there appears to be a general view amongst publics that polls are a 'good' thing, even if those views are not necessarily predicated on any real understanding of polling methodology and design (Traugott and Kang 2000). Instead, there appears to be a certain amount of taking on trust that poll data has been generated by fair means and that they are 'truthful', or perhaps the public actually care less about poll data veracity and are more interested in the fact that they purport to say something about the public's broad assessment of the various parties as a way of forcing politicians to take account of public opinion. But Crewe (2001) argues forcefully that accuracy in polling design does matter precisely because of both bandwagon and boomerang effects. Reflecting on the persistent over-inflation of the British Labour Party support base over several elections, including the general election of 2001, he suggests that:

> Assuming that the true Labour lead over the Conservatives was about 10 percentage points throughout the campaign, well-designed polls based on random samples. . .would have reported Labour leads of between 7 and 13 per cent; a probable Labour victory, but not an inevitable one; a clear Labour majority, but not a landslide; an election to play for, not a foregone conclusion.
>
> (Crewe 2001: 664)

In other words, both Labour and Conservative supporters might have turned out in greater numbers and, if not changed the result, then certainly affected the scale of the win. Although Labour's majority fell from 179 in 1997, to 167 in 2001, to win so commandingly in a back-to-back election was not predicted (Norris 2001a). For Crewe, part of the fundamental problem in Britain's opinion polling organizations, with one or two exceptions, is that they consistently over-represent Labour supporters in their polls. There are several reasons for this quirk in polling methodology, but principal amongst them could be a greater reluctance for respondents to 'admit' they support the Conservatives and/or a higher refusal rate amongst Conservative supporters to participate in polls.

Whilst opinion polls are undoubtedly important in providing a sense of the electoral mood, they have been so spectacularly wrong in too many crucial calls — a good recent example being the exit poll debacle in some American cities in the 2000 Presidential election contest — to be given much predictive authority. Fletcher's (1996) work on polling suggests that the use of polls is not necessarily helpful in the democratic enterprise as their myriad failures — to take into account the intensity of individual preferences, to give the same credence to informed and uninformed opinion alike, and their tendency to discuss single issues in isolation — militates against their having any real utility. Similarly, although less negatively, Herbst (1993) suggests that the use of polling data as a stand-in for public opinion produces a form of communication which is wide but not deep, that is, it can provide superficial data about many things but very little of any depth. And if politicians and candidates are unhappy with the ways in which the media frame political stories during election campaigns, opinion pollsters are equally frustrated with the casual hijacking of their data to provide the basis of some spurious story, especially where polling companies have been careful to ensure that data were as reliable and sober as possible. Broughton (1995) suggests that the news media's insistence on simplification means that the contingent nuances of much poll data are ignored by journalists keen on putting out sensational copy and this propensity contributes to the fact that polls are seen as increasingly unreliable predictors of voting behaviour. However, it is probably not just the media who are implicated in missing the polling point but the electorate itself who will not necessarily tell the truth when asked about their voting intentions in a polling interview.

Whilst the supporters of exit polls (for example, Merkle and Edelman 2000) argue that improvements in poll design will encourage greater reliability, the increasing numbers of non-respondents in successive elections makes it hard to see how their validity *can* be improved. Importantly, though, polls carried out by the media (as opposed to those commissioned by political parties themselves) *do* provide an independent snapshot of views, albeit those which people are willing to share but which do not necessarily reflect what they intend to actually do. And at some level, they do enable the public to have a voice in political debate, to make a statement, albeit in composite form, about the larger political picture. In a recent 'kiss and tell' video diary, Amanda Platell, the ex-media aide to William Hague, suggested that despite the media's insistence on an impending Labour landslide, the Tory 'war room' continued to be relatively positive during the campaign until the *Guardian* published a poll which showed a devastatingly stark endorsement of Tony Blair. Up to that point, the *Guardian*'s poll had always shown a more even balance between the two parties and the publication of that particular poll, very close to polling day itself, marked the beginning of the end for the campaign team (Platell 2001). However, perhaps Lavrakas and Traugott err a little on the side of generosity when they cede symbolic power to the polls, although they are careful to insist that it is only the 'good' poll which can articulate the mood of the people.

When the media report on methodologically sound election polls, they make perhaps their single greatest contribution to democracy. In doing this, they send the *symbolic message* that it is the will and preferences of the entire population of individual citizens that the polity exists to serve, symbolized nowhere better than by a good-quality survey's representative sample of the public.

(2000: 4)

But of course, despite their limitations, one might argue that more *is* better, that more information, albeit sometimes of dubious quality is better than less, especially during election campaigns when having good information is crucial to enable the proper exercise of individual democratic rights. It could be argued that the data provided in polls can assist the political parties as well as the electorate, by gauging the acceptability of certain kinds of policy (or not) and thus the electorate can sometimes actively shape the policy agenda (Meyer 1989; Hickman 1991).

However, polls have their detractors as well as their supporters and from very early on in the career of the opinion poll, its validity as a barometer of *anything* meaningful has been questioned (Blumer 1948). Not least this is because of the ephemeral and contested nature of the very concept being promoted, that is, the reality of *public opinion* itself (see Price 1992; Herbst 1993; Huffington 1998; Salmon and Glasser 1998). A significant element of the mistrust of poll data relates to a point discussed earlier, that is, the extent to which respondents to polls really know anything about policy differences (see Delli-Carpini and Keeter 1996). Specifically, have they given spontaneous views at the time their opinions are canvassed and have they actually thought deeply about the issues on which they are now being asked to comment (Luskin 1987)?

It is precisely the lack of deliberation that most citizens give to the political process which has encouraged some commentators to seek more sensitive ways in which the public might be encouraged to think more carefully about their political choices (see Fishkin et al. 2000; and the section below on deliberative polls). Indeed, there have been consistent calls, in the UK especially, for the publication of opinion polls to be banned during an election campaign. As early as 1967, the (UK) Speaker's Conference on Electoral Reform supported such a ban (Denver 1989), arguing that polls affect voter behaviour and trivialize elections through reducing them to a mere horse-race with only marginal attention given to the serious issues at stake. However, the British government refused to accept the proposal, as have successive governments to the present day, although in Australia, there was until quite recently specific legislation (the Broadcasting Act 1942: section 1.1.6: subsection 4) which enforced a ban on the media's reporting of election issues and party promotion precisely because of the media's putative power as an influential force on public opinion (Winter 1993).

Opinion polls: the next generation

However, there have been efforts to try and mitigate some of the disadvantages of the large-scale opinion poll whilst preserving the benefits of having a means of engaging in public/political discourse. For example, the 'choice' questionnaire was developed by a team of Dutch researchers who introduced relevant information about policies whilst ostensibly conducting an 'ordinary' opinion survey (Neijens 1987). The pollsters intended to better inform the public they were surveying about specific policy positions amongst the parties, although we do not know whether any bias was introduced into their statements of 'fact'! In the 1990s, three more novel methods were devised. *Citizen Juries* were pioneered at the Jefferson Centre in Minnesota and imported to Britain and used by, amongst others, the Institute for Public Policy Research (Coote and Lenagham 1997). In Britain they comprised 'ordinary' members of the public who had responded to a nationwide invitation to participate, and who then formed juries to listen to 'evidence' relating to a particular issue, such as crime or education or health. The evidence was presented by individuals putting forward competing arguments and facilitated by a chair. Once all the evidence had been presented, the jury then discussed what they had heard and came to a judgement about the issue.

Televoting was created by Ted Becker and Christa Daryl Slaton, whereby they interviewed a random sample of people, asked them to take part in a follow-up interview and gave them material to read in between interviews (Slaton 1992). The purpose was to identify whether giving people 'homework' forced them to take a more considered and informed approach to subsequent discussion and, ultimately, personal decision-making.

However, a particularly involving model was developed at the University of Texas and attributed to James Fishkin, and this was the ***deliberative poll*** which was initially established for use in the 1996 Presidential elections (see Price 2000). On that occasion, this new polling format brought together 459 American citizens using a probability sample, to debate a specific set of issues with the aim of both enabling different opinions to be put forward but also to encourage the sharing of perspectives with a view to pushing forward solutions. This first poll was dubbed the National Issues Convention (NIC) and provided the model for successive deliberative polls both in the USA and elsewhere.

If part of the ethos of public journalism (Merritt 1995; Rosen 1996), that is, journalism *for* the public good as opposed to for commercial gain, is to enable different publics to know more about one another, then moves towards a greater use of deliberative polling must also be for the good. Strategies which allow smaller groups of publics to express views and 'speak' to each other and thence to wider publics, might be a useful addition to the more conventional large-scale polls, as part of a wider framework for improving functional democracy. However, the appeal of these more considered public discussions — which find their mirror in the UK with People's Parliament, Citizens Juries and the Labour government's development of (the much lampooned) political 'focus group' — needs to be tempered with an understanding of their limitations (Price 2000). Whilst the traditional large-scale poll tends to elide differences by compositing responses into a simple binary measure of 'for' or 'against', the sampling methodology of the more reliable ones does at least tend towards representativeness. However, as Herbst and Beniger (1995) argue, whilst randomized sampling makes their creators' claims for representativeness more credible, the structure and context of most polls ensures fast and usually ill-considered responses to a prescribed list of topics. The deliberative poll, with its much smaller numbers, cannot make a similar claim for representativeness. But in the end, the reliability placed on the findings of each will, as always, depend on the individual perspectives of the polls' different readers and their desire to find resonance with and corroboration for their own views.

The active voter

In Just et al.'s work (1996) on the relationship between citizens, politicians and the media, they found that despite the various blandishments, biases and economies of truth promoted by both the politicians and the media, the citizen showed herself to be capable of rejection and (re)interpretation of media-ted messages. However, access to and interest in, different sources of information about the political process was important in making final decisions about voting, so that 'as citizens build constructs of the candidates, their information environment makes a difference in the range of considerations they bring to bear.' (Just et al. 1996: 233) In other words, information and knowledge-rich individuals have, or at least make use of, more resources from which to draw when making voting decisions. However, 'more' in this sense does not necessarily mean different, given the conglomeratization of media industries which is leading to more sources saying fewer different things. Interestingly in Just et al.'s work, they found that citizens were much more likely to make assessments of political candidates on the basis of their personal attributes than their political affiliation and these assessments are made primarily via the various forms of communication made available by the mass media.

But such apparent ambivalence is not necessarily either a problem for, or symptomatic of, the undecided voter. Some commentators (Marcus 1988; Hochschild 1993) in fact suggest that just such an open-minded citizen, capable of taking in new information, considering and evaluating it and then 'changing' her mind, is precisely what is required for the proper functioning of a democratic society. To ignore new data which might challenge preconceived notions simply promotes rigid thinking and inertia. In Miller's (2000) terms, to make such informed decisions, no matter how contrary to one's original position, is to practice the ideal of deliberative democracy. However, to be 'open' to new ideas is not the same as being politically ambivalent. Most voter studies, including that of Just et al. (1996), eventually admit that political partisanship remains the most stable predictor of voting behaviour, despite the millions of dollars spent on media advertising during election campaigns to persuade people out of their existing views. Even 'established' predictors such as gender and age — received wisdom being that older women were more likely to vote for right of centre parties — are no longer seen as useful, as the gender gap appears to be closing (Kaufmann and Petrocik 1999). Women and men seem to be shifting in opposite directions, albeit at different speeds, not least because today's 'older generation' are the grown-up children of the radical 1960s.

The active audience and public access broadcasting

While most of the previous discussion has focused on the ways in which audiences consume and make sense of the media's promotion of political messages, both those pushed by journalists and those pushed by the parties, this final section considers the ways in which audiences actively engage in media-ted public/political space.

Traditionally, the most common ways in which we, as citizens, get to participate in the political process is by using our vote at elections and, as discussed above, by becoming involved in opinion poll research and other political surveys. But the increasing use by politicians of broadcast media has meant that members of the public are now more likely to meet national politicians as part of a broadcast (TV or radio) studio debate, than their own constituency MP in their own home town (see Coleman and Ross 2002). Politicians much prefer to get their messages across to a wider audience in ways which are both more immediate and 'natural' as well as less likely to be 'interpreted' by media professionals themselves. But do these public interventions in political debate really count as democratic participation in the public sphere in a way which Habermas (1989) would recognize? In some ways, the answer to the question is circumscribed by the particular structure of the programmes under discussion, by the openness of the competition for participation and the extent to which the balance of participants is not overtly loaded in favour of the elites, to the detriment of the public.

For some commentators, the reality of television programming means that no matter the intent, the outcome is always an infotainment show aimed at maximizing the viewers' enjoyment rather than a 'reasonable' debate between reasonable people aimed at pushing the process forward. However, as Livingstone and Lunt (1994: 32) argue, an 'apparent lack of structure and control of argumentation may signify communicative conflict rather than emotional noise.' In other words, a non-linear set of arguments offered by a variety of individuals may not necessarily connote a communication vacuum but, on the contrary, could mean a robust exchange of equally valid views. There is no requirement, in a democracy, for consensus: what is required instead is respect for different points of view and decisions which the majority can accept. In their work on audience participation programmes, Livingstone and Lunt (1994: 179) suggest that this relatively new type of show confounds allocation to either of two associated genres which also involve the public, that is, as subjects for news or as participants in game shows. They suggest therefore that the audience participation show is 'intergenre', forcing a reconsideration of the relationship (and relative status) between the power elite and the citizenry.

In Coleman and Ross' (2002) work with participants of the radio phone-in program, *Election Call*, which was broadcast during the British general election campaign in 2001, the great majority of callers were very pleased with their involvement in the show. More generally, they were positive about the show's contribution to a genuine political debate which actually engaged 'ordinary' people for a change. Whilst women were slightly more cautious than men about the extent to which audiences are generally open to change, part of their satisfaction with their participation in the show was precisely that they were given access to air the question they wanted to ask (and be taken seriously in doing so). In addition, their status as *citizen* forced whichever politician sat in the chair that day to at least attempt an answer, albeit superficially in many cases. In the view of many regular voters, politicians are too often allowed to 'get away with it' by interviewers who are too cosy and too obsequious, although from the point of view of those who interview politicians, this is not an outcome they desire but rather what the politicians wilfully orchestrate (Williams 1980; Moyser and Wagstaffe 1987; Puwar 1997). Lang and Lang (1983) in fact argue that during the Watergate scandal, it was precisely the public outrage, encouraged by the televised proceedings and enabled by the media's diligent investigations and subsequent public exposure, which eventually brought down the politicians involved. Similarly, the media's dogged pursuit of the 'truth' of the 'Monica Lewinsky' scandal ten years later, and the televised exposure of Bill Clinton's clear inability to tell a convincing story accelerated his public disgrace and departure. What is so surprising is that successive generations of politicians fail to realize that the relationships they enjoy with journalists are only ever as constant as their reputations.

So public access broadcasting does fulfil an important function for democracy by providing a public forum in which public views and opinions can, potentially at least, have influence, if not on the decisions of politicians then perhaps on the voting decisions of the listening audience. Such a forum can be seen, *pace* Heller (1978), as constituting an 'extra-political' power base, where broadcasters 'help' politicians to check the pulse of the nation. The *Election Call* participants in Coleman and Ross's (2002) study believed that democracy *had* been served by the programme because of the range and diversity of the questions and because they had 'had their say' and held the politicians to account. At the very least, such a programme provides an arena in which views can be exchanged and considered, albeit on a rather linear basis comprising a series of discrete one-to-one interactions and without the explicit intention of achieving consensus. Rather the goal was to encourage a dialogue between publics and politics whereby the latter at least listen to the former, fulfilling the minimum criteria of critics such as Fraser (1990) and Mouffe (1992) for interaction rather than resolution. This is probably the best outcome possible in an environment in which political elites will always dominate the debating position, but where the citizen can at least become activist rather than audience for a few moments.

Conclusion

The extent to which you believe that the media can affect public beliefs about political parties and processes will depend on other, more general beliefs about cause and effect, agency and action and the extent to which we believe that, as individuals, we can be influenced in ways which we do not readily recognize or acknowledge. As we have seen in early chapters, the effects of media messages on audiences, including those posted by government and other political players, continues to be a subject which considerably exercises researchers, that is, whether the media have any effect, and if so, what that effect is, and so on. Broadly, though, views on the specific influence of politically oriented media messages on public perceptions and voting behaviour fall into two main camps. Many political communication scholars suggest that such messages and campaigns have minimal impact on *change* although they do have the effect of *confirming* and often entrenching existing political proclivities.

The effect of political communication and communicators, then, is to perform a kind of ritualistic affirmatory performance which is more symbolic than real. Political actors articulate predictable arguments, routine antagonisms are regularly televised but many consumers are already secure in their political beliefs. Whilst there is obviously some shifting of position in response to new information or new policies being promoted by different parties, political belief is usually more enduring than the politicians who front political parties (Butler 1989; Butler and Kavanagh 1997; King 1997).

But politicians and their advisors, on the other hand, as well as professional pollsters, suggest a rather different effect, arguing that even at the eleventh hour, a good election campaign message can pull off a vital shift in voting beliefs and therefore behaviour, at least amongst wavering voters (Gould 1998; Holmes and Holmes 1998; Finkelstein 1998).

The *actual* impact of political communication on public belief probably lies somewhere along the continuum of all-nothing and will be different for each person. The relationship of political news coverage and the public is highly complex and not readily amenable to simplistic theories which frame that influence in absolute terms and at least some election studies are developing analyses which go beyond that simple binary. The growing literature on public access broadcasting and other opportunities for the public to engage with politicians also suggests that, not only are many citizens more interested in the political process than politicians and the media generally acknowledge, but that they appreciate the mediated space offered to them to more actively engage in the democratic process. Thus the media *can* perform a positive role in democratic societies by empowering publics to take up their rights to political participation, it's just that they don't seem to offer those opportunities very often.

Further reading

Fletcher, F.J. (1996) Polling and political communication, in D. Paletz (ed.) *Political Communication in Action*. Cresskill, NJ: Hampton Press.

Lavrakas, P.J. and Traugott, M.W. (eds) (2000) *Election Polls, the News Media, and Democracy*. New York and London: Chatham House Publishers.

Lippman, W. (1922) *Public Opinion*. New York: Harcourt Brace.

Nightingale, V. and Ross, K. (eds) (2003) *Critical Readings: Media and Audiences*. Maidenhead: Open University Press.

Ross, K. (2002) *Women, Politics, Media: Uneasy Relations in Comparative Perspective*. Cresskill, NJ: Hampton.

6 | FAN AUDIENCES: IDENTITY, CONSUMPTION AND INTERACTIVITY

As the community enlarges and as reaction time shortens, fandom becomes much more effective as a platform for consumer activism. Fans can quickly mobilize grassroots efforts to save programs or protest unpopular developments.

(Henry Jenkins 2002: 161)

Introduction

The changing ways in which 'the audience' has been conceptualized by media researchers over the past decades — from passive sap to interactive critic — finds a parallel, to some extent, in the ways in which 'the fan' has also changed shape, a parallel which holds the same kinds of contradictions for fans as it does for audiences. This chapter explores what it means to be a fan, from both the perspectives of researchers and fans, and sometimes from the fan researcher point of view as well. It discusses the different genres which have been especially attractive to fans, and looks particularly at women-focused fan texts such as soaps and at women-oriented media such as 'women's films'. Importantly, it discusses the ways in which fans' knowledge and interest in particular texts has been harnessed by the industry itself, so that fans have become producers of the very texts they love to consume!

The fan in the imaginary

As the highly important work of deconstructing traditional (oppressive) stereotypes promoted by media has been carefully undertaken (notably but not exclusively by Stuart Hall 1988, 1992); as the wholly necessary and vital challenges to the **meta-narratives** of race, class and gender have contributed to a growing critique of normative social theory; as unmasking the processes of global media have become an important part of the post-modern project, so notions of group and community, belonging and not belonging, have become sharpened and problematized. Postmodernism has brought with it, amongst its many treasures, a suitably post-modish disdain for any hint of a collective consciousness: we are none of us anything less than blissfully atomistic/atavistic individual consumers. But, as much as 'we' might wish to change the ways in which 'society' talks about individuals, for example, by rejecting the term 'race' on the grounds that continuing its use enables it to enjoy a false legitimacy, such notions nonetheless still *do* have meaning in the social world and for the social actors with whom we work. Fans *do* think of themselves, in very significant ways, as sharing a common interest in the object of the fanship, that is the particular programme of which they are fans. Similarly, the work undertaken by Ross with niche audiences such as ethnic minority viewers and disabled listeners found exactly this same kind of desire to belong to and speak with one voice, regardless of all the other attributes which individuals do *not* share (see Ross 1996, 2002).

To be sure, fans and fan communities are in a constant state of flux, with new groups emerging and dissolving in a constantly changing fan landscape, a process accelerated by the burgeoning of more interactive media such as email, listservs and the internet. But the point is that most fans *do* see themselves as part of a larger fan community even if their own fandom is an experientially 'private' and individual activity, undertaken alone. Despite their own singular enjoyment of the **fan artefact** in question, that is, *Star Trek* or *Xena* or *Neighbours*, the fan knows that around the country (or even the globe when you consider the popularity of some US and Australian soaps) millions of other people are deriving pleasure from the same texts.

It is the dissonance between the lived fan experience of 'ordinary' people and the fan theory produced by cultural critics which manifests in the theory/practice gap which so often diminishes the real utility of academic research to make sense of the real world. Much (but not quite all — see, for example, Harris and Alexander 1998; Jenkins 1992b) academic writing on the subject of fans is at arm's length distance, where 'the fan' is studied as an object which is entirely 'other' to the researcher and where the ability to name the fan as 'other' gives the 'I/researcher' a certain superiority. This is especially the case when the characterization of the fan from the non-fan's (researcher's) point of view, is inflected with a slight sense of disdain. As Ang (1991) points out, researchers often fail to take account of insiders' (fans) sense of audiencehood, rejecting their sense of community because the concept runs counter to their own received orthodoxies of fan as social isolate (see below). The other crucial problem with academic accounts of fans, where the academic in question is not a fan, is that 'outsiders' are unable to always grasp the highly nuanced discourse of fans, so that much of the subtlety, especially of fan writing, is missed or ignored (Green et al. 1998).

The fanatic fan

When we consider that the provenance of the term 'fan' is 'fanatic', we are usefully reminded of the way in which the fan is often demonized in popular culture, regarded as aberrant and often hysterical. Davidson (1973) argues that early debates about TV fan behaviour were relatively benign, with articles appearing in teen magazines throughout the 1970s which offered advice and support to readers about how to join and even start up fan clubs. But by the beginning of the 1980s, articles began to be published which positioned the fan in an altogether more sinister light. For example, *People Weekly* ran an article with the headline, 'Desperate to fill an emotional void, some fans become dangerous to their idols' (cited in Freedman 1981). Such language characterized the ways in which the media began to frame fans and the more 'fanatic' forms of fan behaviour (Harrington and Bielby 1995). Of particular and salacious interest was the fan stalker, and high-profile celebrity victims of such fanatic behaviour have consistently hit the headlines (Schindehette 1990).

Stereotypes of fans and fan culture have a long history in media portrayal. Lewis (1992: 137) suggests that in contexts where fans are particularly dysfunctional, for example when they indulge in extreme behaviour such as stalking their 'idol', the characterization of the fan includes '. . . lack of social recognition and popularity [which is] held accountable for the intensity of his or her star obsession'. Fandom is thus seen as an individual *and* as a collective pathological response to what is commonly termed, the **star system** (Grossberg 1992). The star system is founded on the principle that for fans to exist, there must be stars for them to adore, be they pop stars, films stars, sports stars or other types of popular personality who capture the imagination.

While many people may enjoy and fête particular stars or movies, the pathological model of the fan frames her/him as more than simply appreciative of a particular star or series. They are often characterized as isolated losers who don't fit into 'normal' life and relations and who are abidingly different to 'ordinary' people: the trekkies (or, more accurately, 'trekkers') who attend conventions are mostly viewed in this way by the more rational 'us' who look upon such activities with smug superiority. Into such a model of fandom slides the stalker who sometimes even kills the object of adoration (Schickel 1985). Notorious fans such as Mark David Chapman (who killed John Lennon) are invoked as exemplary examples of this kind of pathological loon.

The teenage pop fan

Jenson (1992) also identifies and questions the other typical fan, the screaming and hysterical teenager (usually female) shouting and crying at pop concerts. Whilst the loser/fantasist is compelled in her obsession by her isolation from 'normal' society, the pop fan is provoked by the **contagion** of crowds, acting out in order to stay within the scene. Either way, the fan has lost control, although girl fans who have since grown up understand now, if not then, the commercially orchestrated hysteria which is a necessary condition for the purchase of products such as concert tickets, records and associated 'groupie' merchandise. The anonymous fan in Ehrenreich et al.'s work, quoted below, reflects ruefully on the exploitation of her younger self:

> Looking back, it seems so commercial to me, and so degrading that millions of us would just scream on cue for these four guys [the Beatles] the media dangled out in front of us. But at the time, it was something intensely personal for me and, I guess, a million other girls.
>
> (anon. fan cited in Ehrenreich et al. 1992: 99)

In an interesting counter to the more traditional view of female fans and male idols, that is, that the former are driven to frenzied sexual desire by the latter, Ehrenreich et al. (1992) suggest that sexual attraction is not always or even ever the principal motivator. In their work with former Beatles fans, it became clear that many identified with rather than lusted after the Fab Four, wanting to experience the freedom and disregard for authority which the group exemplified: 'I liked their independence and sexuality and wanted those things for myself' (anon. fan cited in Ehrenreich et al. 1992: 103). In this way, the screaming and crying which became emblematic of pop concerts in the 1960s could be re-assessed as expressions of desperate hope for a generation screaming to be freed from post-war austerity and repressed sexual conduct.

Whilst the objects of some fans' desires were and still are entirely sexual, this is not the only story in town. And in any case, as Cline (1992) argues persuasively, many of the descriptions of (female) fan adoration for male bands, were written by male journalists playing out their own babe fantasies.

Women and girls were as likely to be appalled as sanguine at the suggestion that they needed to strip or even prostitute themselves in order to obtain an autograph or a 'chat' with their idol. Such analyses which privilege (hetero)-sexual over other kinds of attraction cannot, in any case, deal adequately with the reality of, say, same-sex fandom or homoerotic enthusiasm for 'straight' women singers or other stars.

The fan as cultural moron

The conceptualization of the fan as either social inadequate or deviant obsessive is only made possible by an insistence, on the part of the researcher/cultural critic, that they are different to 'us'. But if the cult object is opera or wine or the paintings of Claude Monet, then the fan becomes instantly rebranded as enthusiast or even connoisseur. As Jenson (1992: 19) neatly questions, what are the differences 'between fans like "them" and aficionados like "us"'? The answer could lie in the class-culture nexus, where the latter 'do' high art and culture which attracts the cognoscenti, whereas the former 'do' low art and low culture which attracts fan(atic)s. In other words, the hierarchy of cultural forms (see Levine 1988) is simply given another form of expression: appreciating Mozart requires an educated and refined understanding (rational) but attending a Metallica concert requires only a low-grade intellect and good lungs (emotional).

As with other theories of **cultural capital**, the continuum of taste locates 'high' and what Fiske terms 'official' culture at one end, juxtaposed with low, 'popular' culture at the other. However, within these socially prescribed 'taste' categories, the same kind of product discrimination is taking place which reveals the extent to which fans (low) and connoisseurs (high) are remarkably similar (the same, even?) in their habits, particularly in their desire to constitute authenticity — this is a 'real' fan, this is a genuine Ming. They are also united in their interest in collecting artefacts associated with their particular passion, although, as Fiske (1992) points out, fans' collections are likely to be about maximizing volume — Hey, I've got two sets of the first series of Superman comics! — whereas aficionados are more likely to want exclusivity and unique pieces.

The fans who comprised the subject matter for a number of studies in the 1980s easily recognized the effort on the part of cultural 'elites' to down-value their so-called lesser pleasures. They therefore attempted to claim a greater legitimacy for the objects of their own desires by the appropriation of high culture descriptors (Tulloch and Alvarado 1983). But unlike the Keats scholar who uses her expertise to find deeper meaning in the original text, Fiske

(1992) argues that the fan uses her intimate knowledge of the fan-text as a way of superimposing additional layers of meaning onto the original. Thus, perhaps what really distinguishes the fan from the expert is the fan's lack of deference to the object of attention and her belief in her right to appropriate and subvert the text and the object for her own pleasure. For example, alternative *Star Trek* storylines created by women fans often position Kirk and Spock in a sexual relationship with each other, or frame women characters in leadership roles (see below for an elaboration of this point). In the process of over-layering, embellishing or even subverting the text entirely, the fan claims an intellectual integrity and validity to her work of reclamation and appropriation, giving it a value in her own life, at least, even if such endeavours go unrecognized by others. This kind of tampering with the goods would, for the connoisseur's collectible, not only be sacrilegious but would significantly degrade its monetary value

The snobbishness with which fans are routinely described by non-fan commentators is perfectly captured by the surprise made explicit in Griggs' (1991: 12) evaluation of the typical fan of (and letter-writer to) the cult show, *Twin Peaks*: '. . . these people are educated, these people are upscale — these are not letters from the masses. Everything's punctuated correctly, the grammar and spelling are right.' On the other hand and working in the opposite direction, some researchers try to upscale fans of low-taste genres. For example, in their work with the audiences for the cult film *Judge Dredd* (dir: Danny Cannon, 1995), Barker and Brooks (1998) argue that the action film fan is not the mindless yob depicted by the media but is someone who can appreciate the aesthetics of the genre as well as the plentiful supply of blood and gore.

The fan of so-called low culture and 'purely' entertainment texts have long endured the opprobrium of critics not just because of the disdain for the **trash aesthetic** but because consuming such products is seen as mindless and thus a waste of otherwise important time. Brunsdon (1989) suggests that soap fans are particularly despised not just because they cannot, apparently, distinguish between fantasy and reality and are therefore worthy of our ridicule, but also because the object of the fan's desire is simply 'bad' television. Fans will sometimes say this themselves, with embarrassment! (See Ang 1985; McIlwraith et al. 1991; Alasuutari 1992.)

For Grossberg (1992: 51), however, the simple dyad of **cultural superiority/ inferiority** is no longer really tenable because, 'standards for aesthetic legitimacy are constantly changing', so that what was once popular may yet become high art. And given the current wave of trash TV and continuing success of voyeuristic programmes such as *Big Brother* and *Survivor* around the world, perhaps the third millennium is witnessing the relentless slide of 'culture' and 'taste' into a global soup of low-demand entertainment, where the only intellectual work necessary is deciding on the most comfortable viewing position.

The ability of fans to co-opt and subvert texts is described by Grossberg (1992) as the 'subcultural' model, suggesting that members of such sub-cultures are usually a small segment of the larger and mostly passive fan audience, individuals who want to do more than simply consume the fan product. For Grossberg, though, trying to identify what distinguishes a 'fan' from a mere 'consumer' is a difficult task and looking for answers in either the nature of the text/cultural form *or* the audience is likely to prove unproductive. Instead, he analyses the relations and interplay between the two where he describes the particular bond which ties cultural form and audience together as the 'sensibility'. By looking at the sensibility instead of focusing on either cultural form or audience, Grossberg is then able to suggest that what makes fans different to other (ordinary) consumers is that for the former, the text really *matters*, it is invested with a definitional importance through which the fan gains a sense of personal identity and of community (with other fans).

Moreover, not only does the cultural form matter intensely, but the level of **affect** generated for the fan enables other aspects of the fan's everyday life to be determined, in terms of importance, in relation to this central preoccupation with the text. This process of fandom producing identity is also taken up by Hinerman (1992), who argues that for (mostly women) fans who participate in extreme forms of adoration, such as those who believe that Elvis is still alive, such beliefs and fantasies serve to legitimate the individual's sense of self in the face of a hostile and uncaring world. To some extent, this is to endorse the pathological view of the fan as social isolate, although Hinerman's theory is more complex and more generous, giving the fan the benefit of the psychological doubt by arguing that Elvis fantasies perform a recuperative function for women, providing hope and confidence to live a better life.

A similar line — fan as agency — is taken by Dell (1998), who suggests that the development of fan movements is often a proactive response to changing social and economic environments over which people have little control. As Harris (1998a) argues, contemporary society has become more fractured, with more obvious discrepancies between the haves and the have-nots. This is clear from, say, current debates around pay, where directors of large corporations award themselves huge salary increases whilst 'the workers' struggle to achieve small percentage-point increments. Thus membership of fan groups can be viewed as a positive strategy to balance work-based alienation with community-based social interaction. From such a view, it is often the pleasures of group membership itself rather than the fan object which provides the real satisfaction to individuals, as Hobson discusses in her work on *Crossroads* below.

Gender and soaps

Research around audiences for soap opera span more than half a century, with early studies by Arnheim (1944) and Warner and Henry (1948) identifying the 'typical' consumer (of radio soaps) as working-class women with little education or possibilities for advancement. However, another study, by Herzog (1944) in the same period found that women across all class positions enjoyed soaps although, typically, the consumer was married, between the ages of 18 and 35 with a high school education and living in a rural area (cited in Brown 1994: 68). Herzog's analysis of soap consumers was more 'positive' than other studies, suggesting that audiences used soap opera to teach them about aspirational middle-class values and behaviours. Later studies (see, for example, Compesi 1980), which also adopted a *uses and gratifications* approach, began to conceptualize soap audiences as being more educated than previous studies had suggested but still characterized them (women) as being socially lacking or isolated, watching soaps for escape.

By the 1980s, much 'mainstream' work on soap fans still maintained that there was a causal relationship between social interaction and sociability in the real world with the extent of soap watching (Rubin 1985), again suggesting that soap watching functioned as a surrogate friend for social inadequates. But what was often absent from these somewhat positivist and generally harsh analyses of the soap fan was any real sense of the discursive possibilities for interaction with other viewers based on their shared appreciation for particular shows. This analytical gap was puzzling since there was often a thread running through such studies that viewers *did* talk about shows with other people and that there was a great deal of pleasure derived both from individual consumption but also the post-broadcast discussion with friends, family and/or workmates.

However, two notable exceptions to this tendency were the work of David Buckingham (1987) on the British soap *EastEnders* and Dorothy Hobson (1982) on *Crossroads* (see below for a discussion of her work). Buckingham, for example, argued that young audiences were highly 'knowing' about the constructed nature of news programmes and able to achieve a critical distance:

> While the pleasure of passing moral judgement on the characters is to some extent premised on a belief in the psychological coherence and plausibility of their actions and motivations, the pleasure of questioning and even ridiculing the artificiality of the programme is clearly based on an awareness that it is, precisely, a fiction.
>
> (Buckingham 1987: 200)

Buckingham and Hobson both argued that viewers' pleasure in the text was enhanced by the likelihood of discussing episodes with their friends (see below for further elaboration of this point).

Arguably, it was the interest of researchers who wanted to explore the genre as a specifically gendered practice, aimed at women and enjoyed by women, that marked a shift in the way in which the audience for soaps began to be perceived (Brunsdon 1981; Geraghty 1981; Hobson 1982; Ang 1985). It thus became possible and even desirable to think about 'popular' texts as foci for serious scholarly analysis and with that shift came an understanding of the significance of popular culture in the lives of 'ordinary' people. It is ironic that up until that point, mass communication theorists had mostly concentrated on researching those aspects of mass culture which attracted relatively minor audiences such as news genres (print and broadcasting). It becomes almost irresistible to speculate that if more women researchers had been working in the field earlier on, the range of cultural products opened up for analysis might have been more diverse. Perhaps even some of the 'theories' which emerged from early media studies might have been subtly nuanced for differences in personal attributes such as gender, class and age.

One of the first ethnographic studies of women and soaps was carried out by Dorothy Hobson (1982) on the British series *Crossroads*. In a significant departure to the more usual research mode, Hobson went to women's homes and recorded the conversations she had with them about their viewing experiences of and responses to the show. A critical component of the research was the relation of the researcher to the research community: in this case, Hobson aligned herself with her participants as a fellow fan and was thus able to enjoy candid discussions as a consequence of a shared and knowing interest. What Hobson found were viewers who enjoyed the show but were often embarrassed to admit they watched, or defensive about their guilty pleasure, expressing an internalized disdain for the series which they had 'learnt' from cultural critics.

However, not all fans are quite so apologetic about their watching behaviours and don't necessarily berate themselves for their enjoyment of 'trash' culture. Harrington and Bielby (1995) suggest that, unlike fan behaviour, which seeks to challenge the normative renditions of femininity embodied in traditional texts such as science fiction narratives, soap fans in their study derived genuine pleasures from the original texts as they are broadcast and exist. Far from wanting to construct alternative stories and characters in order to subvert sex-role stereotyping, soap fans' principal enjoyment is precisely in experiencing the affect and emotion provoked by the storylines. Crucially, Harrington and Bielby's work with soap fans reveals the importance of personal agency and autonomy. It allows that soap fans do not necessarily watch their favourite shows in guilty disgrace but will gain an additional buzz from the fact that they are deliberately watching TV when they have a number of other things that they *could* and perhaps *should* be doing (but are not!) instead.

Focusing on the same genre but using a different approach, Ang's study (1985) of *Dallas* found that most viewers who participated in her study found the show to be 'realistic' and congruent with their own lives and experiences. Given that Ang's respondents were Dutch women who had responded to her request, in *Viva* magazine, to write to her with their reactions to the show, the (probable) mismatch between viewers' own lives in mainstream Dutch society and the glamorous lifestyles affected by the *Dallas* families was likely to be quite stark. How then, to account for the perception of realism in those narratives? Whilst the female audiences for other soaps, such as Hobson's *Crossroads* viewers, also comment on the realistic storylines and identify with the personal problems and predicaments of characters, such forms of identification are understandable since they will often share a similar social milieu. With the *Dallas* viewers, though, this was clearly not the case.

Ang's answer to this apparent conundrum was to theorize a notion of 'emotional realism', so that the pleasures of affect for audiences were derived from a shared sense of personal tragedy, allowing them to empathize at an emotional level with the pain associated with familiar renditions of domestic dysfunction: Southfork might have had gold taps and marble halls, but Sue Ellen still had a bullying and abusive husband. The ubiquitous elements of power and control are thus seen to be as present in wealthy households as in poorer ones, and family members are vulnerable to the same vicissitudes of life as everyone else, even if they have more resources available to deal with adversity. A more contemporary study on women's consumption of the Martha Stewart cookery programmes (Mason and Meyers 2001: 801) showed a similar trend, with fans appreciating the lavish and expensive lifestyle offered by Martha, but where the 'domestic fantasy of class mobility privileges appearance over substance and substitutes the look of luxury for the unattainable class ascension'. As with Ang's fans, women are not cultural dupes unable to distinguish between reality and fantasy, but rather enjoy particular cultural products both for their intrinsic self as well as for the vicarious pleasures they afford. Indeed, Thomas (2002) suggests that fans of 'quality' programmes such as *Inspector Morse* will often identify precisely with the values inscribed in such dramas, so that the texts become part of viewers' own personal narratives.

Work on women and soaps in the 1990s has both continued the **ethnographic turn** as well as returned to more structured research modes. As with earlier studies, researchers have been keen to credit audiences with sophisticated deconstruction and interpretative skills and to try and understand their viewing behaviours and pleasures as forms of active engagement rather than passive dislocation. In her work on women soap opera fans, Brown (1994) is keen to insist that fanship networks have the potential (and reality) of providing sites of resistance for women to engage in critical discourses about sex-role stereotyping and expectations. She argues, as have others, that the process of ostensibly discussing plotlines and character development in their favourite soap can actually enable women to use those narrative themes as a springboard for much wider debates about their own lives and those of other women they know.

The potential of a safe rehearsal of one's own life choices through the discussion of soap characters' circumstances is an important function for audiences, where the shared experience of bad luck or outcome provides strong identifications between audience and character. Viewers thus 'use television's narratives to comment upon and come to understand events in their lives, thereby providing themselves with a certain pleasure and perhaps relief . . .' (Wilson 1993: 86).

Developing the idea of the **tertiary text** (see Allen 1985; Buckingham 1987), that is, where viewers create meaning from texts through a process of interpretation rather than passively consuming the superficial storyline, Brown (1994) attempts to give the balance of power in meaning-making to audiences rather than the text. The crucial point about the notion of the tertiary text or the reception/response model of the active audience, is that the viewer/reader is not expected to uncover a hidden truth but rather interprets and remixes the material she is watching in order to make it meaningful to her in the context of her own life circumstances. In other words, the viewer renders storylines and narratives meaningful by relating them to their own lives or the lives of people they know. And it is the retelling of episodes and the discussion of plotlines with others which give fans an additional pleasure. What Brown discovered was the way in which women can actively enjoy doing something which is deemed 'unacceptable' both by the taste police but also by men, enabling them to experience subversive pleasure. Borrowing from the **encoding/decoding** model of active reception, the enjoyment and valuation of low status activities such as soap-watching can be seen as a subversive act, resisting the dominant (patriarchal) social discourse. So women appropriate a particular form of cultural capital for themselves, rescuing it (in this case, soaps) from the snobbish grasp of the elite taste-makers and reinserting it into their lives as a meaningful and useful activity.

The pleasure that women experience while watching soap operas can have to do simply with the enjoyment of the activity . . . however, the pleasure that women experience when talking about soap operas and constructing their own spoken text is often resistive pleasure. They use it not only to set boundaries for themselves where they can discuss their own cultural concerns but also to resist aesthetic hierarchies concerned with knowledge, accepted cultural capital and domination by men.

(Brown 1994: 112)

But it is the narrative produced by audiences which constitutes the primary site of resistance, not the primary text itself which is more usually encoded in line with the dominant conventions of a patriarchal status quo. However, some scholars have argued that soap opera itself is a subversive genre since its staple ingredients of broken marriages, casual sex, unintended pregnancies, domestic violence and petty crime are directly antithetical to the socially acceptable norms of romantic love contained within the domesticated marriage arrangement (Lovell 1981) and good citizenship. Thus fans could see soaps as blueprints for behaviour or at least as providing alternative models, thus encouraging life to mimic art.

On the other hand, the ways in which soap 'problems' are resolved, both narratively and usually in 'real' life, are often through an appeal to familiar renditions of 'acceptable behaviour'. The pregnant school girl or the woman who kills her abusive partner is not celebrated in soap texts but rather becomes the focus for a hegemonic discourse which inevitably positions them as deviant. Whilst this is not to argue for actively promoting underage sex or the killing of one's partner, soap storylines are sometimes a little reckless in the ways in which they 'solve' the social problems which they have constructed. Although some soap texts have taken a rather more considered approach in their elaboration of less 'conventional' lifestyles and choices such as gay relation-ships, there remains an underlying normative sub-text which relegates those subject positions to the periphery of 'acceptable' behaviour.

Women and film

As well as analysing the female fans of TV soaps, the other medium which has interested many researchers in terms of gender has been film, with ground-breaking works such as those produced by Laura Mulvey (1975), which suggested that the film audience is irrevocably gendered and the film text as primarily coded for a male gaze. In her work, she argued that the way in which film texts 'work' is to encourage audience identification with the male lead — and at the time very few leads were women — and therefore to view women in film as objects of the male gaze. She suggested that the drive towards identifi-cation with the male hero was equally strong for women as for men, so that all audience members were encouraged to take the position of voyeur and to commodify women actors as objects of desire.

Elsewhere, the principal focus for much early academic study of women and film was textual analysis and deconstruction (see Kaplan 1983; Feuer 1984; Kuhn 1984; Modleski 1984; Brunsdon 1986), but part of the development of 'seeing' film through a gendered frame included researchers who wanted to look beyond the text and their own interpretation, towards the views of the audiences of those materials (see, for example, Gamman and Marshment 1988; Pribham 1988).

Taylor's (1989) work in the late 1980s sought precisely to rupture the firm hold that 'the text' had on film researchers and the dangers inherent in theories which irrevocably situated women and men in fixed subject positions based on identifiable sex characteristics. In her work with women fans of *Gone With The Wind* (dir: Victor Fleming, 1939), she showed the multiplicity of readings that audiences could bring to a single cultural product, let alone a genre. She also identified the importance of historical specificity in understanding changing responses to texts, since the women she interviewed in the late 1980s had seen the film when it was first made and brought a critical distance to their readings of the film then and now.

Similarly, Bobo (1988) set out explicitly to problematize the static and unitary position of women and men as audience by focusing on black women's experiences of Steven Spielberg's adaptation of Alice Walker's important book, *The Color Purple* (dir: Steven Spielberg, 1985). In her work with black female audiences, she found that, contrary to the mostly critical tenor of (white) feminist analyses of the film, many found pleasures in the text. This was not only because Walker's narrative was an authentic and resonant one for them, but because they wanted to identify with strong black women characters and such opportunities for positive identification were rarely available elsewhere.

Such studies have been significant because they place the female spectator at the centre of the analysis in ways which give her importance in her own right, as possessing agency, rather than being simply 'positioned' by the text. Stacey's (1994) more recent work also has a women-watching-women focus. She analysed hundreds of letters and questionnaires which she received from British women who had been regular cinema-goers during World War 2 and in the post-war period (1940s and 1950s) in order to identify the pleasures they derived from Hollywood films of that era. Crucially, Stacey was aware of the paucity of research then available which focused specifically on the relationship between women audiences and the women stars on whom they gazed, and the pleasures for women in looking at female actors intended to appeal to male viewers.

Women, films and consumption

Producing media specifically targeted at women audiences has a long and distinguished pedigree. As Stokes (1999) points out, even in the early days of the movies in the 1920s, the industry acknowledged that women comprised the majority of movie-goers. Not only did this mean that a high proportion of films produced in that period were genre films made to appeal to women audiences, especially melodrama and romance with a preponderance of female characters (see Lynd and Lynd 1929; Haskell 1987), but that the studios 'delivered' women consumers to advertisers via strategic placement of women-oriented products such as toiletries in the films themselves as well as in the more conventional space of the commercial break (Eckert 1978). The overt acknowledgement of such films' female address can be seen in the wording of many flyers during that decade and the following one. The caption for one such film used the exhortations, 'Girls! You'll learn How to Handle 'Em!' (cited in Stokes 1999: 49), making clear the film's intention to show women how to get and keep her man.

Fuller (1996) suggests that such was Hollywood's perception (if not the verifiable reality) that women comprised the majority film audience, that women's films became the principal mechanism whereby film news and associated tie-ins was distributed. So forthcoming film openings and events which would be attended by film celebrities were trailed in fan magazines and women's magazines, together with movie reports. Clearly, then, the industry itself perpetuated its own business interests by focusing what Fuller describes as the main 'discursive apparatus' of cinema, that is materials and publicity promoting its products, towards those media forms most popular with women. It is interesting then, that the rather cynical impetus for the original production and distribution of fan magazines, that is to 'sell' women to advertisers, including to the movie industry itself in the form of ticket sales, has been so successfully subverted by fans themselves who have appropriated the medium to meet their own very different ends. As we discuss in Chapter 6, the fan magazine or fanzine has been transformed from a vehicle pushed by the industry to sell its products, to a vehicle which is controlled entirely by fans themselves.

It is beyond the scope of this chapter and indeed the book more generally, to offer a sustained analysis of why Hollywood's fascination with women audiences in the early decades of the last millennium has been so spectacularly absent for most of its closing ones, but that reality does provide puzzling food for thought. When Anne Thompson (1991) wrote a leader in *Variety* magazine, asking why Hollywood continued to resist making movies with a strong female appeal when they are cheaper to make and more profitable when successful, she received a range of responses from studio executives. The bottom line, however, was that studios now target the under-25s as their principal audience believing that young women are more willing to watch a male-oriented film, than men are to watch more female-centred material. Thus the purchasing power (through film choice decisions) was now perceived to reside with men rather than women.

But at least one studio executive argues that there are other factors at play which are less rational and commercial but which, fortunately for the industry, still produce 'positive' outcomes at the box office. One of them is that many senior male studio executives prefer to work on male-oriented genres such as action movies because these are what they prefer to watch and which inevitably have male leads (cited in Thompson 1991: 191). Whilst this may well be the case, there is a very obvious question to ask: why did the much more male-dominated and conservative studio system of the 1920s and 1930s nonetheless decide to target women as the principal audience, whilst the contemporary industry with many more senior women executives, so blatantly ignores them?

For Krämer (1998), a hopeful answer could lie in the box office success of a film such as *Titanic*, which he suggests could usher in a more savvy understanding of the commercial pull of female-oriented films. Unfortunately, the signs since Krämer posited this rosy future are not that good. In 2002, the top five grossing films in North America were *Spider Man*, *Star Wars*, *Harry Potter*, *Lord of the Rings* and *Signs*, none of them notable for their strong women leads!

Fans, fantasy and science fiction

The other genre which has attracted significant research interest has been science fiction and other kinds of fantasy text. Of course, although many media scholars agree that most texts are broadly polysemic and thus open to a number of different interpretations, the kinds of texts which often interest fans, or at least which interest the fans who interest academic researchers, often share particular characteristics. Whilst long-running serials such as the British *Coronation Street* and the American *Dallas* have spawned any number of fan groups, memorabilia and fanzines, it has arguably been science-fiction texts which constitute the most sustained and long-standing interest for fans, from *Star Trek* to *Xena: Warrior Princess*.

In Fiske's (1992) terms, fantasy texts are more 'producerly' than others, because their very unreality allows for a much greater range of interpretations. They incorporate inconsistencies, contradictions and ambivalences which provide any number of credibility or narrative gaps which the fans can then fill in myriad ways. In Penley's (1991) work on the women fans of *Star Trek*, for example, she suggests that the fantasy genre offers considerable licence for fans since real-life issues can be rehearsed in unreal contexts, making them safe vehicles to try out ideas and 'realities'. Another attraction of fantasy and science fiction texts for fans (and researchers) is the meta-polysemic nature of the narratives. For example, *Star Trek* allows a diversity of reading positions for the futurist, the buddy or the happy family member (Jenkins 1992b), providing something for everyone and encouraging different forms of identification, both contextual but also at the level of character. It is therefore possible to identify with the male hero figure of Captain Kirk, or to appreciate the imagination of the show's writers, or to enjoy the simple pleasures of good triumphing over evil. Attributing a certain religiosity to *Star Trek* narratives, Jindra (1999) argues that for many fans of the show, the inherent insistence on the triumph of good over evil, its emphasis on scientific development and technological innovation provides a manifestation of their own positive hopes for a better future.

It is precisely the familiar and 'folksy' articulation of 'goodness' and the repetitive motifs of moral(izing) humanity which, for Jindra's fan audiences, provide 'guidance in a pluralistic, often meaningless postmodern world' (1999: 218). But the crucial point about *Star Trek* is not the obeisance of fans to a particular sense of morality but rather the seduction of a vision of a better tomorrow, what Jindra's terms a 'folk philosophy'. Whilst this might seem a rather grand claim for what is, after all, a very tame and by contemporary terms, quite old-fashioned show, it is possible to use such a term because the show's creator, Gene Roddenberry, was himself a practising humanist. Storylines were punctuated with his own homespun philosophy and vision which, put simply, was that human beings can and must control their own future.

Of course, there is a paradox here since humanism explicitly rejects conventional religious belief as mere superstition, and some *Star Trek* fans have been keen to distance the show from any religious association (cf Sanda and Hall 1994), although this is surely to frame the notion of 'religion' within an extremely narrow definition (Greil and Robbins 1994). But the way in which some fans have appropriated Vulcan 'teachings' as the basis for an entire philosophy and worldview (Jindra 1999) is an interesting example of fans' desire to find deeper messages and meanings within entertainment texts. However, as Marsalek (1992) observes below, there is considerable attraction in a philosophy which is based on inclusion and aims to make life better for everyone.

The "*Star Trek*" universe is a celebration of pluralism encompassed in the Vulcan philosophy of IDIC — Infinite Diversity in Infinite

Combinations. "*Star Trek*" advances a commitment to self-determination, freedom, equality and individual rights. The *Enterprise* crews are dedicated to using reason, science and logic . . . in understanding the universe, solving problems and improving the human condition.

(Marsalek 1992: 53)

The British show, *Doctor Who*, has a similar range of address forms. As part of their work on science fiction audiences, Tulloch and Jenkins (1995) explored audience reactions to *Doctor Who* amongst two distinct groups. One of the groups comprised people who were attending a 'para' science fiction convention and who had what the authors describe as a technical/technological and graduate/professional background, while the other comprised a university-based 'literary' science fiction club.

In broad terms, Tulloch and Jenkins (1995) suggests that the former group were particularly interested in the special effects and gadgets and the extent to which the storylines and actions were realistic, given existing technological knowledge. However, these fans were also interested in the narrative sophistication of the text and the teacherly quality of 'The Doctor's' benevolent approach to supporting the underdog through knowledge transfer. The 'literary' group, on the other hand, were much more interested in the discursive content and context of science fiction programmes, using their knowledge of 'original' works (that is, the historical referents for later science fiction series) to critique the texts which they then inspired.

This latter group's fondness for the *Doctor Who* series, which surprised the researchers, seemed to be based on their interpretation of the text as 'charming' and an appreciation of the humour contained in scripts as the principal 'estranging' device which allowed the series to be viewed as within the science fiction genre. In the end, Tulloch and Jenkins argue that science fiction texts such as *Star Trek* and *Doctor Who* engage fan audiences at many different levels, and for any number of reasons, so caution is needed when trying to categorize 'types' of fan on the basis of their alleged interest and/or background.

Fans and cultural production

While all of us, simply by virtue of being members of audiences, work with the texts we read, watch and listen to, in order to produce meaning and pleasure, fans often take this engagement a step further, becoming what Harris (1998a: 4) describes as 'specialised audiences with very intensified relationships to content.' When fans go on to produce texts which are then circulated, sometimes within a fan community and sometimes more widely, Fiske (1992) calls this process a 'shadow cultural economy'. Following Bourdieu (1984) in describing culture as an economic system, individuals, 'invest and accumulate capital' (Fiske 1992: 30–31). In other words, cultural capital is a form of asset, like education, but which we use to maintain or enhance our social status rather than our bank balance. Fans who want to do more than simply 'consume' the text will often turn to producing a fan artefact, be it a story, a song, a webzine or even the embodiment of a screen character. For example, businesses will sometimes sponsor look-alike and sound-alike competitions, where fans have an opportunity of not just adoring but actually pretending *to be* the object of their attachment.

More common, though, are the fans who write their own material such as scripts or produce their own stories and images. In becoming a consumer/producer, then, the fan ceases to be a passive disciple but rather becomes a proactive collaborator. Finding that theories of fandom are often too restricted in their analytical choices, Jenkins (1992) argues that part of what distinguishes fans as a particular set of textual consumers is the way in which their cultural activity, especially their 'production', is socially organized and celebrated. Thus:

> Fans produce meanings and interpretations; fans produce artworks; fans produce communities; fans produce alternative identities. In each case, fans are drawing on materials from the dominant media and employing them in ways that serve their own interests and facilitate their own pleasures.
>
> (Jenkins 1992: 214)

Crucially, for Jenkins, the cultural production of fans is multi-layered and often directed towards serving the interests of their particular fan community but cannot necessarily be read off to symbolize what is 'going on' in the minds of the fans towards the fan object. What such products can do, perhaps, is demonstrate the versatility of the human imagination to rework material made for one purpose into one which serves an altogether different one, to reinvent the wheel but with different tyres. The appropriation of fan texts in order to deconstruct and reassemble them or to embellish them or even to create parallel but relevant texts, is an important feature of fans' cultural production. This act of 'reworking' is one of the more creative ways in which fans critique fan texts, '. . . posing what could or should have happened in place of what did' (Baym 1998: 124).

More extremely, fans believe that artists or series become 'theirs' by dint of their excessive (fanatic) following and support, as Hobson (1982) discusses in her study of the audiences for the early British soap opera *Crossroads*. For example, fans will often use the possessive 'our' when describing particular characters, such as 'our Bet' [Bet Lynch in *Coronation Street*, played by Julie Goodyear]. Such is their involvement with and in the text that fans do not allow distance between the adored object and themselves, believing that they 'know' the particular character(s) better than the scriptwriter and that therefore they can write more authentic lines (Fiske 1992). Such fan criticism is often accompanied by alternative storylines offered by fans (Hobson 1990), sometimes exaggerating the dramatic potential of a particular plotline and sometimes offering a more sober alternative.

Perhaps the most long-lived form of fannish cultural production is the fan magazine otherwise known as the fanzine. As early as 1973, for example, there were 88 different *Star Trek* fanzines in circulation and once films began to emerge at cinemas and the TV programmes were syndicated, a further (new) set of audiences were created, generating yet more fanzine contributors, peaking at more than 400 amateur publications by 1980 (Jenkins 1995). The progress of the 'zine' has developed from the relatively crude and unsophisticated hand-typed circular, through offset-printed and professionally produced artefacts to the web-based materials currently available, although examples of earlier models are still in circulation. However, whilst the mode of production might have changed, the essential characteristics of the fanzine in terms of its content has remained the same, blending fiction and non-fiction writings on the cult object and often subverting original plotlines and narratives to produce entirely differently nuanced and even entirely original narratives.

Focusing specifically on science fiction fan writing, Bacon-Smith (1992) suggests that the authors and editors are predominantly women, writing and producing for a predominantly female audience. Gender is important here because, Jenkins (1992a) argues, what female fans are doing when they engage in specific cultural production around, say, *Star Trek* is reworking the text in order for the narrative drive and character development to speak to their own, female concerns, concerns which were almost entirely ignored in the original show. In addition, fan writing enables women to become involved in fan culture in constructive and creative ways. Such a rationale is almost certainly true for science fiction fanzines, since the primary fanship community for this particular genre is predominantly male, especially as attendees at conventions.

Thus, the one place where women *can* exert some control in and gain pleasure from their fandom outside of their enjoyment of the text itself is through their own cultural production of associative texts. For women fans of *Star Trek*, their pleasures in the text were often complicated by their views on how women characters appeared in the show. The discursive rhetoric of the show often stressed equality but most women who appeared were little more than decorative foils to the male leads, their status as sex object reinforced by the display of their bodies sheathed in short-skirted and body-hugging uniforms.

Rejecting charges of sexism, though, one of the *Star Trek's* fan liaison personnel, Richard Arnold, insisted that the philosophy of the show was more important than the gender of the lead characters (Arnold, cited in Lalli 1992: 321). But one might argue that, on at least two counts — gender and role — this is a rather glib and patronizing comment to make. Ironically, when women were presented in positions of authority, it was usually in the context of being alien and thus generally 'bad' in relation to the 'good' *Enterprise* crew. In other situations, women who exhibited more assertive or even aggressive tendencies, especially in relation to male characters, were portrayed as unnatural and as having lost or suppressed their 'real' feminine self (Jenkins 1995).

Thus much fan fiction written by women subverts these gender stereotypes and writes women back into the picture, literally, by narrativizing their potential for leadership, courage and ability as well as romanticizing their relations with their colleagues. Not only does the writing of these alternative stories provide an emancipatory pleasure in its own right, to envision a more equitable society, but the sharing (and then discussion) of these narratives via fanzine or online distribution represents a movement 'from domestic isolation towards community participation' (Jenkins 1995: 203). So fan fictions express something more than mere textual subversion and transformation, they can also have a revolutionary impact on self-esteem.

However, care needs to be taken that Bacon-Smith's (1992) insistence on the emancipatory potential of fan communities does not lock women into the prison of victimhood by obliterating the importance of their own creative out-put. Gillian (1998: 184) describes these women-flavoured and women-controlled spaces as 'wild-zones', '. . . a women-centered cultural space in which reinterpretations of the text can occur' and where such activity, importantly, occurs *away from* the dominant culture industry. So, even as women (and men) fans may have boring and routinized lives and seek comfort in the welcoming embrace of a fan community, their involvement is not just about solace, it can also be about excitement and agency.

Following de Certeau (1984), Jenkins (1992a) uses the term 'textual poaching' to describe these activities of cultural appropriation. Fans use the narratives of programmes and series as mere springboards for character development and elaboration, often in ways which are highly unlikely to ever be written for 'real'. Fans can challenge the restricted mores of industry norms by revisioning relationships and storylines which speak in the register of liberation and enlightenment. However, such transgressive writings are not without their own protocols and boundaries, mostly adhering to the conventions which have developed around the particular fan community in which they operate, building on previous fan writing and articulating perspectives which are already codified. Brown (1994) identifies a range of story types written by women about female heroes in fanzines, especially related to *Star Trek*: 'Mary-Sue' stories revolve around assertive young women joining others on the ship's bridge, resolving conflict, saving the world and ultimately dying. The 'Lay-Spock' or 'Lay-Kirk' stories are hopefully self-explanatory! 'Hurt-comfort' stories usually feature a central character being tended to by a caring colleague.

Stories about men, especially the Kirk and Spock characters from *Star Trek*, are almost always about aspects of homoerotic desire and fulfilment, often bracketed together under the broad label of 'slash fiction'. The provenance of 'slash' lies in the tendency to use a forward stroke mark to denote same/sex relationships and has historically, but not always exclusively, focused on male-on-male sexual and emotional relationships (Jenkins 1992a). Interestingly, as with soap storylines which are often left deliberately open-ended in order to allow for the re-appearance of characters who have apparently disappeared, 'moved away' or even died, fanzine plotlines and characters also enjoy this lack of closure. It enables writers to resurrect characters and narratives written by others some months or even years later.

A variation on the theme of cultural (re)production through written form is that of 'filking', a term coined by fans to describe fan music-making, usually inventing songs which are performed in character. Unlike fan writing, though, filking is intended to be a collective as opposed to individual activity. It developed as a sub-genre of science fiction fandom where the songs were designed to be sung 'collectively and informally by fans gathered at science fiction conventions.' (Jenkins 1992a: 217) Importantly, a central element to filking is an interest in reifying the status of the fan, specifically in relation to the non-fan (non-entity). In a neat parody of an elite discourse which positions fan culture as weird, strange and aberrant, filk lyrics sing about the mundane and boring conformity of mainstream society, juxtaposing the fans as consumers and purveyors of pleasure and joy against the forces of grey ordinariness.

The 'con'

The convention ('con') is a locus of considerable fan activity, often providing the principal mechanism through which fans get to meet and socialize with each other on a regular basis. Most cons comprise any number of different elements, including screenings, distribution of fan-produced materials, masquerade halls, games room, art gallery and retail outlets, as well as allotted times for 'filking' (Jenkins 1992a). For Porter (1999) and her fans, there is an almost transcendental quality attached to their attendance at *Star Trek* conventions, where they can meet other people who share precisely the same devotion to the show and where this one common interest can unite an otherwise entirely disparate group of individuals. Not only are the more meaning-loaded differences in class, race and gender rendered largely irrelevant in the context of a convention, but the egalitarian dream it sells is the manifestation (in the imagination of the participating fans at least) of the longed-for better life promised by, say, the *Star Trek* discourse.

Drawing on her observations at a number of *Star Trek* conventions in mid-1990s North America, Porter (1999: 246) suggests that attendance at such events can be viewed as a 'secular inheritor of religious pilgrimage'. In other words, attendees attach deep and significant meaning to just 'being there', as if the convention represents, and perhaps is even experienced as the lived, metaphysical embodiment of nirvana. Importantly, given the level of personal ridicule which many *Star Trek* fans experience, even from close family members, the opportunity to enter a world where their fan interest is not only normal but welcomed and embraced is clearly seductive. In the convention context, then, the fan is free to love *Star Trek* without apology and meet many other individuals who feel exactly the same way. She can thus get to swap her usual habitus of isolated weirdo for a share in a collective identity which is entirely positive and inclusive.

But if attending conventions allows you to express your 'real' self, it can also make available the opportunity to be someone else entirely, in the same way that attendance at conferences or going away on holiday without a partner allows the invention of a different, perhaps more daring, persona to emerge. It is precisely the **liminality** of the *Star Trek* convention, the celebration of fantasy as pseudo-reality, which encourages the adoption of altered states, especially where the new mantle allows an otherwise repressed trait to gain expression. As Turner (1977) argues, liminoid contexts (such as that offered by the *Star Trek* convention) allow individuals to exhibit their full personality in ways which are often precluded by the requirement to live and work in environments which are over-determined by normative rules of behaviour and interaction.

The shape of fans to come

The emerging technology of the internet has produced a step-change in the ways in which fans practise their fandom (see Chapter 7 for an extended discussion of the internet and audiences). During the 1990s, many fans moved over to cyberspace with enthusiasm, quickly realizing the medium's potential to share discussions, writings and ideas amongst a significantly wider and always expanding cyber fan community. In Baym's (1998) study of one of the first and most successful computer-based fan groups — Usenet's *rec.arts.tv.soaps* (r.a.t.s.) — set up in 1994, she argues that from the start, r.a.t.s challenged the orthodox view of soap fans as uneducated: most r.a.t.s members were educated professionals who used r.a.t.s while at work (see also Nightingale and Ross 2003). Such internet fan communities also challenge the gender stereotypes which surround the internet since 75 per cent of r.a.t.s. members in Baym's study were women.

As with other work on fans, Baym's work also found that much of the enjoyment which women derived from being involved in an internet fan community was the opportunity it afforded for social discourse and interaction, albeit computer-mediated. From her 'observation' of fan-talk in r.a.t.s., Baym (1998: 113) suggests that the interactions she witnessed can be categorized in terms of goal attainment, where members' various satisfactions include: '. . . the creation of a performance space with the potential status and recognition that entails, and perhaps most provocatively, the opportunity to engage in public discussion of normally private socioemotional issues.'

Whilst much of the discussion around fans and computer-mediated communication (CMC) and fans suggests that fansites are places of of pleasurable engagement, MacDonald (1998) signals a warning about inferences of unalloyed collegiality. Her work with *Quantum Leap* fans demonstrates that women fans of the show were strongly encouraged to form their own discrete newsgroup because other (male) members resented the 'silliness' of their postings, their interest in the physical attributes of the principal male characters and their long and complex discussions of the relationships with which the lead characters were involved. Interestingly, the women who have developed the women-only list are now fiercely protective of its privacy and change its name regularly to further police the boundaries of their safe space. Scodari (1998) also signals a cautionary note, suggesting that cyberfandom can close down as well as open up discussion.

Along with other aspects of social life, the internet has made a significant impact on the way in which fans can communicate with each other, no longer needing to wait weeks for the latest 'zine' to appear, but merely a few minutes or hours to receive feedback on a plot perspective or new storyline suggestion. In 2000, there were 1200 sites relating to *Star Trek* and at least 200 sites dedicated to the much more contemporary *Xena* fan (Pullen 2000) with a variety of material included on their pages, including some sites dedicated to fan fiction. Most major stations have created specific websites for their most popular shows which include chatrooms, plot summaries, biographies of and interviews with the main stars.

Whilst much of this material has traditionally only been available to fans through membership of official fan clubs, the internet has, to some extent, transformed what it is to be a fan, no longer a sad loser with no friends, but an ordinary internet surfer who happens to like *Star Trek*. As Pullen (2000) points out, the internet is blurring the boundaries between fandom and exploitation as the film and broadcast industries increasingly consider internet audiences as the prime market for their products and target their merchandizing strategy accordingly. *Xena: Warrior Princess* is a good case in point.

Xena debuted in 1995 and is syndicated through MCA/Universal Pictures. The show featured Lucy Lawless as the eponymous hero and Renee O'Connor as her sidekick, Gabrielle. The show has generated hundreds of websites including the 'official' MCA/Universal homepage which encourages the purchase of any number of *Xena*-associated products and merchandize. Pullen (2000) argues that most of the *Xena* websites incorporate clearly marked codes for gender and sexuality, mostly falling into the categories of lesbians, straight women and straight men. She suggests that in the early days of the sites' development, there was considerable hostility amongst the three groups of fans towards each other but over time this animosity appears to have disappeared and sites of one group will often include hyperlinks to the others.

There is also a much more discursive cross-over now than happened in the early years of the show's existence. Currently, the lesbian sites most commonly focus on aspects of the show relating to the relationship between Xena and Gabrielle or what is often quite coyly described as 'the subtext', although this relationship is also an important element for many heterosexual fans as well. However, perhaps unsurprisingly, the 'subtext' is never mentioned in the official site although its bulletin board does contain postings where fans themselves discuss the sexual chemistry between the two principal actors, often through heated exchanges between the 'yes she is' and the 'no she isn't' factions. For a further discussion of the ways in which the internet has and will continue to transform the way in which researchers think about and work with audiences, see Chapter 7.

Conclusion

This chapter has focused on a particular kind of textual consumer, the fan. It has looked at the ways in which 'fans' have been conceptualized at both the generic, societal level as mostly deviant, weird and sometimes dangerous, and as foci for media research. Most of the significant studies of fans and fan culture discussed above (and elsewhere) use ethnographic approaches in order to explore meaning-making from the perspective of fans themselves, how they interact with the objects of their interest, how they subvert textual narratives and rework them for their own and others' pleasures and how fan cultures operate as 'interpretive communities' (following Fish 1980).

The important point about the ethnographic turn in audience studies with fans and fan communities is that the researcher is interested in exploring not just the text itself, but the ways in which the text is used as a catalyst for other activities and pleasures in the everyday lives of viewers and listeners. It attempts to answer, both consciously and unconsciously, the criticisms which have been levelled at more *positivist* or less nuanced accounts of audience reception, attempted to fracture assumptions about hegemony (the uncritical and mani-pulated consumer), homogeneity (the undifferentiated 'mass' audience) and singularity (attention to consuming as a discrete activity) by showing precisely the multi-layered and complex relations that fan audiences have with the text and with each other.

Crucially, ethnographic studies attempt to situate media consumption within the wider context of personal, domestic and social life. They seek to show the dynamics of viewing and listening and to make visible the otherwise *in*visible strategies at work in the interpretative process which often includes cultural *production* as well as cultural *consumption*. Here the consumer is also pro-ducer, the reader is also writer. Such a model promotes conceptions of audiences who are empowered and creative not just passive and dull. By working with audiences in their own homes, watching social exchange within domestic environments, observing the delicate power-plays over the remote, watching a chat-room thread develop, exploring the place of media in domestic life, a much clearer picture emerges about the importance (or not) of particular media in particular social lives.

Because of the desire to really get 'inside' the reader/reception nexus, most ethnographic studies are small-scale and do not overtly attempt to generalize from their modest sample base to wider populations. However, the richness of the resulting data and the insights which are revealed about processes rather than outcomes provide important clues in expanding our understanding of the meaning of (different) texts for (different) audiences and especially, fans. As Hills (2002) points out, very persuasively, the study of fans is irrevocably a study of contradictions, where fan culture can provide fora for mutual celebration but also spaces for private thought. We can idealize the notion of a fan community whilst also recognizing the enforced nature of hierarchical structures. Fans can both challenge and intensify commodification. Some writ-ing about fans is somewhat romanticized in perspective (see Moores 1993 for a useful critique of this propensity), especially in relation to the extent to which audiences really *can* hijack the juggernauts of corporate capital and patriarchal self-interest to suit their own ends. However, identifying acts of resistive reading and the forms of cultural production with which fans are engaged, nonetheless remain persuasive and attractive.

Further reading

Baym, N.K. (2000) *Tune In, Log On: Soaps, Fandom and Online Community*. Thousand Oaks, London, New Delhi: Sage.

Hill, A. (1997) *Shocking Entertainment: Viewer Response to Violent Movies*. Luton, England: John Libbey Media.

Hills, M. (2002) *Fan Cultures*. London and New York: Routledge.

Jenkins, H. (1992) *Textual Poachers: Television Fans and Participatory Culture*. New York and London: Routledge.

Stokes, M. and Maltby, R. (eds) (2001) *Hollywood Spectatorship: Changing Perceptions of Cinema Audiences*. London: British Film Institute.

Thornham, S. (ed.) (1999) *Feminist Film Theory: A Reader*. Edinburgh: Edinburgh University Press.

7 | NEW MEDIA, NEW AUDIENCE, NEW RESEARCH?

The audience fights back

Audience studies have come a long way over the past 50 years, from the early models of a passive and duped consumer in thrall to government propaganda, to the *Xena* fan in Kentucky who 'talks' to her friend in Calcutta in real time and sends alternative storylines to the *Xena* production team by email attachment. The previous chapters have attempted to show the great diversity of audience research contexts and foci, the different ways in which the concept of 'audience' has been appropriated to serve particular purposes at particular times for particular people, from broadcasters, to pollsters, to cultural critics. Whilst the second half of the twentieth century saw a significant growth in audience studies, with the actual concept of 'the audience' moving through the arc of passive sap to interactive player, it was arguably the 1990s which saw the most significant shift in thinking about the audience with the widespread incursion of the internet into everyday lives and culture and the explosion in talk and reality TV shows.

Whilst cultural theorists throughout the 1980s began to show the ways in which consumers were not simply accepting media messages but were actively negotiating and even resisting the dominant codes embedded in cultural products, the 1990s saw the talk/back show assume genre status, where audiences were encouraged to not only have their say, publicly, about things they saw, read or heard in the media, but encouraged to participate in shows where they were the stars (Livingstone and Lunt 1994). The game show was already a popular format but the unexpected success of the *Oprah Winfrey Show* (subsequently shortened to 'Oprah' to signify the intimate appeal of the eponymous presenter), spawned an entirely new genre which has become loosely known as 'confessional TV', where 'ordinary' people vie with each other to relate the most harrowing life experience, to disclose the most debauched fantasy, to reveal the most embarrassing anecdote (Decker 1997; Illouz 1999; Wilson 2001).

The audience subject and the audience object suddenly became interchangeable: each was also the other. And the most recent manifestation of these real-people-as-entertainment shows is 'reality' TV (see Fetveit 1999), exemplified, as noted in Chapter 1, by shows like *Big Brother* where viewers become voyeurs looking at and listening to a microcosmic world where a faux intimacy is traded in exchange for a fleeting leap at fame (Cathode 2000; Sigismondi 2001; van Zoonen 2001). We, as audience, are both consumers of the spectacle but also players in the game since shows like *Big Brother* require audience participation to decide who stays in the game and who is relegated to the also-ran benches. Not all shows in this genre include this element of audience interaction but *Big Brother's* production team quickly realized that audiences not only enjoyed the voyeuristic opportunity which they were afforded by the regular 30-minute programme slot, but were hitting the 24/7 webcam in even greater numbers (see also Roscoe 2001).

Wired world: interactivity and the audience

As *Big Brother* exemplifies, developments in genre are paralleled by changes in technology and it is arguably this latter change which has already and will continue to refocus and reshape the way in which research with audiences is undertaken. As McQuail (1997: 129) argues, the fast pace of technological change is heralding nothing short of a revolution: '. . . the typical audience role can cease to be that of passive listener, consumer, receiver or target. Instead it will encompass any of the following: seeker; consultant; browser; respondent; interlocutor; or conversationalist.' The development of the world wide web and its gradual journey to becoming a mass medium requires us to rethink both the audience and the medium. The concomitant development of cyber cafes, telecentres and community-based facilities in even the most remote parts of world, means that the *potential* of the medium to attract a mass audience is considerable. What phone-in radio slots, TV talk shows and other audience-based programming have started, in terms of encouraging a more genuinely *interactive* audience — as opposed to simply an *active* one which uses its power to switch channels or shout at the TV — has been carried through with spectacular results to the internet.

The great leap forward which the internet allows, in terms of 1–2–1-communication, is 'talking' with others in real *and* virtual time, where the send/respond mode of email, chatroom or newsgroup, mimics the turn-taking of regular conversation between two or more people, but expanded exponentially. For our purposes, audiences and fans of particular media such as *Star Trek* or *Xena* or even whole genres such as soaps can all 'talk' to and with each other, messaging about a favourite episode or a character or asking about information or even writing new storylines. And not only does the internet mean a reconsideration of 'the audience' in terms of its global base, albeit that most media sites which are used by fan audiences have English as the common language, but the very identity of the audience itself, who it actually comprises, can be easily hijacked by the proclivities of internet users to take on new and multiple identities and personalities (Barnes 2001). Whilst Baym (2000) points out that the internet did not invent fan groups, its development has not only encouraged fan communities to proliferate and transcend geographical boundaries, but has also enabled fans of even the most obscure show or film or text, to get in touch with each other and communicate about the object of their desire.

And of course, it is not simply that fans are talking to each other. The media industry wants to talk to audiences because they understand the commercial implication of the 'ordinary' person's creative activities. Jenkins (2002) has claimed that through the collaborative activities in which they engage, audiences are gaining greater power in the entertainment industries. The capacity to operate websites and develop and display their creative efforts has given fans a presence in the mediascape. Jenkins attributes this increased power to three trends: the new tools available to fans; the existence of subcultures online that promote DIY production; and economic trends that favour horizontal integration. The outsourcing and subcontracting activities of entertainment companies lead them to encourage enthusiasts and fans to engage in creative research and development and product trials.

> The horizontal integration of the entertainment industry — and the emergent logic of synergy — depends on the circulation of intellectual properties across media outlets. Transmedia promotion presumes a more active spectator who can and will follow these media flows.
>
> (Jenkins 2002: 10)

Jenkins describes fan culture as dialogic not disruptive, affective rather than ideological, and collaborative rather than confrontational (2002: 13). He has also claimed that they are examples of the 'intelligent communities' anticipated by Pierre Levy's evolutionary and utopian theory of **cyberculture** (Levy 1997).

Levy is fascinated by the ways technologies developed by human beings to make living easier, change the ways people orient themselves to the natural world. In Levy's account, the purpose of technologies is control — of living species, of matter, of messages and of human groups, and he traces the evolution of technologies of control from archaic principles based on phenomenology, though molar principles devised for the exercise of mass control, to molecular technologies that focus on control organized at the most basic level of existence: gene-by-gene; atom-by-atom; bit-by-bit (Levy 1997: 41). Because human groups evolve *in* technology, technologies actually produce spaces for the expression of human creativity, and here too, Levy has developed an evolutionary model to explain the accumulation of spaces that characterize the different ways of knowing in digital culture (1997: 175).

Levy suggests that as of the year 2000, a knowledge space has come into being that makes it possible for people to engage with 'knowledge in all its diversity'. He anticipates that identity will be 'distributed and nomadic' rather than defined by 'belonging'; meaning will be created by 'the involvement of beings in worlds of signification; the spaces we inhabit will be 'metamorphic' — possessing the capacity to change in line with 'collective becomings', and time will be experienced subjectively, and by the mutual 'adjustment and co-ordination of rhythms.' (1997: 175) Explaining the complexity of Levy's vision for cyberculture is beyond the scope of this glimpse at his work but it has been introduced here as a context for explaining the significance of the net-work in which fans and enthusiasts engage. Levy's theory has been used to validate the activities of fans and others in cyberspace, and to explain their commitment to a collaboration that is enjoyed for its own sake, and for the increased knowledge it produces, rather than for profit.

The particular type of net-work that is of interest when studying audiences is *collaboration*. Jenkins refers to it as the 'DIY culture' of the internet, but it is also enshrined in the philosophy of **shareware** and the commitment to freedom of information that is pervasive in cyberculture. Another dimension of internet engagement is the construction of multiple personalities for net-engagement. As Markham (1998) has shown, the anonymity of the internet is used in a variety of ways, from being a means of opening opportunities for engagements with others to searching for stealth and the capacity to attack the remaining 'strongholds' of secrecy on the internet.

Banks (2002) explores the range of collaborative initiatives which a games-development company he was involved with used to solicit information and development advice from potential gamers. This involved marshalling infor-mation from both 'data miners' (in this case, train enthusiasts) and from operational experts (like games enthusiasts). He explains that it is now usual for games developers to enlist the help of games enthusiasts in the development process — in the marketing as much as in the innovation phases. To do this, they actively network sites habituated by people who are likely to be interested in their proposed product development. Since the developers are also likely to be avid gamers, producers and enthusiasts, they act as something like opinion-leaders in cyberspace, talking up the game prior to its release.

Banks (2002: 198) explains that this collaborative process recognizes the diverse interests of players and that its aim is to embrace within the game the main roles players adopt to make the gaming experience more enjoyable for each other. He notes that these identities include: 'consumers, producers, maven, and community leaders' The one player can be all of these things simultaneously. Some of these identities are generated by the game itself, but some are related to typical player/enthusiast/producer activities. For example, Banks notes that two types of enthusiast were enlisted to assist with the production process — games enthusiasts and train enthusiasts. This allowed two different types of knowledge to be merged and incorporated into the game, alongside the knowledge and experience of the company as a games developer. The train enthusiasts developed the detailed knowledge of trains required for the development of realistic 'skins', thus making the game more visually variable, more authentic in look, and more interesting, whilst the gamers contributed the knowledge of rhythm, levels and transitions that make gaming exciting. Engagement with the game itself produces 'mavens' (experts or connoisseurs) who offer support and guidance to new players. Since filter sites are likely to have been established by either the company or the gamers, these sites become the places where community among fans is established and community-leadership developed. The central game site therefore fosters the establishment of satellite sites which provide specialized 'audience' services on behalf of the game itself.

The net-*work* to which Banks draws attention is complex and specialized. Producers, gamers and enthusiasts bring different skills to the production process. The collaborative process involves the company in sometimes sensitive communicative engagements with both gamers and enthusiasts, since the knowledge of the enthusiasts is not always helpful in making the game exciting, interesting and involving to play, and the expert knowledge of gamers about what makes a good game will not necessarily fit the requirements for realism that are inherent in the game. The development company may make creative decisions that annoy or upset some of the co-collaborators, and then will need to trouble-shoot in the filter sites to make sure that disaffection with the company does not persist. It is in this context that Jenkins' description of the sentimental nature of audience engagement is most in evidence, since people will not engage with products that do not give them a buzz.

The other high profile production area in which media consumers become media producers — and thus again force a reconsideration of who is the object in media research — is the area of internet news. At the time of writing this conclusion (2003), the war in Iraq had just begun. Before and during the war, many anti-war proponents were desperate that an alternative source of news be available to mitigate the more blatant manifestations of the Anglo-American propaganda machine. The traditional media cover their tracks by presenting the work of the journalist as transparent. Reports read as though who the journalist, and which side of the conflict they are reporting from, has no influence on the news distributed. In the interests of easier reading, the news media aim to make the processes of production invisible and to erase all evidence of the work of production from the finished product. This is called 'professional practice'. But professionalism separates knowledge production from its users, and situates audiences outside the news creation circle — as marginal to the events reported. The decontextualization of information and the immobilization of audiences practised by mainstream media constitutes fertile ground for the growth of a sense of manipulation by the media. Luhmann has suggested that:

> The system's coding and programming, specialised towards selection of information, causes suspicion to arise almost of its own accord that there are background motives at work.
>
> (2000: 38)

In a complex argument, Luhmann (2000) has suggested that the news media, by their very nature, create suspicion about the events they report. The dependence of audiences on news media generates several paradoxical positions. For example, the more numerous the accounts of an event, the less certain people feel about the information available to them; the more suspicious people become, the more they turn back to the media for answers. So, uncertainty breeds increased dependence on the media. The mainstream media maintain a web of meaning that allows the unusual or cataclysmic to be framed and understood. But, in a counter-intuitive way, the media decontextualize information by making it 'news', and by doing so, recontextualize the reported event as contemporary history. Misrepresentations can therefore be very long-lived. The more that is known about how news is produced, the more certainty grows that there is a hidden or concealed truth, or that some sort of manipulation is occurring. Luhmann claims that this conviction of manipulation is caused by the ways news is produced, by the fact that in order to know anything, audiences have to engage with the available news production. The media's web of meaning is more permanent and pervasive than the memories of frail human beings, and media archives outlive the life spans of most individuals.

The internet therefore has introduced a new possibility to the news environment — the possibility that news can be made by audiences/publics rather than by the professionals.

In recent years another approach to finding out the 'behind-the-scenes' news has been gaining ground — once again in the context of the internet. Net-news enthusiasts set out consciously to subvert the complacency of mainstream news. One of the most attractive aspects of the independent net-news environment is its inclusiveness. That inclusiveness is based on a radical vision of net-*working* that abolishes the passive status of audience and replaces it with a participatory model of authorship. The open publishing movement (see for example *www.indymedia.org/*; *www.cat.org/*; or *www.kuro5hin.org*) provides a good example of such net-*work*. The 'open publishing' sites are designed to record and display the news provided by participants/audiences. While it is tempting to see this participatory authorship as a rekindling of organic community in the context of the internet, Levy's analysis of the technological evolution that has produced the possibility of independent net-news, points to a different explanation. The audiences for net-news are mass audiences and they are globally dispersed. They participate on the basis of their local knowledge and in their capacity as eye-witnesses to events. Net-news is networked to city-based clubs, student, political and/or religious associations.

This 'open publishing' movement self-consciously challenges the mainstream media by telling stories they have overlooked or ignored. It encourages participants to submit news stories as they are happening — using mobile or pay phones, **SMS messages**, video footage, digital photographs or written copy. The stories are uploaded immediately onto the site and published almost instantly. For this reason, the stories are often very short as the event takes shape in the net-environment on a 'bit-by-bit' basis. Rather than being professionally 'reproduced' as a published event, the open publishing versions of events allow the experiences, observations and reflections of a lot of people to provide a pattern of the event that readers can explore and self-consciously shape into meanings.

For example, the site, *www.indymedia.org*, claims open publishing provides opportunities for people 'to instantaneously self-publish their work on a globally accessible website. The Indymedia newswire encourages people to become the media by posting their articles, analysis videos, audio clips and artwork directly to the web site'. In an article accessed through the open publishing sites, Arnison has published a manifesto that usefully summarizes the open publishing project situating it in relation to a range of mainstream media shortcomings (Arnison 2000). In comparison with the game development described above, these independent news sites can be seen to be taking up satellite positions around mainstream news sites, actively challenging for management of critical reflection by news audiences.

The problems Arnison identifies in mainstream news production can be summarized under three themes: the secrecy of the media; their attitudes to audiences; and the non-transparency of the production process. Open publishing seeks to redress the perceived shortcomings summarized below:

1. *Secrecy*: the mainstream media, and the transnational corporations that control them, can be seen as ensuring that audiences remain ignorant of their operation and intent. This is achieved by treating some information as confidential and secret, by privatizing strategic information, and by not sharing with people the long term commercial strategies they are pursuing. This secrecy is directly related to the commercial nature of the media and is contrasted to the openness of open publishing, where participants are encouraged to take and share information, evaluate submissions and make sure that other people are kept informed about important stories submitted to the site. Both production and distribution are therefore devolved to the audience.

2. *Audiences*: the mainstream media are believed to underestimate the capacity of ordinary people to make the news, so open publishing encourages site visitors to communicate meaningfully about the events they witness; to *be* the media. This is contrasted with the exclusion of audiences from the production process in mainstream media; by a refusal to listen to audience views; and by the use of audience research to maintain the myth of audience stupidity. The denigration and neglect of audiences by the mainstream media is contrasted with the repeated assertion of audience expertise, and of the value of voluntary and combined human action as an alternative to the mainstream media. People are considered to be proving the mainstream media wrong by participating in the site.

3. *Non-transparency of the production process*: the mainstream news production process is criticized for the secrecy that covers up the news production process and its impact on the telling of news stories. It is also claimed that the mainstream media systematically neglect or misrepresent certain news themes, issues, topics and perspectives — like environmentalism and the negative reporting of the anti-globalization movement, and fail to disclose that their reporting has hidden agendas. The stories filed on open publishing sites reflect a preoccupation with the global issues around which contemporary identity is shaped: globalization itself; the environment; protection of endangered species; human rights and free speech; and the production of news.

In the independent news net-working context, audiences are invited to move to centre-stage and to be media stars by producing their own news stories based on their eye-witness accounts or 'inside' information. The news items offer more intense reactions, and arguably better-informed evaluation of the events reported than most mainstream press reports. Audiences also have the power to be even more selective in their choice of what they should notice. The open publishing sites nevertheless appear to face some difficulties in maintaining their operations.

A considerable problem faced by the 'indymedia' approach to news production concerns the pace and rhythm of news. Where the mainstream media create news as an ongoing, but managed, flow of events, independent net-news is patterned by the occurrence of reported events and the presence, in-time and on-site (both real and virtual), of its participants. The sites therefore have to develop the capacity to handle at times dramatic fluctuations in intensity of usage, linked to levels of audience/producer interest and capacity to generate newsworthy comment. As noted in Chapter 3, mainstream media produce both programming flow and predictions of audience continuity as a managed and controlled flow of exposures. The volunteer and voluntary status of the indymedia site participants means that news flow is almost impossible to control. Most sites have had to invent some constraints, designed to protect the site and to keep it operational. A third problem is one of discrimination — how to discriminate between more and less interesting reports, and reports that consist of little more than swearing or lewd suggestions.

In response to these operational problems, Dru Oja Jay (2001) has formulated three proposals 'towards a transparent and collaborative editorial framework'. These include a 'filtering and editorial process'; a proposal that more editorial comment and a better ratings system be used; and thirdly a system for open editing and revision by site visitors. The *ratings system* referred to in this context is the evaluations site visitors generate about the articles posted on the site. The ratings categories Dru Oja Jay suggests are conventional (relevance, fairness, factuality, prose, novelty and soon) and incorporate a hint of adherence to mainstream journalism practice. The suggestion for the establishment of filter sites to help site visitors to navigate is interesting for its placement of editorial authority — outside the context of the site, yet linked to sites maintained by others. In this sense, the solution proposed to the problem of editing is more networking rather than centralized managerial control. *Sidebar listings* offer access to networks of more specialized sites for particular discussion *threads*.

The open publishing sites are sites in the process of *becoming*. They are an open (unfinished) net-work, and of interest to the study of audiences and media because they are a mass audience initiative. Even though many site participants and site links indicate connection to established political parties — particularly environmentalist and left activist groups — the site itself works on the pattern of 'immanence' described by Levy in that the participants are a 'molecular group' — a fluid community — always moving and reflecting the changing moods and concerns of mass audiences; chasing stories, engagements, interests and interactions through a complex web of work and pleasure.

New medium, new research approaches?

What the internet and other new information and communication technologies provoke, is not simply a revisioning of the audience as a researchable group whose 'members' might live in every corner of the earth, but a reconceptualization of media research methods and approaches. Most research methods used with audiences have assumed an embodied human subject who can be interviewed, questioned, watched or experimented on. This has largely been because audience studies have tended to be relatively small-scale, often local or at best national, and have often involved face-to-face interaction between the researcher and the researched via some kind of qualitative method such as an unstructured or semi-structured interview. Admittedly, some audience studies have looked only at the artefacts produced by consumers such as letters and fanzines rather than the producers themselves, but most audience-oriented work has tended to work on an interpersonal basis. But what if the new foci of our interest are virtual audiences, albeit with a human persona somewhere behind the cyber front? Whilst online communication, as Turkle (1995) reminds us, is clearly not the same as 'live' encounters, users of the internet nonetheless can and do use the medium to:

> ...create social environments that facilitate the process of human communication in ways that are similar to face-to-face contexts. However, the lack of physical presence alters both conditions of attendance and the methods for interpersonal correspondence.
>
> (Barnes 2001: 11)

Whilst Gauntlett (2000) is perhaps a little harsh in his assessment that media (and audience) studies were in terminal decline and were rescued by the advent of the world wide web, it is unarguably the case that studies of cyberculture had begun to grow as a sub-genre during the 1990s. Silver (2000) suggests that, as with other new areas of technological study, research on cybercultures began with a few commentators (journalists rather than academics) looking at this emergent technology as another, and a novel, aspect of popular culture before the academic community began to grasp its importance, both to culture but also to communication. For Silver, the second research phase was what he terms 'cyberculture studies' (2000: 19), where the focus was on analysing virtual communities and identities. The phase in which he suggests we are *now* engaged is the next step, 'critical cyberculture studies', which embraces a number of different strands including design elements of sites, digital discourses and governance issues. It is different to the two previous phases because it adopts a critical/analytical rather than merely descriptive stance towards ICTs.

So, do we need new approaches and methods to study these new audiences or can we adapt the 'old' ones to work in these new media contexts? What kinds of research are being undertaken with internet users and audiences and to what extent are *really* different questions being asked of this new medium? For example, much internet-based research is carried out by market research organizations who want to find out how many 'hits' a site has had in a given period, usually so that the site owner can claim popularity and charge higher advertising rates. Such studies usually analyse log files but of course, the number of 'hits' is not the same as the number of *individual* users accessing the site and in any case, such data provides very little information about user profiles in terms of why that site was chosen, what the user liked/disliked about it, whether s/he will return and so on.

This kind of superficial audience/user research is not dissimilar to that carried out by broadcasters who use panels of viewers to determine how many people watch a particular station or a particular show. Such simple on/off measures can say very little about user enjoyment or relevance or even if the individual actually watched the show as opposed to having the TV switched on as background noise only. And so it is with researching online audiences, but where the reality of browsing (not dissimilar to the TV channel-switcher hunting to find something of interest on which to settle and concentrate) is embedded in the very architecture and language of the medium itself. So, although the media *are* different, some of the techniques are broadly the same, albeit that research methodologies and approaches themselves are susceptible to flux and change, often moving in response to media developments, as well as shifts in philosophical, ethical and cultural politics. And, of course, new media such as satellite and the internet are rarely intended to displace more traditional media (see Baym 1993), since site owners are often the same groups of people and institutions who own more conventional media and for whom nothing is gained by reducing parts of their empire.

But there *are* distinctive elements of the internet, both in terms of the text/image as well as users/audiences, which create genuinely novel research opportunities as well as requiring genuinely novel research methods. Mitra and Cohen (1999) for example, argue that web-based text has a number of special characteristics including global reach and audience, *intertextuality* and non-linearity, all of which demand a more complex research design than a study of more traditional visual artefacts such as TV programmes, photographs or newspapers. The 'text' itself is qualitatively different from other written and visual products. The ways the 'reader' accesses web-based material also differ, not least because of the use of links which work in an elastic time/space zone rather than the more rigid boundaries of hard copy pages or screened images.

The various ways in which users/audiences interact with the internet also requires a different research mindset since communication is often on a huge scale when users could be involved in any number of chatrooms, bulletin boards, listservs and newsgroups. Because of the scale of the internet, designing a research study on web-based communication can seem daunting. Fortunately a number of tools are now being developed which will at least enable a mapping process to take place on small sections of the web, to track discourse through an analysis of particular discursive threads. Warren Sack, for example, has developed 'Conversation Map' which is software that analyses the content of and relationship between messages to a newsgroup and then displays the result in graphical form, attempting to show the complex relationships between messages, audiences and texts. Another piece of software, the 'Loom' tool has been developed by Judith Donath et al. (1999) to show the importance and role of individual users in a particular community or group, where dots represent individual postings in a visual representation of the 'community'.

These kinds of tools usefully represent these relationships in visual and perhaps more intelligible form. With them, patterns and inter-relationships that would otherwise be hard to grasp conceptually, become analysable. However, such tools are quantitative in nature and incapable of providing much of a sense of who the users are or why they are involved in the first place. For this level of analysis, there still needs to be engagement with the person behind the statistic. Even though mapping tools are highly sophisticated, there are already a number of studies where the researcher is also a participant in a chatroom, newsgroup or listserv in a more personal way (Cherny 1999) and where the research 'texts' become the printed out hard copy of posted discourse, in which the researcher is also a player who sometimes prompts particular discursive themes via their own postings. These texts, although much more impersonal than letters, nonetheless convey a sense of *real* discourse and of a real person 'writing' the texts. In such cases, we still need to engage the human user to make sense of the internet's importance to ourselves in our real world.

Studying the internet audience

In one of the most comprehensive analyses of online users and the sense they make of 'being' online, the boundaries between reception and production are found to be constantly blurred, not only by the study's participants but by the author herself. Annette Markham's extended and highly reflexive account of both her findings and her method (see also Nightingale and Ross 2003), not to mention her evolving self, render problematic the notion that the internet must inevitably change the way in which we conduct audience research (Markham 1999). Markham's account, whilst fascinating and insightful about the 'virtual' and disembodied nature of computer mediated communication (CMC), ultimately shows us that despite the consistent disavowal of corporeality, online users themselves are only too aware of the biological reality of their actual, embodied selves. Having already stated that, at least in text-based (as opposed to image-based) sites, the CMC must necessarily be real text, that is, 'live' individuals actually keyboarding *real* messages, regardless of any fantasy aspect of the message's content, Markham is clear that individuals know that their online lives are different to their offline existence. No matter what kinds of games users play online, no matter what guises they assume, or what kinds of gender shape-shifting they display, they still have to perform the basic functions of life such as eating and sleeping which constantly remind them of their humanity:

> Talking with . . . users has taught me something very meaningful: people know they are not really transcending their physical world; their body is the place where they live. . . all the people I have met, anyway, know that there comes a time when the computer must be shut down and the needs of the body must be met.
>
> (Markham 1999: 222)

So while Markham's online ethnography does indeed offer the contemporary researcher some interesting food for thought, especially in relation to the role of the researcher in a research context where the boundaries between participation and observation are even more blurred than in 'traditional' research, she none-theless acknowledges that achieving 'truth' online is just as tricky as its offline counterpart. One additional complication, for example, is the lack of environ-mental clues and cues which online research erases. This drawback is perhaps not that dissimilar to the impersonal receipt of a postal questionnaire or the conduct of an unannounced telephone interview, since in both these latter examples, the researcher has access to limited interpersonal feedback. As Markham readily concedes, 'After a few weeks of second-guessing the honesty of their [her online participants] words, I realized that, online or offline, all of us make sense of our experiences and tell the stories of our lives in self-centred and self-understood ways' (1999: 210). In other words, 'truth' is always con-tingent, always fluid, and researching online simply brings that reality into sharper relief since much of the discourse relating to internet use, at least in terms of communication (rather than simply information seeking) centres on precisely the fluidity of user identities.

Whilst it may be, as some of Markham's interviewees insisted, that online identities are as real as offline ones and that a person's virtual text is simply a substitute for their actual voice, if all these identities and voices are constructions (which they *must* be as they are consequences of deliberate human agency), then their veracity is as open-ended in cyberspace as in 'real' time. *All* human communication is artifice and if we are simultaneously consuming and producing, sending and receiving, then the possibilities for interpretation are endless and it is the researcher, of course, who finally arbitrates meaning: it is *our* truth which prevails.

Researching online audiences, as users, producers and consumers of media, certainly requires a different understanding of who the audience is/are but does not necessarily require us to use wholly different research tools. Even in a sophisticated online research study such as the ethnography undertaken by Markham, the primary research tool was still 'interviewing' individual users by setting up a real-time interview. And, when she and the interviewee were both online and in direct communication, Markham keyboarded her questions and waited for a text reply. She was 'writing' the same question she was simultaneously articulating in her head, and her interviewee was 'responding' in the traditional question/answer mode. Whilst this *method* of interviewing is currently only possibly via the internet, its format is very familiar. Without doubt, we *are* in a different research context in the early years of the twenty-first century, with definitions of audience being in their usual state of flux, but we need to ensure that our enthusiastic embrace of ICTs is an inclusive one so that we develop knowledge in a context that builds on the past to make our future rather than insisting that everything about what's new is also novel:

> My understanding of what it means to be online is growing more conservative as each day passes. I am struck by the normalcy of my conversations with others, in the interviews and online. I am amazed that I don't find more weird stuff and more exotic transmutations of the body and mind online . . . we academics who write about the transcendence of the body, the fragmentation of identity in cyberspace, the hyperreal etc. may be making too much of the entire phenomenon.
>
> (Markham 1999: 221–2)

The audiences for electronic media such as the internet are people who continue to use and regularly consume more traditional media such as TV, radio, film and newspapers. Although the internet enables, potentially at least, a much broader sample base either through posted invitations to take part in research studies or else by the provision of online research instruments, the methods used to access audiences are likely to be in the familiar format of a questionnaire or a real-time interview in person or by telephone. To be sure, the internet *does* produce different kinds of text to interrogate, such as chat-room and newsgroup discussions, web page content and design, navigation and architecture strategies and so on, but work with the consumers and producers of internet texts will inevitably rely on traditional research tools designed with human subjects in mind. Internet researchers have also discovered that despite the novelty of the technology, individuals look to the internet to satisfy fairly traditional needs such as information, entertainment and interaction. What is different now, though, is that the internet seems able to fulfil a range of complex needs which had been thought to be satisfied only via traditional media. Flanagin and Metzger (2001: 175) suggest, from their study of nearly 700 inter-net users, that, '. . . the Internet is a multidimensional communication tech-nology used to fulfil well-understood needs in novel ways.' However they also argue that in general, new technologies are employed in ways similar to older media to meet a set of enduring needs. So the internet might be seen, in audience research terms at least, as providing a new medium through which to explore the complexities of 'old' communication.

It is important not to romanticize the internet as always and everywhere a force for 'good'. Whilst early supporters of the web celebrated its facility to offer not only a quasi-community in which to affirm membership but also a safe space in which to 'try out' different identities (see Rheingold 1993; Turkle 1995), later commentators such as Scodari (1998) have been much more cautious about the web's allure. In particular, the overt and covert 'rules' that limit and delimit user involvement continue to cause concern, as does the increasing availability of pornographic material and images (Arnaldo 2001; McBain 2002; Taylor and Quayle 2003). Interestingly, as has emerged from more 'traditional' studies of media consumption, web user demographics show very clear ethnic and gender skews in terms of access (NTIA 1999), involvement and content. In other words, the 'old' forms of differential access to media based on personal characteristics such as gender and age as well as geography (the North-South divide) are replicated with this new medium, provoking any number of studies on the 'digital divide' (Norris 2001b; Katz and Rice 2002; Warschauer 2003).

Not only has there been concern over access to ICTs but also over content, especially in a context of conglomerization and corporate ownership of large parts of the internet. So, over the past two or three years, a significant number of new internet sites have been set up to provide alternative forums for users to discuss issues of concern to them, sites which have been constructed for a variety of political, ethnically-specific and/or gender-specific audiences (see, for example, Harcourt 1999). Such sites include fan sites as discussed in Chapter 6 as well as politicized sites such as those set up by women and women's groups, which are specifically interested in exploiting the internet's potential for united (local and global) action, education, sharing of information/ideas and campaigning (see Green and Adam 2001; Moran 2002) and those promoting alternative political viewpoints, especially in the wake of 9/11 (see, for example, *www.opendemocracy.com* and *www.rawa.com*).

The diverse character of contemporary audience net-work demonstrates the ways the information age is changing what it means to be an audience. Audiences are no longer passive receivers of media texts. They have outgrown the models proposed in 'active reception'. Audiences are learning how *to be* the media, how to net-*work*. This means that their activities as audiences are becoming increasingly diverse, and moving beyond the entertainment arena. The range of activities reminds us that the development of cyberculture is not uniform — and that it is a work in progress. Net-audience research suggests the importance of moving beyond the fan and enthusiast dimensions of mainstream media audience research and to leave behind the preoccupation with activities that were principally of interest in relation to mainstream media production.

In net-activism and collaborative networking, we see people engaged in complicity, opposition or symbiosis with mainstream media in order to achieve specific outcomes. Net-work is more obviously purposive than much television viewing. These audience activisms are in a sense 'additive' in that they redress the omissions of mainstream media. By doing so they also happen to challenge the hegemonic views of dominant cultures. They aim to increase the diversity of views circulating in the public sphere, and pursue counter-hegemonic aims as much through production and creative effort as through rhetoric and argumentation. The rhetoric, as Meadows (2002: 157) points out is the case with indigenous communication in Australia, 'must be authorised in some way by the audience from which it emerges'.

Being an audience is now a much more active and interactive experience than in the broadcasting era. As noted in previous chapters, the information age has brought about fundamental changes in the ways people approach the media and in their engagements with media texts. As people notch up experience of interactive media, and particularly as they begin to enjoy the more intense media engagement available in interactive media environments, dissatisfaction with the constraining 'molar' qualities of mainstream broadcasting is likely to increase. It is hard to resist the sense that interactive media are poised to dramatically disrupt the familiar programming patterns of mass broadcasting.

But the internet is still only one medium amongst many and in mass communication terms — and therefore, importantly, in terms of the medium's ability to have a significant effect on social action — it is a medium still in its infancy. Its reach is still substantially less, especially in the developing world, than more traditional media such as TV, radio and the press. If notions of the digital divide can be a little overplayed — many of even the poorest villages in India and Africa are online — it is nonetheless the case that individual and regular access to the internet is still an activity primarily undertaken by users in the developed world. So, although there were 400 million internet users by the end of 2000, across nearly 200 countries, the USA alone accounted for one-third of all users and a collection of 15 industrialized nations including the USA, Japan, the UK, Australia, China, Taiwan and Western European countries accounted for 78 per cent of all users (Juliussen and Juliussen 2001). And while we celebrate the web's utility and ask ourselves how we ever managed without it, we should not forget the commercial interests that are heavily implicated in the success and the future shape of ICTs. The contours of technological development are determined by the industry's main players and, as Roscoe (1999: 682) pertinently remarks, 'New technologies are often feature-rich and able to be put to a wide range of uses, but the need to cut costs soon reduces the capabilities, as features that are not "ainstream" are removed.'

Of course what the web *does* problematize very neatly are the thin lines, not to mention the cross-overs, between audience, consumer, producer and user. If we log on to the internet, are we also *using* a medium? When we browse a website, are we also *consuming* a text? If we listen to an online concert, are we also part of a (larger) live audience? If we send an email to a TV programme director, are we also *producing* an artefact? We are clearly engaged in *all* these processes if we are interactive web users and perhaps the web's most profound contribution to audience studies is precisely to force a reconsideration of orthodox renditions of audience-hood and thus move us to a position where we can be seen as members of different audiences at different times for different media, sometimes with others, sometimes alone. Audience-hood is not a per-manent identity, but a constant shifting in and out of audience formations that allow us to access particular materials that help us shape our identities and our environments.

Developments in media and communication technology such as the internet, interactive TV and WAP phones as well as shifts in media content (for example, reality-based TV) are providing exciting new media contexts and new audience formations for the audience researcher to explore. Interrogating the relationships which audiences now enjoy with different kinds of media and different kinds of texts will produce new ideas and thinking about 'the audi-ence', not least exposing the inherent contingency and fluidity of the concept itself. If Staiger (2000) goes a little far in her insistence that the common-sense understanding of 'audience' is simply an academic construction, we do need to be sensitive, as researchers, to the specifics of context when researching audiences, so that our theoretical contributions are underpinned by actual audience experience and not just our own imaginings. We look forward to the growth of audience studies and we hope this book, in its own way, has made its own small offering to that development.

The audience is dead. Long live the audience.

Further reading

Castells, M. (1998) *End of Millennium*. Maiden, MA and Oxford: Blackwell.

Evans, P. and Wurster, T.E. (2000) *Blown To Bits: How the New Economics of Information Transforms Strategy*. Boston, Massachusetts: Harvard Business School Press.

Harcourt, W. (ed.) (1999) *Women @ Internet*. London and New York: Zed Books.

Levy, P. (1997) *Collective Intelligence: Mankind's Emerging World in Cyberspace*. (Trans. Robert Bononno) Cambridge, Massachusetts: Perseus Books.

Markham, A. (1999) *Life Online: Researching Real Experience in Virtual Space*. Walnut Creek, SA: Altamira Press.

GLOSSARY OF KEY TERMS

Affect — the word 'affect' has at least three meanings. In this book it is used primarily to describe ways the media exert influence on individuals, cultures and society — whether directly or indirectly, by the manipulation of sentiments or socio-cultural control. Additionally, its psychological meaning (referring to the human affects: excitement, joy, startle, anguish, humiliation, disgust, rage and terror) is used in Chapter 2.

Anomie — loss of a sense of belonging as a result of social and cultural change, resulting in inability to find ways of active cultural participation that are rewarding to the person. The term is widely used in studies of deviance.

Attack ads — short political broadcasts which attack the opposition parties rather than extol the virtues of one's own party.

Catharsis — literally meaning cleansing or purifying: in the context of media/violence debate, meaning that the act of *watching* violence provides a release from negative desires to *commit* violence and allows those negative/aggressive feelings to evaporate and for the individual to feel 'cleansed'.

Contagion theory — individuals are encouraged to act in ways which are not necessarily 'natural' or within their usual repertoire, because of the actions of the people around them.

Cultivation analysis — theory that people who watch a lot of television are more likely to share the beliefs of the dominant group in a given society, that is that they become acculturated to accept the dominant codes of behaviour.

Cultural capital — the personal accumulation of cultural knowledge and information which, without having an obvious monetary value, nonetheless has value in terms of social standing (class), mobility and hierarchy. A deficit in cultural capital is often deemed a disadvantage in one's ability to progress in society at all levels.

Cultural superiority — used in the context of discussing high and low cultural products, where the former is said to be superior to the latter.

Culture theory approach — an approach to the study of audiences that emphasizes the cultural origins of texts and discourses, and the cultural contexts in which people find themselves being audiences.

Customer relationship marketing — an approach to marketing that foregrounds the importance of relationships established between manufacturer/merchant and customer. The process is informed by statistical analysis and development of software programming that analyses choices made by customers.

Cyberculture — term used to describe the culture produced by the universalizing but non-totalizing nature of cyberspace. It universalizes by linking people regardless of who or where they are, but is non-totalizing in the sense that its communicative mode is one-to-one or one-to-few but not one-to-all.

Data mining — a process of searching for information from large databases of information, whether publicly or privately collected.

Deliberative poll — discursive and complex form of opinion poll which has a more sustained public involvement which deliberates over potential policy positions and comes up with 'solutions'; attributed to James Fishkin, University of Texas, in 1996.

Diaspora — where peoples of the same or very similar cultural or ethnic background are settled in places outside their geographical place of origin, for example the African Diaspora; often implies forced resettlement or living away from 'home'.

Discriminant analysis — form of statistical analysis that identifies variables which are good at discriminating on the basis of choices made.

Encoding/decoding — theory of text/audience which suggests that texts are encoded by the person/people who originated them with a specific (dominant) meaning, which the audience then decodes, but where the dominant meaning is not always 'read' in the way the author intended.

Ethnographic turn — approach to research which focuses on the meanings made by the group or individual who is being researched, usually requiring long-term study of small groups or communities, to fully understand the range of meanings they produce; an approach which builds theory from an empirical base.

Fan artefact — product which fans produce such as a story or poem for a magazine (fanzine) or an invented song (filk) or a page on a website.

Gesellschaft — refers to the way that a sense of belonging is experienced in complex, competitive, achievement-oriented societies. It is contrasted with the term **gemeinschaft**, which refers to the ways belonging is experienced in small-scale, traditional, organic societies. *Gesellschaft* is an affiliative process and *gemeinschaft* is a mechanical process. Where the individual voluntarily seeks affiliation with others we see *gesellschaft* in operation, where the individual is mechanically allocated rights and responsibilities at birth, *gemeinschaft* is in operation. Both terms are German words, introduced by the sociologist Emile Durkheim in the early twentieth century as part of his account of the phenomenon of *anomie*, or identity loss, that occurs in modern societies.

Hegemony — theory of power and dominance which suggests that the dominant group in a given society circulates an ideology or a 'correct' way of understanding the world, which it 'encourages' everyone else to support; a shared set of values and views assumed to exist amongst people in a given society.

Homology — suggestion of similarities between phenomena based on relationship between elements of content.

Horse-race — used in the context of political elections, where the focus in debate is on issues of gamesmanship, which party is ahead, and which political strategies are being most successful in influencing potential voters. The focus on the *process* of election campaigns is then seen as preventing debate on *policy* to be articulated, leaving the electorate ignorant of the real differences between the various political options.

Information warehousing — the collection, storage and maintenance of large quantities of data for sale to commercial and public institutions.

Inherited audience — the audience which has been watching an earlier programme on a particular day at a particular time, where it is assumed that a 'carry-over' atmosphere will encourage those viewers to stay a little longer to watch the next programme on the same channel.

Intertextuality — cross-referencing from one artefact to another, for example the way in which a film has an additional layer of meaning if the audience has also seen and therefore understands the in-jokes or in-references to other films or media artefacts which are woven into the narrative.

Intervening variable — unobservable conceptual factors, like 'needs' or 'gratifications', that affect the outcomes in communicative exchanges.

Liminality — on the threshold of consciousness, almost hidden but just observable — often used to describe sub-themes or sub-texts which lie just beneath the surface of the 'overt' story, text or image.

Left criticism — criticism rooted in political economic analysis derived from Marx's analysis of capitalism.

Lobby hack — usually pejorative term used to describe the corps of journalists who routinely work in parliamentary lobbies.

Media dupe — person susceptible to media messages because they believe everything they read/hear/listen to, without discrimination or thought.

Mediascape — umbrella term to describe the complex and numerous media elements which comprise modern life in the twenty-first century.

Mediatization — taking an event and changing it into a story for mass distribution. It is an approach to the control of information practised by mass media, which involves capturing the moment (using photography, sound bite or video images, for example), and recontextualizing it for mass distribution.

Meta-narrative — grand theories around the primary, distinctive and different characteristics which human beings possess, such as race, class, gender, disability, sexuality, which comprise the building blocks to understanding how society works.

Molar technologies — technologies, like the mass media, which depend on the actions of masses of units (or people in the case of audiences) to have an effect.

Naming/othering — process whereby a more dominant group has the power to name the less dominant groups as different (and usually inferior) to 'us', that is the power to name as 'other'.

Naturalistic research paradigm — qualitative social science research that investigates pre-existing groups of people, or naturally occurring events (that is does not use sampling techniques to generate research population).

Newszak — phrase used to suggest the bland media landscape offered by mainstream broadcasting, as in supermarket 'muzak'.

Political economy approach — research approach that begins from analysis of relevant political and economic matters, and identifies their social and cultural consequences.

Polysemy — describing the multilayered nature of most media texts which are capable of more than one reading/meaning-making by audiences.

Positivism — broad theoretical view which focuses on outcomes and outward direction rather than on internal, motivational and psychological processes. The term 'positivist' is often used pejoratively to describe someone who refuses to believe anything unless it is demonstrably capable of being 'proved' (touched, seen, verified).

Propaganda event — an instance of an attempt to persuade audiences to a particular course of action by promulgation of part-truths, use of emotional language, or misleading construction of arguments.

Protonarratives — archaic story elements used to structure media messages — particularly news and drama.

Semiotics — the study of signs, codes, discourses and myths to deconstruct the meaning of messages.

Senate races — US national elections which elect Senators to Congress, similar to the election of MPs to the Westminster Parliament.

Shareware — intellectual property for which the originator has waived his/her copyright and with which they encourage free use and improvisation.

Sidebar listings — options offered to internet site visitors for site navigation, usually listed down the side of the website.

SMS messages — text messages sent by mobile phone.

Star system — way of describing Hollywood's (box-office-derived) interest in stars and celebrity rather than stories.

Structures of domination — ways in which political and economic institutions authorize and allocate resources to benefit those who control such institutions, thereby perpetuating a hierarchy of domination by the elites over everyone else.

Tabloid turn — describes the way in which newspapers have become more interested in entertainment than information and thus the quality of the content is said to have degraded.

Tertiary text — interpretation of underlying textual meaning in any given text, created by audience members in response to personal experiences and often articulated through conversation with others.

Third-person effects — idea that other people are affected by, say, media violence but that 'we' are too clever to be so influenced.

Threads — exploratory and improvisatory online discussion topics generated by individuals which form continuous themes for discussion amongst the wider list membership.

Trash aesthetics — according to a particular cultural product such as a film or TV programme, with low (trash) values, usually pejorative term, although some film-makers have tried to turn this sense of bad taste into a cult genre.

Uses and gratifications — theory of audience which suggests that audiences use media for their own purposes and pleasures, positing active agency rather than inert passivity amongst viewers.

REFERENCES

Abercrombie, N. and Longhurst, B. (1998) *Audiences*. London, Thousand Oaks, New Delhi: Sage.

Ahmed, K. (2003) Age limits for children on violent video games, *Observer*, 29 December.

Alasuutari, P. (1992) 'I'm ashamed to admit it but I have watched Dallas': the moral hierarchy of television programmes, *Media, Culture & Society*, 14(3): 561–82.

Allan, S. (1999) *News Culture*. Buckingham: Open University Press.

Allen, R. (1985) *Speaking of Soap Operas*. Chapel Hill: University of North Carolina.

Althusser, L. (1971) *Lenin and Philosophy*, London: New Left Books.

American Society of Newspaper Editors (1998) *ASNE Journalism Credibility Project*. http://www.asne.org/works/jcp/jcpmain.htm.

Anderson, B. (1983, 1991) *Imagined Communities: Reflections on the Origin and Spread of Nationalism*, Revised edn. London and New York: Verso.

Ang, I. (1985) *Watching 'Dallas': Soap Opera and the Melodramatic Imagination*. London: Methuen.

Ang, I. (1991) *Desperately Seeking the Audience*. London and New York: Routledge.

Ansolabehere, S., Behr, R. and Iyengar, S. (1991) Mass media and elections: an overview, *American Politics Quarterly* 19: 109–39.

Ansolabehere, S., Iyengar, S. and Simon, A. (1997) Shifting Perspectives on the Effects of Campaign Communication, in S. Iyengar and R. Reeves (eds) *Do the Media Govern? Politicians, Voters and Reporters in America*. Thousand Oaks, London, Delhi: Sage.

Antorini, Y.M. (2003) The essence of being a child in M. Lindstrom and P. Seybold (eds) *Brandchild: Remarkable Insights into the Minds of Today's Global Kids and Their Relationships with Brands*. London and Sterling, VA: Kogan Page.

Appadurai, A. (1997) *Modernity at Large: Cultural Dimensions of Globalization*. Minneapolis and London: University of Minnesota Press.

Arnaldo, C.A. (ed.) (2001) *Child Abuse on the Internet: Ending the Silence*. New York: Berghahn Books.

Arnheim, R. (1944) The world of the daytime serial, in P.F. Lazarsfeld and F.M. Stanton (eds) *Radio Research: 1942–1943*. New York: Duell, Sloan and Pearce.

Arnison, M. (2000) Open publishing is the same as free software. Revision 1.14. Date: 2002/09/28 12:56:27, *maffew@cat.org.au*.

Atkin, C. (1983) Effects of realistic TV violence vs. fictional violence on aggression, *Journalism Quarterly*, 69: 615–21.

Bacon-Smith, C. (1992) *Enterprising Women: Television Fandom and the Creation of Popular Myth*. Philadelphia: University of Pennsylvania Press.

Ballard, M.E. and Lineberger, R. (1999) Video game violence and confederate gender: effects on reward and punishment given by college males, *Sex Roles*, 41: 541–58.

Banks, J. (2002) Gamers as co-creators: enlisting the virtual audience – a report from the net face, in M. Balnaves, T. O'Regan and J. Sternberg (eds) *Mobilising the Audience*. St Lucia, Brisbane: University of Queensland Press.

Barban, A.M., Cristol, S.M. and Kopec, F.J. (1987) *Essentials of Media Planning: A Marketing Viewpoint*, 2nd edn. Lincolnwood, IL.: NTC Business Books.

Barker, C. (1999) *Television, Globalization and Cultural Identities*. Buckingham: Open University Press.

Barker, M. (1989) *Comics: Ideology, Power and The Critics*. Manchester: Manchester University Press.

Barker, M. (1997) The Newson Report: a case study in 'common sense', in M. Barker and J. Petley (eds) *Ill Effects: The Media/Violence Debate*, 2nd edn. London and New York: Routledge.

Barker, M. (1998) Critique: audiences 'Я' us, in R. Dickinson, R. Harindranath and O. Linné (eds) *Approaches to Audiences: A Reader*. London and New York: Arnold.

Barker, M. and Brooks, K. (1998) *Knowing Audiences: Judge Dredd, its Friends, Fans and Foes*. Luton: University of Luton Press.

Barnes, S. (2001) *Online Connections: Internet Interpersonal Relationships*. Cresskill, New Jersey: Hampton Press.

Barnhurst, K.G. and Mutz, D. (1997) American journalism and the decline in event-centred reporting, *Journal of Communication*, 47(4): 27–53.

Bauserman, R. (1998) Egalitarian, sexist and aggressive sexual materials: attitude effects and viewer responses, *The Journal of Sex Research*, 35(3): 244–53.

Baym, N.K. (1993) Interpreting soap operas and creating community: inside a computer-mediated fan culture, *Journal of Folklore Research*, 30(2/3): 143–76.

Baym, N.K. (1998) Talking about soaps: communicative practices in a computer-mediated fan culture, in C. Harris and A. Alexander (eds) *Theorizing Fandom: Fans, Subculture and Identity*. Cresskill, NJ: Hampton Press.

Baym, N.K. (2000) *Tune In, Log On: Soaps, Fandom and Online Community*. Thousand Oaks, London and New Delhi: Sage.

Becker, L.B. and Dunwoody, S. (1982) Media use, public affairs knowledge and voting in a local election, *Journalism Quarterly*, 67: 708–22.

Benedict, H. (1992) *Virgin or Vamp: How the Press Covers Sex Crimes*. New York: Oxford University Press.

Bennett, S.E., Flickinger, R.S., Baker, J.R., Rhine, S.L. and Bennett, L.M. (1996) Citizens' knowledge of foreign affairs, *Press/Politics*, 1(2): 10–29.

Bennett, T., Emmison, M. and Frow, J. (1999) *Accounting for Tastes: Australian Everyday Cultures*. Cambridge: Cambridge University Press.

Bennett, W.L. (1997) Cracking the News Code: Some Rules That Journalists Live By, in S. Iyengar and R. Reeves (eds) *Do the Media Govern? Politicians, Voters and Reporters in America*. Thousand Oaks, London, Delhi: Sage.

Berger, J. (1976) *Ways of Seeing*. Harmondsworth: Penguin.

Berger, J. and Mohr, J. (1982) *Another Way of Telling*. London and New York: Writers and Readers Publishing Co-operative Society.

Bernhardt, J.M., Sorenson, J.R. and Brown, J.D. (2001) When the perpetrator gets killed: effects of observing the death of a handgun user in a televised public service announcement, *Health Education and Behavior*, 28(1): 81–94.

Beville, H.M. Jr. (1988) *Audience Ratings: Radio, Television, and Cable*. Hillsdale, New Jersey, Hove and London: Lawrence Erlbaum and Associates.

Blomquist, D. and Zukin, C. (1997) *Does Public Journalism Work? The 'Campaign Central' Experience*. Washington DC: Pew Center for Civic Journalism; Hackensack, NJ, *Record*, May.

Blumer, H. (1933) *Movies and Conduct*. New York: Macmillan.

Blumer, H. (1948) Public opinion and public opinion polling, *American Sociological Review*, 13(5): 542–49.

Blumler, J. and Katz, E. (eds) (1974) *The Uses of Mass Communicaitons: Current Perspectives on Gratifications Research*. London and Beverly Hills: Sage.

Blumler, J.G. and Gurevitch, M. (1995) *The Crisis of Public Communication*. London and New York: Routledge.

Bobo, J. (1988) The Color Purple: black women as cultural readers, in E.D. Pribram (ed.) *Female Spectators: Looking at Film and Television*. London: Verso.

Bogaert, A.F., Woodward, U. and Hafer, C.L. (1999) Intellectual ability and reactions to pornography, *The Journal of Sex Research*, 36(3): 283–91.

Bourdieu, P. (1984) *Distinction: A Social Critique of the Judgement of Taste*. Cambridge: Harvard University Press.

British Crime Survey (2002) London: HMSO.

Brody, S. (1977) *Screen violence and film censorship – a review of research*. London: Home Office Research Unit.

Broughton, D. (1995) *Public Opinion Polling and Politics in Britain*. London: Prentice-Hall.

Brown, M.E. (1994) *Soap Opera and Women's Talk: The Pleasure of Resistance*. Thousand Oaks, London, New Delhi: Sage.

Brunsdon, C. (1981) *Crossroads*: notes on a soap opera, *Screen*, 22: 32–7.

Brunsdon, C. (1989) Text and Audience, in E. Seiter, H. Bochers, G. Kreutzner and E. Warth (eds) *Remote Control*, London: Routledge.

Brunsdon, C. (ed.) (1986) *Films for Women*. London: British Film Institute.

Brunsdon, C. and Morley, D. (1978) *Everyday Television: 'Nationwide'*. London: BFI.

Buchanan, B. (1991) *Electing a President: The Markle Commission's Report on Campaign '88*. Austin: University of Texas Press.

Buckingham, D. (1987) *Public Secrets: EastEnders and its Audience*. London: British Film Institute.

Buckingham, D. (1993) *Children Talking Television: The Making of Television Literacy*. London: The Falmer Press.

Buckingham, D. (1996) *Moving Images: Understanding Children's Emotional Responses to Television*. Manchester UK: Manchester University Press.

Bureau of Justice Statistics (1998) *Serious violent crime levels continued to decline in 1997*. http://www.ojp.usodj.gov/bjs/glace/frmdth.txt (accessed 20 September 2002).

Burns, T. (1997) The impact of the national press on voters in 1997. Paper presented to the *Political Studies Association* specialist conference on Elections, Public Opinion and Parties, Essex, September.

Butler, D. and Stokes, D.E. (1974) *Political Change in Britain: The Evolution of Political Choice*. London: Macmillan.

Butsch, R. (2000) *The Making of American Audiences: From Stage to Television, 1750–1990*. Cambridge, New York, Melbourne, Madrid: Cambridge University Press.

Cantor, J. (1994) Confronting children's fright responses to mass media, in D. Zillmann, J. Bryant and A.C. Huston (eds) *Media, Children and the Family: Social Scientific, Psychodynamic and Clinical Perspectives*. Hillsdale, NJ: Lawrence Erlbaum.

Cappella, J.N. and Jamieson, K.H. (1997) *Spiral of Cynicism: The Press and the Public Good*. New York: Oxford University Press.

Carey, J. (1988) *Communication as Culture*. Boston, MA: Unwin Hyman.

Carey, J. and Kreiling, A. (1974) Popular culture and uses and gratifications: notes towards an accommodation, in J. Blumler and E. Katz (eds) *The Uses of Mass Communications: Current Perspectives on Gratifications Research*. London and Beverly Hills: Sage.

Carroll, N. (1996) *Theorizing the Moving Image*. Cambridge: Cambridge University Press.

Castells, M. (1996) *The Rise of the Network Society*. Oxford and Malden, MA: Blackwells.

Castells, M. (1998) *End of Millennium*. Oxford and Malden, MA: Blackwells.

Cathode, R. (2000) In praise of dirty washing: Channel 4 after "Big Brother", *Sight and Sound*, 10(1): 9.

Cherny, L. (1999) *Conversation and Community: Chat in a Virtual World*. SCLI Publications.

Cline, C. (1992) Essays from Bitch: the women's rock newsletter with bite, in L. Lewis (ed.) *The Adoring Audience: Fan Culture and Popular Media*. London: Routledge.

Cohen, S. (1972) *Folk Devils and Moral Panics*. London: McGibbon and Kee.

Cole, J. (1996) *The UCLA Television Violence Monitoring Report*. Los Angeles: UCLA, Center for Communication Policy.

Coleman, S. and Ross, K. (2002) *The Public, Politics and the Spaces Between: Election Call and Democratic Accountability*. London: Hansard Society.

Compesi, R.J. (1980) Gratifications of daytime TV serial viewers, *Journalism Quarterly*, 57: 155–85.

Comstock, G., Chaffee, S., Katzman, N., McCombs, M. and Roberts, D. (1978) *Television and Human Behavior*. New York: Columbia University Press.

Cook, J. (1978) Behaviouralism in political science, in R. Beehler and A.R. Drengson (eds) *The Philosophy of Society*. London: Methuen.

Cook, T.E. (1998) *Governing with the News: The News Media as a Political Institution*. Chicago, London: University of Chicago Press.

Cooper, J. and Mackie, D. (1986) Video games and aggression in children, *Journal of Applied Social Psychology*, 16: 726–44.

Coote, A. and Lenagham, J. (1997) *Citizens' Juries: Theory into Practice*. London: Institute of Public Policy Research.

Crary, J. (1994) Modernising Vision, in L. Williams (ed.) *Viewing Positions: Ways of Seeing Film*. New Brunswick, New Jersey: Rutgers University Press.

Crewe, I. (2001) The opinion poll: still biased to Blair, *Parliamentary Affairs*, 54(4): 650–65.

Crothers, C. (1987) *Robert K. Merton*. London and New York: Tavistock Publications and Ellis Horwood Limited.

Cumberbatch, G. and Howitt, D. (1989) *A Measure of Uncertainty: the Effects of the Mass Media*. London: John Libbey.

Curran, J., Gurevitch, M. and Woollacott, J. (eds) (1971) *Mass Communication and Society*. London: Edward Arnold.

Davidson, S. (1973) Feeding on dreams in a bubble gum culture, *Atlantic Monthly*, 232 (October): 62–72.

Davies, K.A. (1997) Voluntary exposure to pornography and men's attitudes toward feminism and rape, *The Journal of Sex Research*, 34(2): 131–7.

Davison, W.P. (1983) The third-person effect in communication, *Public Opinion Quarterly*, 47:1–15.

de Certeau, M. (1984) *The Practice of Everyday Life* (trans. S. Randall). Berkeley: University of California Press.

Decker, J.L. (1997) *Made in America: Self-Styled Success from Horatio Alger to Oprah Winfrey*. Minneapolis: University of Minnesota Press.

Dell, C. (1998) 'Lookit that Hunk of Man!': subversive pleasures, female fandom and professional wrestling, in C. Harris and A. Alexander (eds) *Theorizing Fandom: Fans, Subculture and Identity*. Cresskill, NJ: Hampton Press.

Delli-Carpini, M.X. and Keeter, S. (1991) Stability and change in the US public's knowledge of politics, *Public Opinion Quarterly*, 55: 583–612.

Delli-Carpini, M.X. and Keeter, S. (1996) *What Americans Know About Politics and Why It Matters*. New Haven, Conn: Yale University Press.

Denver, D. (1989) *Elections and Voting Behaviour in Britain*. London: Philip Allan.

Dill, K.E. and Dill, J.C. (1998). Video game violence: a review of the empirical literature, *Aggression & Violent Behavior*, 3: 407–28.

Dominick, J.R. (1984). Videogames, television violence and aggression in teenagers, *Journal of Communication*, 34: 136–47.

Donnerstein, E., Slaby, R.G. and Eron, L.D. (1994) The mass media and youth aggression, in L.D. Eron, J.H. Gentry and P. Schlegel (eds) *Reasons to Hope: A Psychosocial Perspective on Violence and Youth*. Washington DC: American Psychological Association.

Dran, E. and Hildreth, A. (1995) What the public thinks about how we know what it is thinking, *International Journal of Public Opinion Research*, 7: 128–44.

Duck, J.M. and Mullin, B.A. (1995) The perceived impact of the mass media: reconsidering the third-person effect, *European Journal of Social Psychology*, 25: 77–93.

Dunleavy, P., Margetts, H., Smith, T. and Weir, S. (2001) Constitutional reform, New Labour in power and public trust in government, *Parliamentary Affairs*, 54(3): 405–24.

Durkheim, E. (1930) *Rules of Sociological Method*. Paris: F. Alcan

Eckert, C. (1978) The Carole Lombard in Macy's Window, *Quarterly Review of Film Studies*, 3(1): 1–21.

Ehrenreich, B., Hess, E. and Jacobs, G. (1992) Beatlemania: girls just want to have fun, in L. Lewis (ed.) *The Adoring Audience: Fan Culture and Popular Media*. London: Routledge.

Elliot, P. (1972) *The Making of a Television Series: A Case Study in the Production of Culture*. London: Constable.

Entman, R.M. (1989) How the media affect what people think: an information processing approach. *Journal of Politics* 51: 347–70.

Evans, P. and Wurster, T.E. (2000) *Blown To Bits: How the New Economics of Information Transforms Strategy*. Boston, MA.: Harvard Business School Press.

Feshbach, S. (1955) The drive-reducing function of fantasy behavior, *Journal of Abnormal and Social Psychology*, 50: 3–11.

Fetveit, A. (1999) Reality TV in the digital era: a paradox in visual culture?, *Media, Culture and Society*, 21(6): 787–806.

Feuer, J. (1984) Melodrama, serial form and television today, *Screen*, 25(1): 4–16.

Finkelstein, D. (1998) Why the Conservatives lost, in I. Crewe, Gosschalk and J. Bartle (eds) *Political Communications: Why Labour Won the General Election of 1997*. London: Frank Cass.

Firmstone, J. (2002) *Discerning Eyes: Viewers on Violence*. Luton: University of Luton Press.

Fish, S. (1980) *Is There a Text in this Class? The Authority of Interpretive Communities*. Cambridge, MA and London: Harvard University Press.

Fisher, J. (2001) Campaign finance: elections under new rules. *Parliamentary Affairs* 54(4): 689–700.

Fisher, W.A. and Grenier, G. (1994) Violent pornography, antiwoman thoughts, and antiwoman acts: in search of reliable effects, *The Journal of Sex Research*, 31(1): 23–38.

Fishkin, J., Luskin, R. and Jowell, R. (2000) Deliberative polling and public consultation, *Parliamentary Affairs*, 53(4): 657–66.

Fiske, J. (1992) The cultural economy of fandom, in L. Lewis (ed.) *The Adoring Audience: Fan Culture and Popular Media*. London: Routledge.

Fiske, J. and Hartley, J. (1978) *Reading Television*. London: Methuen.

Flanagin, A.J. and Metzger, M.J. (2001) Internet use in the contemporary media environment, *Human Communication Research*, 27(1): 153–81.

Fletcher, F.J. (1996) Polling and Political Communication, in D. Paletz (ed.) *Political Communication in Action*. Cresskill, NJ: Hampton.

Fowles, J. (1999) *The Case for Television Violence*. Thousand Oaks, London, New Delhi: Sage.

Franklin, B. (1997) *Newszak and News Media*. London: Arnold.

Fraser, N. (1990) Rethinking the public sphere: a contribution to the critique of actually existing democracy, *Social Text*, 25/26: 56–80.

Freedman, J.L. (1984) Effects of television on aggressiveness, *Psychological Bulletin*, 96: 227–46.

Freedman, J.L. (2002) *Media Violence as Scapegoat: Scientific Evidence of its Effect on Aggression*. Toronto: University of Toronto Press.

Freedman, L.Z. (1981) Desperate to fill an emotional void, some fans become dangerous to their idols, *People Weekly*, 15, 20 April.

Gamman, L. and Marshment, M. (eds) (1988) *The Female Gaze: Women as Viewers of Popular Culture*. London: The Women's Press.

Gauntlett, D. (1995) *Moving Experiences: Understanding Television's Influences and Effects*. London: John Libbey.

Gauntlett, D. (1998) Ten things wrong with the 'effects' model, in R. Dickinson, R. Harindranath and O. Linné (eds) *Approaches to Audiences: A Reader*. London and New York: Arnold.

Gauntlett, D. (ed.) (2000) *Web.Studies: Rewiring Media Studies for the Digital Age*. London: Arnold.

Geraghty, C. (1981) The continuous serial: a definition, in R. Dyer et al. (eds) *Coronation Street*. London: British Film Institute.

Gerbner, G. (1967) Mass media and human communication theory, in F.E.X. Dance (ed.), *Human Communication Theory*. New York: Holt, Rinehart and Winston.

Gerbner, G. (1972) Violence in television drama: trends in symbolic functions, in G.A. Comstock and E.A. Rubinstein (eds) *Television Social Behavior: Vol 1, Media Content and Control*. Washington DC: Government Printing Office.

Gerbner, G. (1993) Testimony to the US House of Representatives Subcommittee on Crime and Criminal Justice. Hearing on Violence on Television, 15 December, 1992.

Gerbner, G. (1995) Marketing global mayhem, *Javnost/The Public*, 2(2): 71–6.

Gerbner, G. and Gross, L. (1976) Living with television: the violence profile, *Journal of Communication*, 26(2): 173–99.

Gerbner, G., Morgan, M. and Signorielli, N. (1995) Violence on television: the cultural indicators project, *Journal of Broadcasting and Electronic Media*, 39(2): 278–83.

Gillespie, M. (2000) Transnational communications and diaspora communities, in S. Cottle (ed.) *Ethnic Minorities and the Media*. Buckingham and Philadelphia: Open University Press.

Gillian, C. (1998) War of the world: Richard Chaves, Paul Ironhorse and the female fan community, in C. Harris and A. Alexander (eds) *Theorizing Fandom: Fans, Subculture and Identity*. Cresskill, NJ: Hampton Press.

Goldenberg, E.N. and Traugott, M.W. (1987) Mass media effects in recognizing and rating candidates in U.S. Senate elections, in J. Vermeer (ed.) *Campaigns in the News: Mass Media and Congressional Elections*. New York: Greenwood Press.

Goldman, E. (1948) Poll on the polls. *Public Opinion Quarterly*, 8: 461–7.

Gorna, B. (2003) *In Their Own Words*. London: Social Policy Institute.

Gould, P. (1998) Why Labour won, in I. Crewe, Gosschalk and J. Bartle (eds) *Political Communications: Why Labour Won the General Election of 1997*. London: Frank Cass.

Goyder, J. (1986) Surveys on surveys: limitations and potentialities, *Public Opinion Quarterly*, 50: 27–41.

Gray, A. (1987) Behind closed doors: video-recorders in the home, in H. Baer and G. Dyer (eds) *Boxed In: Women and Television*. London: Pandora.

Gray, H. (1995) *Watching Race: Television and the Struggle for 'Blackness'*. Minneapolis: University of Minnesota Press.

Graybill, D., Kirsch, J. and Esselman, E. (1985) Effects of playing violence versus non-violent video games on the aggressive ideation of aggressive and nonaggressive children, *Child Study Journal*, 15: 199–205.

Green, E. and Adam, A. (eds) (2001) *Virtual Gender: Technology, Consumption and Identity*. London, New York: Routledge.

Green, S., Jenkins, C. and Jenkins, H. (1998) Normal female interest in men bonking: selections from The Terra Nostra Underground and Strange Bedfellows, in C. Harris and A. Alexander (eds) *Theorizing Fandom: Fans, Subculture and Identity*. Cresskill, NJ: Hampton Press.

Greenberg, B.S. (1974) Gratifications of television viewing and their correlates for British children, in J.G. Blumler and E. Katz (eds) *The Uses of Mass Communications: Current Perspectives on Gratifications Research*. Beverley Hills and London: Sage Publications.

Greil, A.L. and Robbins, T. (1994) *Between Sacred and Secular: Research and Theory on Quasi-Religion, Religion and the Social Order*. Greenwich, Conn.: JAI Press.

Griffiths, M. (1999). Violent video games and aggression: a review of the literature, *Aggression & Violent Behavior*, 3: 203–12.

Griggs, R. (1991) Peaks freaks seek to keep weak show, *Mediaweek*, 29 April.

Gronroos, C. (1994) Quo vadis marketing? Towards a relationship marketing paradigm, *Journal of Marketing Management*, 10: 347–60.

Grossberg, L. (1992) Is there a fan in the house?: The affective sensibility of fandom, in L. Lewis (ed.) *The Adoring Audience: Fan Culture and Popular Media*. London: Routledge.

Gunter, B. (1985) *Dimensions of Television Violence*. New York: St Martin's Press.

Gunter, B. (1987) *Television and the Fear of Crime*. London: John Libbey.

Gunter, B. (1994) The question of media violence, in J. Bryant and D. Zillmann (eds)

Media Effects: Advances in Theory and Research. Hillsdale, NJ: Lawence Erlbaum Associations.

Gunter, B. (2002) *Media Sex: What are the Issues?* London: Lawrence Erlbaum.

Gunter, B. (2003) *Violence on Television: Distribution, Form, Context and Themes.* London: Lawrence Erlbaum.

Habermas, J. (1989) *The Structural Transformation of the Public Sphere: An Inquiry into a Category of Bourgeois Society* (trans. T. Burger with F. Lawrence). Cambridge, Mass: The MIT Press.

Hagell, A. and Newburn, T. (1994) *Young Offenders and the Media: Viewing Habits and Preferences*. London: Policy Studies Institute.

Hall, S. (1980) Coding/Encoding, in S. Hall, D. Hobson, A. Lowe and P. Willis (eds) *Culture, Media, Language*. London: Hutchinson.

Hall, S. (1988) New ethnicities, in K. Mercer (ed.) *Black Film: British Cinema*. ICA document No.7. London: British Film Institute.

Hall, S. (1992) What is this 'black' in black popular culture?, in M. Wallace with G. Dent (eds) *Black Popular Culture*. Seattle: Bay Press.

Hallin, D. (1994) *We Keep America on Top of the World*. London and New York: Routledge.

Halloran, J.D., Elliott, P. and Murdock, G. (1970) *Demonstrations and Communication: A Case Study*. Harmondsworth: Penguin Books.

Harcourt. W. (1999) *Women @ Internet*. London and New York: Zed Books.

Harrington, C.L. and Bielby, D.D. (1995) *Soap Fans: Pursuing Pleasure and Making Meaning in Everyday Life*. Philadelphia: Temple University Press.

Harris, C. (1998a) Introduction, in C. Harris and A. Alexander (eds) *Theorizing Fandom: Fans, Subculture and Identity*. Cresskill, NJ: Hampton Press.

Harrison, M. (1992) Politics on the air, in D. Butler and A. King (eds) *The British General Election of 1992*. London: Macmillan.

Hart, R. (1987) *The Sound of Leadership: Presidential Communication in the Modern Age*. Chicago: University of Chicago Press.

Hartley, J. (1987) Invisible fictions: television audiences, pedocracy and pleasure. *Textual Practice*, 1/2: 121–38.

Hartman, P. and Husband, C. (1974) *Racism and the Mass Media*. London: Davis Poynter.

Haskell, M. (1987) *From Reverence to Rape: The Treatment of Women in the Movies*. Chicago: University of Chicago Press.

Head, S.W. (1954) Content analysis of television drama programs, *Quarterly of Film, Radio and Television*, 9: 175–94.

Hebdige, D. (1979) *Subculture: The Meaning of Style*. London and New York: Methuen.

Heggs, D. (1999) Cyberpsychology and Cyborgs in A. Gordo-Lopez, and I. Parker, *Cyberpsychology*. Houndsmills and London: Macmillan Press.

Heller, C. (1978) *Broadcasting and Accountability*. Monograph #7. London: British Film Institute.

Herbst, S. (1993) *Numbered Voices: How Opinion Polling Has Shaped American Politics*. Chicago: University of Chicago Press.

Herbst, S. and Beniger, J.R. (1995) The changing infrastructure of public opinion, in J. Ettema and D.C. Whitney (eds) *Audiencemaking: How the Media Create the Audience*. Thousand Oaks, London and New Delhi: Sage.

Herzog, H. (1944) What do we really know about daytime serial listeners?, in P.F. Lazarsfeld and F.M. Stanton (eds) *Radio Research: 1942–1943*. New York: Duell, Sloan and Pearce.

Hickman, H. (1991) Public polls and election participants, in P.J. Lavrakas and J.K. Holley (eds) *Polling and Presidential Election Coverage*. Newbury Park, Calif.: Sage.

Hill, A. (2001) 'Looks like it hurts': women's responses to shocking entertainment, in M. Barker and J. Petley (eds) *Ill Effects: The Media/Violence Debate*, 2nd edn. London and New York: Routledge.

Hills, M. (2002) *Fan Cultures*. New York and London: Routledge.

Hinerman, S. (1992) 'I'll be here with you': fans, fantasy and the figure of Elvis, in L. Lewis (ed.) *The Adoring Audience: Fan Culture and Popular Media*. London: Routledge.

Hitchon, J.C. and Chang, C. (1995) Effects of gender schematic processing on the reception of political commercial for men and women candidates, *Communication Research*, 22(4): 430–58.

Hobson, D. (1982) *Crossroads: The Drama of a Soap Opera*. London: Methuen.

Hobson, D. (1990) Women audiences and the workplace, in M.E. Brown (ed.) *Television and Women's Culture*. Newbury Park, CA: Sage.

Hochschild, J.L. (1993) Disjunction and ambivalence in citizens' political outlooks, in G.E. Marcus and R.L. Hanson (eds) *Reconsidering the Democratic Public*. University Park: Pennsylvania State University Press.

Hoffner, C., Plotkin, R.S., Buchanan, M., et al. (2001) The third-person effect in perceptions of the influence of television violence, *Journal of Communication*, 51(2): 283–99.

Holmes, R. and Holmes, A. (1998) Sausages or policeman? The role of the Liberal Democrats in the 1997 general election campaign, in I. Crewe, Gosschalk and J. Bartle (eds) *Political Communications: Why Labour Won the General Election of 1997*. London: Frank Cass.

Honeywill, R. and Byth V. (2001) *I-Cons: The Essential Guide to Winning and Keeping High-value Customers*. Sydney: Random House Australia Limited.

Huffington, A. (1998) Margin of arrogance is huge for pollsters, *Chicago Sun-Times*, 14 October.

Husband, C. (2000) Media and the Public Sphere in Multi-Ethnic Societies, in S. Cottle (ed.) *Ethnic Minorities and the Media*. Buckingham and Philadelphia: Open University Press.

Illouz, E. (1999) That shadowy realm of the interior: Oprah Winfrey and Hamlet's glass, *International Journal of Cultural Studies*, 2(1): 109–31.

Irwin, A.R. and Gross, A.M. (1995) Cognitive tempo, violent video games and aggressive behavior in young boys, *Journal of Family Violence*, 10: 337–50.

Iyengar, S. (1987) Television news and citizens: explanations of national affairs. *American Political Science Review*, 81: 815–31.

Jacobson, G.C. (1992) *The Politics of Congressional Elections*. San Diego: Harper Collins.

Jakubowicz, A. (2001) Australian dreamings: cultural diversity and audience desire in a multinational and polyethnic State, in K. Ross (ed.) (with Peter Playdon) *Black Marks: Minority Ethnic Audiences and Media*. Aldershot, UK and Burlington, USA: Ashgate.

Jay, D.O. (2001) Three proposals for Open Publishing: towards a transparent. Collaborative editorial framework, *Copyleft* 2001, Dru Jay. *dojy@mta.ca*.

Jenkins, H. (1992a) *Textual Poachers: Television Fans and Participatory Culture*. New York and London: Routledge.

Jenkins, H. (1992b) 'Strangers no more, we sing': filking and the social construction of the science fiction fan community, in L. Lewis (ed.) *The Adoring Audience: Fan Culture and Popular Media*. London: Routledge.

Jenkins, H. (1995) At other times, like females: gender and Star Trek fan fiction, in J. Tulloch and H. Jenkins (eds) *Science Fiction Audiences: Watching Doctor Who and Star Trek*. London and New York: Routledge.

Jenkins, H. (2002) Interactive Audiences, in D. Harries (ed.) *The New Media Book*. London: British Film Institute.

Jenson, J. (1992) Fandom as pathology: the consequences of characterization, in L. Lewis (ed.) *The Adoring Audience: Fan Culture and Popular Media*. London: Routledge.

Jindra, M (1999) 'Star Trek to me is a way of life': fan expressions of Star Trek philosophy, in J.E. Porter and D.L. McLaren (eds) *Star Trek and Sacred Ground: Explorations of Star Trek, Religion and American Culture*. New York: State University of New York Press.

Jo, E. and Berkowitz, L. (1994) A priming effect analysis of media influences: an update, in J. Bryant and D. Zillmann (eds) *Media Effects: Advances in Theory and Research*. Hillsdale, NJ: Erlbaum.

Jones, N. (1995) *Soundbites and Spin Doctors: How Politicians Manipulate the Media – and Vice Versa*. London: Indigo.

Juliussen, E. and Petska-Julioussen, K. (2001) *Computer Industry Almanac*. Glenbrook, NV: CIA Inc.

Just, M.R., Crigler, A.N., Alger, D.E., et al. (1996) *Crosstalk: Citizens, Candidates and the Media in a Presidential Campaign*. Chicago: University of Chicago.

Just, M., Crigler, A. and Buhr, T. (1999) Voice, substance and cynicism in presidential campaign media. *Political Communication*, 16(1): 25–44.

Kahn, K.F. and Goldenberg, E.N. (1991) Women candidates in the news: an examination of gender differences in U.S. Senate campaign coverage, *Public Opinion Quarterly*, 55: 180–99.

Kaplan, A. (1983) *Woman and Film*. New York: Methuen.

Katz, E. and Lazarsfeld, P. (1965/1955) *Personal Influence: The Part Played by People in the Flow of Mass Communications*. New York: The Free Press.

Katz, J.E. and Rice, R.E. (2002) *Social Consequences of Internet Use: Access, Involvement and Interaction*. Cambs, MA.: MIT Press.

Kaufmann, K.M. and Petrocik, J.R. (1999) The changing politics of American men: understanding the sources of the gender gap, *American Journal of Political Science*, 43(3): 864–87.

Keane, J. (1991) *The Media and Democracy*. Oxford: Polity Press.

Kellerman, J. (2000) Phases in the rise of the information society, *Info*, 2(6): 537–41.

Kennamar, J.D. (1987) How media use during campaigns affects the intent to vote, *Journalism Quarterly*, 64: 291–300.

Kern, M. and Just, M. (1997) A gender gap among viewers? in P. Norris (ed) *Women, Media and Politics*. Oxford: Oxford University Press.

Kiousis, S. (2000) Boomerang agenda-setting: Presidential media coverage and public confidence in the press. Paper presented at the annual conference of the *International Communication Association*, Acapulco, June.

Klotz, R. (1998) Virtual criticism: negative advertising on the internet in the 1996 senate race, *Political Communication*, 15(3): 347–65.

Koukounas, E. and McCabe, M.P. (2001) Emotional responses to filmed violence and the eye blink startle response: a preliminary investigation, *Journal of Interpersonal Violence*, 16 (5): 476–88.

Krämer, P. (1998) Women first: *Titanic* (1997), action-adventure films and Hollywood's female audience, *Historical Journal of Film, Radio and Television*, 18(4): 599–618.

Krcmar, M. and Greene, K. (1999) Predicting exposure to and uses of television violence, *Journal of Communication*, 49(3): 24–45.

Krcmar, M. and Cooke, M.C. (2001) Children's moral reasoning and their perceptions of television violence, *Journal of Communication*, 51(2): 300–16.

Kuhn, A. (1984) Women's genres, *Screen*, 25(1):18–29.

Kunkel, D., Maynard Farinola, W.J., Farrar, K., et al. (2002) Deciphering the V-chip: an examination of the television industry's program rating judgements, *Journal of Communication*, 52(1): 112–38.

Lalli, T. (1992) Same sexism, different generation, in W. Irwin and G.B. Love (eds) *The Best of the Best of Trek II*. New York: Roc.

Lang, G. and Lang, K. (1981) Mass communication and public opinion: strategies for research, in M. Rosenberg and R.H. Turner (eds) *Social Psychology, Sociological Perspectives*. New York: Basic Books.

Lang, G.E. and Lang, K. (1983) *The Battle for Public Opinion: the President, the Press and the Polls During Watergate*. New York: Columbia University Press.

Lasora, D.L. (1997) Media agenda setting and press performance: a social system approach for building theory, in M. McCombs, D.L. Shaw and D. Weaver (eds) *Communication and Democracy: Exploring the Intellectual Frontiers in Agenda-setting Theory*. Mahwah, New Jersey: Lawrence Erlbaum.

Lasswell, H.D. (1927) *Propaganda Technique in the World War*. New York: Knopf.

Lau, R.R., Sigelman, L., Heldman, C. and Babbitt, P. (1997) The effects of negative political advertisments: a meta-analytic assessment. Paper presented to the annual conference of the *American Political Science Association*, Washington, August.

Lavrakas, P.J. and Traugott, M.W. (eds) (2000) *Election Polls, the News Media, and Democracy*. New York and London: Chatham House Publishers.

Lazarsfeld, P.F. and Kendall, P.L. (1948) *Radio Listening in America*. New York: Prentice-Hall.

Lemert, J.B., Elliott, W.R., Rosenberg, W.L. and Bernstein, J.M. (1996) *The Politics of Disenchantment: Bush, Clinton, Perot and the Press*. Cresskill, NJ: Hampton Press.

Leppert, R. (1995) *The Sight of Sound: Music, Representation and the History of the Body*. Berkeley, Los Angeles, London: University of California Press.

Levi-Strauss, C. (1978) *Myth and Meaning*. London: Routledge and Kegan Paul.

Levine, L.W. (1988) *Highbrow/Lowbrow: The Emergence of Cultural Hierarchy in America*. Boston: Harvard University Press.

Levy, P. (1997) *Collective Intelligence: Mankind's Emerging World in Cyberspace* (trans. R. Bononno). Cambridge, MA.: Perseus Books.

Lewis, J. (2001) *Constructing Public Opinion*. Columbia: Columbia University Press.

Lewis, L. (ed.) (1992) *The Adoring Audience: Fan Culture and Popular Media*. London: Routledge.

Lichter, R.S, Lichter, L.S. and Rothman, S. (1994) *Prime Time: How TV Portrays American Culture*. Washington, DC: Regency.

Lichter, S.R. and Noyes, R.E. (1996) *Good Intentions Make Bad News: Why Americans Hate Campaign Journalism*. Lanham, MD: Rowman and Littlefield.

Liebes, T. and Peri, Y. (1998) Electronic journalism in segmented societies: lessons from the 1996 Israeli elections, *Political Communication*, 15(1): 27–43.

Lindlof, T.R. (ed.)(1987) *Natural Audiences: Qualitative Research Of Media Uses And Effects*, Norwood N.J.: Ablex Publishing.

Lindstrom, M. and Seybold, P. (2003) *Brandchild*. London and Sterling, VA: Kogan Page.

Lippman, W. (1922) *Public Opinion*. New York: Harcourt Brace.

Livingstone, S. and Lunt, P. (1994) *Talk on Television: Audience Participation and Public Debate*. London and New York: Routledge.

Lovell, T. (1981) Ideology and 'Coronation Street', in R. Dyer, C. Geraghty, M. Jordan, et al. (eds) *Coronation Street*. London: British Film Institute.

Lovenduski, J. (2001) Women and politics, *Parliamentary Affairs*, 54(4): 743–58.

Luhmann, N.(2000) *The Reality of the Mass Media*. (trans. K. Cross). Cambridge, UK: Polity Press.

Lull, J. (1990) *Inside Family Viewing*. London: Routledge.

Luskin, R.C. (1987) Measuring Political Sophistication, *American Journal of Political Science*, 31: 856–99.

Lynd, R.S. and Lynd, H.M. (1929) *Middletown: A Study in American Culture*. New York: Harcourt, Brace and Co.

MacDonald, A. (1998) Uncertain utopia: science fiction media fandom and computer mediated communication, in C. Harris and A. Alexander (eds) *Theorizing Fandom: Fans, Subculture and Identity*. Cresskill, NJ: Hampton Press.

Malinowski, B. (1954) Myth in Primitive Life, in *Magic, Science and Religion and Other Essays*. New York: Anchor Books.

Manguel, A. (1997) *A History of Reading*. Hammersmith, London: Flamingo.

Marcus, G.E. (1988) Democratic theories and the study of public opinion, *Polity*, 21: 25–44.

Markham, A. (1999) *Life Online: Researching Real Experience in Virtual Space.* Lanham, Walnut Creek and Oxford: Alta Mira Press.

Marsalek, K. (1992) *Star Trek: humanism of the future, Free Inquiry*, 12(4): 53–6.

Mason, A. and Meyers, M. (2001) Living with Martha Stewart media: chosen domesticity in the experience of fans, *Journal of Communication*, 51(4): 801–23.

Mattelart, A. (2000) *Networking the World 1794–2000* (trans. L. Carey-Libbrecht and J.A. Cohen). Minneapolis and London: University of Minnesota Press.

McBain, M.A. (2002) *Internet Pornography: Awareness and Prevention.* Lincoln, NE: Writers Club Press.

McGuire, W.J. (1986). The myth of massive media impact: savagings and salvagings, in G. Comstock (ed.) *Public Communication and Behavior*, Vol.1. Orlando: Academic Press.

McIlwraith, R., Smith Jacobvitz, E., Kuby, R. and Alexander, A. (1991) Television Addiction, *American Behavioral Scientist*, 35: 104–21.

McLeod, D.M., Detenber, B.H. and Eveland, Jr., W.P. (2001) Behind the third-person effect: differentiating perceptual processes for self and other, *Journal of Communication*, 51(4): 678–95.

McQuail, D. (1994) *Mass Communication Theory: An Introduction*, 3rd edn. London, Thousand Oaks, New Delhi: Sage.

McQuail, D. (1997) *Audience Analysis*. Thousand Oaks, London, New Delhi: Sage.

Meadows, M. (2002) Tell me what you want and I'll give you what you need: Perspectives on Indigenous media audience research, in M. Balnaves, T. O'Regan and J. Sternberg (eds) *Mobilising the Audience*. St Lucia, Brisbane: University of Queensland Press.

Meehan, E. (1984) Ratings and the institutional approach: a third answer to the commodity question, *Critical Studies in Mass Communication*, 1: 216–25.

Meehan, E. (1991) Why we don't count: the commodity audience, in P. Mellencamp (ed.) *Logics of Television: Essays in Cultural Criticism*. Bloomington and Indianapolis: Indiana University Press; and London: BFI Publishing.

Meehan, E. (1993) Heads of household and ladies of the house: gender, genre and broadcast ratings, 1929–1990, in W.S. Solomon and R.W. McChesney (eds) *Ruthless Criticism: New Perspectives in U.S. Communication History*. Minneapolis and London: University of Minnesota Press.

Merkle, D.M. and Edelman, M. (2000) A review of the 1996 voter news service exit polls from a total survey error perspective, in P.J. Lavrakas and M.W. Traugott (eds) *Election Polls, the News Media, and Democracy*. New York and London: Chatham House Publishers.

Merritt, W.D. (1995) *Public Life and the Press: Why Telling the News is Not Enough.* Hillsdale, NJ: Lawrence Erlbaum Associates.

Merton, R.K. (1967) *On Theoretical Sociology: Five Essays, Old and New.* New York: The Free Press; and London: Collier-Macmillan.

Merton, Robert K. (1968) *Social Theory and Social Structure*. New York: The Free Press; and London: Collier Macmillan.

Meyer, P. (1989) Precision journalism and the 1988 elections, *International Journal of Public Opinion Research*, 1(3): 195–205.

Meyers, M. (1994) News of battering, *Journal of Communication*, 44(2): 47–63.

Miller, D. (2000) *Citizenship and National Identity*. Cambridge, UK: Polity Press.

Miller, E.D. (1994) *The Charlotte Project: Helping Citizens Take Back Democracy*. St Petersburg: Poynter Institute for Media Studies.

Miller, W.L. (1991) *Media and Voters: The Audience, Content and Influence of Press and Television*. Oxford: Clarendon Press.

Miller, M., Singletary, M.W. and Chen, S.-L. (1988) The Roper question and television vs. newspapers as sources of news, *Journalism Quarterly*, 65: 12–19.

Mitra, A. and Cohen, E. (1999) Analyzing the web: directions and challenges, in S. Jones (ed.) *Doing Internet Research: Critical Issues and Methods for Examining the Net*. Thousand Oaks, CA: Sage.

Modleski, T. (1984) *Loving With a Vengeance: Mass-Produced Fantasies for Women*. London: Methuen.

Moores, S. (1993) *Interpreting Audiences: The Ethnography of Media Consumption*. London: Sage.

Moran, M. (2002) Womenspeak: online domestic violence consultation project, *Towards Equality*, 12–13 March.

Morin, R. (1996) Tuned out, turned off, *The Washington Post National Weekly Edition*, 5–11 February: 6–8.

Morley, D. (1980) *The 'Nationwide' Audience: Structure and Decoding*. London: British Film Institute.

Morley, D. (1986) *Family Television: Cultural Power and Domestic Leisure*. London: Comedia.

Morrison, D.E. (1998) *The Search for a Method: Focus Groups and the Development of Mass Communication Research*. University of Luton: University of Luton Press.

Morrison, D.E. (1999) *Defining Violence: The Search for Understanding*. Luton: University of Luton Press.

Mouffe, C. (1992) Feminism and radical politics, in J. Butler and J.W. Scott (eds) *Feminists Theorize the Political*. New York and London, Routledge.

Moyser, G. and Wagstaffe, M. (1987) Studying elites: theoretical and methodological issues, in G. Moyser and M. Wagstaffe (eds) *Research Methods for Elite Studies*. London: Allen and Unwin.

Mughan, T. (1996) Television can matter: bias in the 1992 general election, in D.M. Farrell et al. (eds) *British Elections and Parties Yearbook 1996*. London: Frank Cass.

Mulvey, L. (1975) Visual pleasure and narrative cinema, *Screen*, 16(3): 6–18.

Myers, M. (1997) *News Coverage of Violence Against Women: Engendering Blame*. Thousand Oaks, London, New Delhi: Sage.

Naficy, H. (1993) *The Making of Exile Cultures: Iranian Television in Los Angeles*. Minneapolis and London: University of Minnesota Press.

National Telecommunications and Information Administration (NTIA)(1999) *Falling Through the Net: Defining the Digital Divide*, www.ntia.doc.gov/ntiahome/digitaldivide/ (accessed 11 November 2002).

Negrine, R. (1996) *The Communication of Politics*. London: Sage.

Neijens, P. (1987) *The Choice Questionnaire*. New York: The Free University Press.

Neuman, W.R. (1991) *The Future of the Mass Audience*. Cambridge, UK: Cambridge University Press.

Neuman, W.R., Just, M.R. and Crigler, A.N. (1992) *Common Knowledge: News and the Construction of Political Meaning*. Chicago: University of Chicago Press.

Nightingale, V. (1993) Industry measurement of audiences, in S. Cunningham and G. Turner (eds) *The Media in Australia: Industries, Texts, Audiences*. St Leonards, NSW: Allen and Unwin.

Nightingale, V. (1996) *Studying Audiences: The Shock of the Real*. London and New York: Routledge.

Nightingale, V. (1999) Are Media Cyborgs? in A. Gordo-Lopez and I. Parker (eds) *Cyberpsychology*. Houndsmills and London: Macmillan Press.

Nightingale, V. (2003) The 'Cultural Revolution' in Audience Research, in A. Valdivia (ed.) *The Blackwell Media Studies Companion*. Malden and Oxford: Blackwell.

Nightingale, V. and Ross, K. (2003) *Critical Readings: Media and Audiences*. Maidenhead: Open University Press/McGraw Hill.

Nightingale, V., Griff, C. and Dickenson, D. (2000) *Children's Views on Media Harm*, monograph #10. Sydney: Australian Broadcasting Authority and University of Western Sydney.

Norris, P. (2001a) Apathetic landslide: the 2001 British General Election, *Parliamentary Affairs*, 54(4): 565–89.

Norris, P. (2001b) *Digital Divide, Civic Engagement, Information Poverty and the Internet Worldwide*. Cambridge, UK: Cambridge University Press.

Norris, P. (ed.)(1997) *Women, Media and Politics*. Oxford: Oxford University Press.

Norris, P., Curtice, J., Sanders, D., Scammell, M. and Semetko, H.A. (1999) *On Message: Communicating the Campaign*. London, Thousand Oaks and New Delhi: Sage.

O'Regan, T. (2002) Arts Audiences: Becoming Audience-minded, in M. Balnaves, T. O'Regan and J. Sternberg (eds) *Mobilising the Audience*. St Lucia, Brisbane: University of Queensland Press.

Owen, D. (1997) Talk radio and evaluations of President Clinton, *Political Communication*, 14: 333–53.

Paik, H. and Comstock, G. (1994) The effects of television violence in antisocial behavior, *Communication Research*, 21: 516–46.

Patterson, T.E. (1994) *Out of Order*. New York: Knopf.

Pearson, G. (1983) *Hooligan: A History of Respectable Fears*. Basingstoke and London: Macmillan.

Peled, T. and Katz, E. (1974) Media functions in Wartime: the Israeli home front in October 1973, in J. Blumler and E. Katz (eds) *The Uses of Mass Communications: Current Perspectives on Gratifications Research*. London and Beverly Hills, Sage.

Penley, C. (1991) Brownian motion: women, tactics and technology, in C. Penley and A. Ross (eds) *Technoculture*. Minneapolis: University of Minnesota Press.

Perloff, R.M. (1998) *Political Communication: Politics Press and Public in America*. New Jersey: Lawrence Erlbaum Associates.

Perse, E. (2001) *Media Effects and Society*. Mahwah, N.J.: Lawrence Erlbaum Associates.

Pfau, M., Parrott, R. and Lindquist, B. (1992) An expectancy theory explanation of the effectiveness of political attack television spots: a case study, *Journal of Applied Communication Research*, 20: 263–73.

Pinkleton, B.E. and Austin, E.W. (2000) Exploring relationships among media use frequency, media importance, political disaffection and political efficacy. Paper presented at the annual conference of the *International Communication Association*, Acapulco, June.

Pinkleton, B.E., Austin, E.W. and Fortman, K.J. (1998) Relationships of media use and political disaffection to political efficacy and voting behaviour, *Journal of Broadcasting & Electronic Media*, 42(1): 34–49.

Plantinga, C. and Smith, G.M. (eds.) (1999) *Passionate Views: Film, Cognition, and Emotion*. Baltimore and London: The Johns Hopkins University Press.

Platell, A. (2001) *The Secret Diary of Amanda Platell* (dir: Amanda Platell, Carlton TV, UK).

Popkin, S.L. (1991) *The Reasoning Voter; Communication and Persuasion in Presidential Campaigns*. Chicago: University of Chicago Press.

Porter, J.E. (1999) To boldly go: *Star Trek* convention attendance as pilgrimage, in J.E. Porter and D.L. McLaren (eds) *Star Trek and Sacred Ground: Explorations of Star Trek, Religion and American Culture*. New York: State University of New York Press.

Prentice, E-A (2003) *War, Lies and Videotape*. Centre for Communication, Culture and Media Studies, monograph #3. Coventry: Coventry University.

Pribham, E.D. (1988) *Female Spectators: Looking at Film and Television*. London and New York: Verso.

Price, V. (1992) *Public Opinion*. Newbury Park, CA: Sage.

Price, V. (2000) Deliberative polling in the 1996 elections, in P. Lavrakas and M.W. Traugott (eds) *Election Polls, the News Media, and Democracy*. New York and London: Chatham House Publishers.

Pullen, K. (2000) I-Love-Xena.com: creating online fan communities, in D. Gauntlett (ed.) *Web.Studies: Rewiring Media Studies for the Digital Age*. London: Arnold.

Puwar, N. (1997) Reflections on Interviewing Women MPs, *Sociological Research Online*, 2(1). http://www.socresonline.org.uk/socresonline/2/1/4.html (accessed 14 November 2001).

Rheingold, H. (1993) *Virtual Communities*. Reading, MA: Addison-Wesley.

Robinson, J.P. and Davis, D.K. (1990) Television news and the informed public: an information processing approach, *Journal of Communication*, 40(3): 106–19.

Roper, B. (1986) Evaluating polls with poll data, *Public Opinion Quarterly*, 50: 10–16.

Roscoe, J. (2001) Big Brother Australia: performing the 'real' twenty-four-seven, *International Journal of Cultural Studies*, 4(4): 473–88.

Roscoe, T. (1999) The construction of the world wide web audience, *Media, Culture and Society*, 21(5): 673–84.

Rosen, J. (1996) *Getting the Connections Right: Public Journalism and the Troubles of the Press*. New York: Twentieth Century Fund.

Ross, K. (1996) *Black and White Media: Black Images in Popular Film and Television*. Cambridge, UK: Polity Press

Ross, K. (2001) All ears: radio; reception and discourses of disability, *Media, Culture and Society*, 23(4): 423–36.

Ross, K. (2002) *Women, Politics, Media: Uneasy Relations in Comparative Perspective*. Cresskill, N.J.: Hampton Press.

Rubin, A.W. (1985) The uses of daytime television serials by college students: an examination of viewing motives, *Journal of Broadcasting and Electronic Media*, 29: 241–58.

Salmon, C.T. and Glasser, T.L. (1998) The politics of polling and the limits of consent, in C.T. Salmon and T.L. Glasser (eds) *Public Opinion and the Communication of Consent*. New York: Guilford Press.

Sancho-Aldridge, J. (1997) *Election '97*. London: Independent Television Commission.

Sanda, J. and Hall, Jr., M. (1994) *Alpha Quadrant Membership Manual*. Madison, Wisc.: Sanda and Hall.

Sanders, D. and Norris, P. (1997) Does negative news matter? The effect of television news on party images in the 1997 British general election. Paper presented to the *Political Studies Association* specialist conference on Elections, Public Opinion and Parties, Essex, September.

Saunders, K.W. (1996). *Violence as Obscenity: Limiting the Media's First Amendment Protection*. Durham: University of North Carolina Press.

Scammell, M. (1990) Political Advertising and the Broadcasting Bill, *Political Quarterly*, 61(2): 200–13.

Scammell, M. (1998) The wisdom of the war room: US campaigning and Americanization, *Media, Culture and Society*, 20(2): 251–75.

Scammell, M. and Semetko, H.A. (1995) Political Advertising on Television, in L.L. Kaid and C. Holtz-Bacha (eds) *Political Advertising in Western Democracies*. Thousand Oaks, London, New Delhi: Sage.

Scheff, T.J. and Scheele, S.C. (1980) Humor and catharsis: the effect of comedy on audiences, in P.H. Tannenbaum (ed.) *The Entertainment Functions of Television*. Hillsdale, N.J.: Lawrence Erlbaum Associations.

Schickel, R. (1985) *Intimate Strangers: The Culture of Celebrity*. Garden City, New York: Doubleday.

Schindehette, S. (1990) Vanna White and Teri Garr ask the courts to protect them from fans who have gone too far, *People Weekly*, 14, 16 July.

Schlesinger, P. (1991) *Media, State and Nation: Political Violence and Collective Identities*. London, New York and Delhi: Sage.

Schlesinger, P., Dobash, R.E., Dobash, R.P. and Weaver, C. Kay (1992) *Women Viewing Violence*. London: British Film Institute.

Schutz, A. (1998) Audience perceptions of politicians' self-presentational behaviors concerning their own abilities, *Journal of Social Psychology*, 138(2): 173–88.

Scodari, C. (1998) No politics here: age and gender in soap opera cyberfandom, *Women's Studies in Communication*, 21(2): 168–87.

Scott, D. (1995) The effect of video games on feelings of aggression, *Journal of Psychology*, 129: 121–32.

Sherry, J. (2001) The effects of violent video games on aggression: a meta-analysis, *Human Communication Research*, 27(3): 409–31.

Sigismondi, A. (2001) The format of success: why "Big Brother" succeeded in Europe but failed in the US, *Television Quarterly*, 32(1): 30–4.

Silver, D. (2000) Looking backwards, looking forwards: cyberculture studies 1990–2000, in D. Gauntlett (ed.) *Web.Studies: Rewiring Media Studies for the Digital Age*. London: Arnold.

Sissors, J.Z. and Bumba, L. (1996) *Advertising Media Planning*, 5th edn. Lincolnwood: NTC Business Books.

Slaton, C.D. (1992) *Televote: Expanding Citizen Participation in the Quantum Age*. Westport, CT: Praeger.

Skinner, B.F. (1973) *Beyond Freedom and Dignity*. Harmondsworth: Penguin.

Smith, S.L. and Boyson, A.R. (2002) Violence in music videos: examining the prevalence and context of physical aggression, *Journal of Communication*, 52(1): 61–83.

Smith, S.L., Nathanson, A.I. and Wilson, B.J. (2002) Prime-time television: assessing violence during the most popular viewing hours, *Journal of Communication*, 52(1): 84–111.

Smulyan, S. (1994) *Selling Radio: The Commercialization of American Broadcasting 1920–1934*. Washington and London: Smithsonian Institution Press.

Smythe, D. (1954) Reality as presented by television, *Public Opinion Quarterly*, 18: 13–21.

Smythe, D. (1981) *Dependency Road: Communications, Capitalism, Consciousness and Canada*. Norwood, N.J.: Ablex Publishing.

Soja, E.W. (2000) *Postmetropolis: Critical Studies of Cities and Regions*. Oxford and Malden, MA.: Blackwells.

Soothill, K. and Walby, S. (1991) *Sex Crime in the News*. London: Routledge.

Sreberny, A. (2000) Media and diasporic consciousness: and exploration among Iranians in London, in S. Cottle (ed.) *Ethnic Minorities and the Media*. Buckingham and Philadelphia: Open University Press.

Stacey, J. (1994) *Star Gazing*. London and New York: Routledge.

Staiger, J. (2000) *Perverse Spectators: The Practices of Film Reception*. New York and London: New York University Press.

Stark, E., Flitcraft, A., Zuckerman, D., et al. (1981) *Wife Abuse in the Medical Setting: An Introduction for Health Professionals*, monograph #7. Washington DC: Office of Domestic Violence, Government Printing Office.

Stokes, M. (1999) Female Audiences of the 1920s and early 1930s, in M. Stokes and R. Maltby (eds) *Identifying Hollywood's Audiences: Cultural Identity and the Movies*. London: BFI.

Stout, K.D. (1991) Women who kill: offenders or defenders?, *Affilia*, 6(4): 8–22.

Strate, J.M., Ford III, C.C. and Jankowski, T.B. (1994) Women's use of print media to follow politics, *Social Science Quarterly*, 75(1): 166–86.

Takeuchi, M., Clausen, T. and Scott, R. (1995) Televised violence: a Japanese, Spanish and American comparison, *Psychological Reports*, 77: 995–1000.

Taylor, H. (1989) Scarlett's Women: *Gone with the Wind and its Female Fans*. London: Virago.

Taylor, M. and Quayle, E. (2003) *Child Pornography: An Internet Crime*. London and New York: Brunner-Routledge.

Thomas, L. (2002) *Fans, Feminisms and 'Quality' Media*. London and New York: Routledge.

Thompson, A. (1991) Studios stick to their guns over sex appeal of pics, *Variety*, 7 January.

Tompkins, J.P. (1980) *Reader-Response Criticism: From Formalism to Post-Structuralism*. Baltimore and London: Johns Hopkins University Press.

Traugott, M. and Kang, M-E. (2000) Public attention to polls in an election year, in P.J. Lavrakas and M.W. Traugott (eds) *Election Polls, the News Media, and Democracy*. New York and London: Chatham House Publishers.

Tulloch, J. and Alvarado, M. (1983) *Dr Who: The Unfolding Text*. London: Macmillan.

Tulloch, J. and Jenkins, H. (1995) *Science Fiction Audiences: Watching Doctor Who and Star Trek*. London and New York: Routledge.

Turkle, S. (1995) *Life on the Screen: Identity in the Age of the Internet*. New York: Simon and Schuster.

Turner, V. (1977) Variations on a theme of liminality, in S.F. Moore and B.G. Beyerhof (eds) *Secular Ritual*. Amsterdam: Van Gorcum.

Turow, J. (1997) *Breaking Up America: Advertisers and the New Media World*. Chicago and London: University of Chicago Press.

UCLA Center for Communication Policy (1998) *1997 TV Violence Report*. Los Angeles: UCLA CCP.

Van Zoonen, L. (2001) Desire and resistance: Big Brother and the recognition of everyday life, *Media, Culture and Society*, 23(5): 669–78.

Vine, I. (1997) The dangerous psycho-logic of media 'effects', in M. Barker and J. Petley (eds) *Ill Effects: The Media/Violence Debate*. London and New York: Routledge.

Warner, W.L. and Henry, S.E. (1948) The radio day time serial: a symbolic analysis, *Genetic Psychology Monographs*, 37: 71.

Warschauer, M. (2003) *Technology and Social Inclusion: Rethinking the Digital Divide*. Cambs, MA: MIT Press.

Weaver, D.G. and Wilhoit, C.G. (1997) The American Journalist in the 1990s, in S. Iyengar and R. Reeves (eds) *Do the Media Govern? Politicians, Voters and Reporters in America*. Thousand Oaks, London, Delhi: Sage.

Webster, J. and Lichty, W. (1991) *Ratings Analysis: Theory and Practice*. Hillsdale, Hove and London: Lawrence Erlbaum and Associates.

Webster, J.G., Phalen, P.F. and Lichty, L.W. (2000) *Ratings Analysis: The Theory and Practice of Audience Research*, 2nd edn. Mahwah, New Jersey and London: Lawrence Erlbaum and Associates.

Wertheimer, F. (1997) TV ad wars: how to cut advertising costs in political campaigns, *Press/Politics*, 2 (summer): 93–101.

West, D. (1993) *Air Wars: Television Advertising in Election Campaigns 1952–1992*. Washington DC. Congressional Quarterly.

Wheeler, M. (1997) *Politics and the Mass Media*. Oxford: Blackwell.

Williams, P.M. (1980) Interviewing politicians: The life of Hugh Gaitskell, *Political Quarterly*, 51(3): 303–16.

Williams, R. (1974) *Television: Technology and Cultural Form*. London: Fontana/ Collins.

Wilson, B.J., Colvin, C.M. and Smith, S.L. (2002) Engaging in violence on American television: a comparison of child, teen and adult perpetrators, *Journal of Communication*, 52(1): 36–60.

Wilson, B.J., Kunkel, D., Linz, D., et al. (1997) Television violence and its context: University of California, Santa Barbara study. *National Television Violence Study*, Vol. 1. Newbury Park, CA: Sage.

Wilson, B.J., Kunkel, D., Potter, W.J., et al. (1998) Violence in television programming overall: University of California, Santa Barbara study. *National Television Violence Study*, Vol. 2. Newbury Park, CA: Sage.

Wilson, T. (1993) *Watching Television: Hermeneutics, Reception and Popular Culture*. Cambridge: Polity Press.

Wilson, T. (2001) On playfully becoming the 'other': watching Oprah Winfrey on Malaysian television, *International Journal of Cultural Studies*, 4(1): 89–110.

Winter, J. (1993) Gender and the political interview in an Australian context, *Journal of Pragmatics*, 20: 117–30.

Wood, W., Wong, F.Y. and Chachere, J.G. (1991) Effects of media violence on viewers' aggression in unconstrained social interaction, *Psychological Bulletin*, 109: 371–83.

Yankelovich, D. (1991) *Coming to Public Judgment: Making Democracy Work in a Complex World*. Syracuse, NY: Syracuse University Press.

Zhao, X. and Chaffee, S.H. (1995) Campaign advertisements versus television news as sources of political issue information, *Public Opinion Quarterly*, 59: 41–65.

Zillmann, D. (1988) Mood management: using entertainment to full advantage, in L. Donohew, H.E. Sypher and E.T. Higgins (eds) *Communication, Social Cognition and Affect*. Hillsdale, NJ: Erlbaum.

INDEX

CRITICAL READINGS: MEDIA AND AUDIENCES

Virginia Nightingale and Karen Ross (eds)

- How have media researchers changed the ways in which the audience is perceived over time?
- How have audiences become fragmented in the search for ratings?
- What next for audience research in the 21st century?

The study of 'audience' is a central concept in both media and cultural studies. Although it has become an academic fashion to turn away from imagining that groups of people can share common purpose or interests, there are still reasons enough for wanting to explore the way in which audiences behave, understand and interact with media texts in all their various forms, not least because of the vast sums of money which are persistently expended by advertisers and broadcasters trying to give 'the audience' what 'it' wants and therefore maintaining or preferably increasing market share.

This collection of readings brings together some of the important developments in the history of audience and media studies and the significant research trajectories which have shaped the field until now. It is sometimes difficult to locate specific examples of audience research or discussions of research practice, as opposed to description, conjecture or critical reflection about audiences, which are in abundant supply: the Reader allows students and lecturers to source original research commentaries and better understand the rationale, findings and forms of analysis undertaken at different points in the field's research-based career.

Contents

Series editor's foreword – Introduction – The passive-active continuum: competing theories of agency and affect – The segmented audience: niche consumers and the ratings agenda – Inter-active audiences: fans, cultural production and new media – Glossary – Index.

288pp   0 335 21150 X (Paperback)   0 335 21151 8 (Hardback)

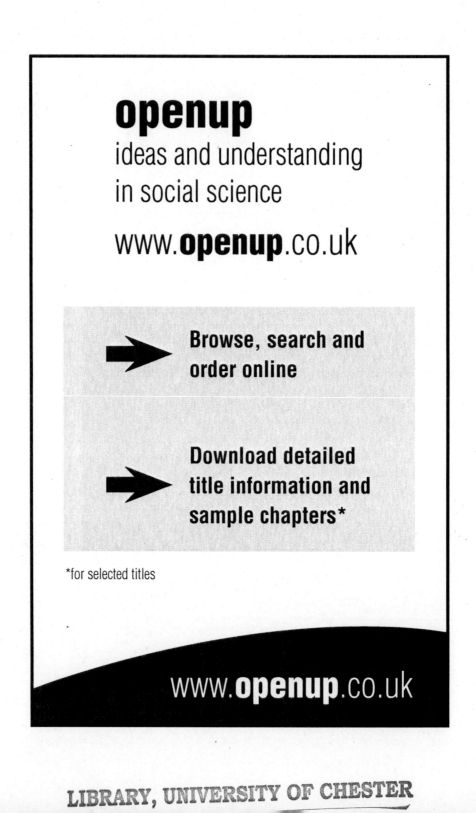

LIBRARY, UNIVERSITY OF CHESTER